Reading Activities
in
Content Areas

Reading
Activities
in
Content
Areas

Dorothy Piercey
Arizona State University

AN
IDEABOOK
FOR
MIDDLE
AND
SECONDARY
SCHOOLS

———————

ALLYN AND BACON, INC.
BOSTON · LONDON · SYDNEY

The author is grateful to those who granted permission to reproduce
the following material: *The Arizona Republic,* for articles and headlines
appearing on pages 19, 80, 81, 166, 168, 170, 173, 184, 188, 189, 212,
215, 219, 300, 338, 356–57, 414, 429, 437, 467, 481–83, 543–44, 546,
569, 570, 573, 575; The Associated Press, for articles on pages 81, 188,
189, 219, 414, 546; *The Phoenix Gazette,* for the article on page 175.
The ads on page 258, courtesy of Barnes Associates, Inc. (left), and The
Pacific Marketing Group (right); page 280, by permission of Metro
Newspaper Service, New York, N.Y.; page 329, courtesy of Norwich
Products; page 343, courtesy of General Mills, Inc.; page 344, courtesy
of The Quaker Oats Company (left) and Kellogg Company (right); ads
on pages 356 and 357 courtesy of Switzer's, Phoenix, and Hart
Schaffner & Marx Retail Stores; pages 488 and 489, courtesy of the
Environment and Health Committee of Single Service Institute; page
543, courtesy of Emperor's Garden; page 544, SENOR T's, Phoenix,
Arizona, U.S.A.

Library of Congress Cataloging in Publication Data

Piercey, Dorothy, 1921–
    Reading activities in content areas.

    Includes index.
    1. Reading (Secondary education) I. Title.
LB1632.P5   428'.4'0712   76-10340
ISBN 0-205-05507-9
Third printing . . . February, 1979

Contents

Preface

Frank Jennings* saw words as things that mold the squalling, squirming blob of homo into sapiens; Susanne Langer† said that between the clearest call of an animal and the most trivial word of man lies a whole day of creation. In other words, language—both the words themselves and the way speakers and writers string words together—is prerequisite to thinking. It is on the backs of words that ideas ride. It is on the backs of concepts that learning rides.

Many ingredients make up successful learning and successful performing. But perhaps the major, the pivotal, ingredient is the ability to manage the specialized language peculiar to a special field whether it is hydroponics, cliometrics, horse breeding, aviation, or biology, general math, geography or any other of the subjects in the curriculum.

Ability to manage the language of a subject area can be developed, and that development is a function of teaching. It is estimated that **80** percent of the learning students are asked to do involves the printed word. Eighty percent of the time reading is the **process** through which students are supposed to accumulate a body of knowledge in each subject area. Some students need assistance with the **process** most of the time; most of them require help much of the time; and even the best students need the teacher's guidance some of the time. When teachers merge the teaching of thinking/reading skills (process) and the teaching of content, students develop and refine their ability to manage the specialized language of each

*Frank Jennings, *This is Reading* (New York: Dell Publishing Co.), 1965.
†Susanne Langer, *Philosophy in a New Key* (New York: Mentor Books), 1948.

field of study, and possibilities for successful learning become probabilities.

Reading Activities in Content Areas offers guidelines for teacher behaviors as well as student activities which foster merging two teaching approaches: process and content. Described in another way, they are behaviors and activities that promote teaching content through its language.

For every person who writes a book, there are scores of other people whose ideas, advice, and materials help bring it to completion. Appreciation is extended to Freddie Antilla, *The Arizona Republic,* The Associated Press, Reta Bardrick, Gordon Berry, Barnes Associates, Inc., Danny Brennecka, Cindy Bryan, William H. Cherry, Melba Constable, Bryan H. Curd, Del Monte Foods, Betty Dianics, Emperor's Garden, Mary Carroll Fox, Shirley Gartin, General Mills, Inc., Green Giant Co., Gregg and Community College Division of McGraw-Hill Book Co., Jerri Gustafson, John P. Haire, Joan Hantla, Hart Schaffner & Marx, Elinor A. Hirsch, Nancy L. Hopkins, The Kellogg Company, Kathryn Lowe, G. & C. Merriam Co., Metro Associated Services, Inc., Barbara J. Mitchell, Mountain Bell, Paulette Mulvin, Jean Myers, National Assessment of Educational Progress, National Live Stock and Meat Board, Norwich Products, Sal D. Olivo, Kay K. Olsson, The Pacific Marketing Group, *The Phoenix Gazette, Popular Mechanics,* The Quaker Oats Co., The Reader's Digest Association, Inc., Michaele R. Roark, Adela Santa Cruz, Madeline Schneck, Scott, Foresman and Co., Angela Seidel, Senor T's, Susan M. Sherman, Single Service Institute, Switzer's, Jean M. Turner, Dorolis Wade, Gary Wolverton, and Gracia M. Zimmerman.

Although there were times when the author wondered if fait would ever be accompli, there were two who never doubted: her friend and mentor, Dr. Daisy Marvel Jones, and her husband, Carl V. Piercey.

D.P.

Introduction

You Have the Know-How

By this stage in your career you are exceptionally proficient in the language of your subject area. It is no longer difficult for you to pick up a textbook or an article and read it through with excellent comprehension.

You know the language of your field, both the words and the way words form thought patterns. You have language-coping skills despite the fact that you may have forgotten the names of those skills long ago. You now exercise them automatically.

Certainly your proficiency is an advantage to you in the classroom. But it is possible that it also could work to your disadvantage. You have become so facile, so knowledgeable that you may tend to forget that there was a time when the language was strange to you, when concepts were difficult and took study.

Words and concepts that are simple to you may present difficulties for your students. Some of the language of your area may be as mystifying to students as the following sentences are to you.

. . . Well, Almost Always

How successful could you be, for instance, in areas represented by these languages?

1. He pied the Roman and relegated it to the hellbox.
2. We'll only be able to shoot TACAN at our destination.

3. It takes know-how to distinguish between an overo and a tobiano.
4. They headed for the tell, hungry to start on what was to be their daily diet for the next five years.

Are you having difficulty coping with the language of some of the sentences? What about your comprehension? Nil?

Many people can understand the sentences, including some of your students. They can cope if they are members of the group whose language it represents: printers, air controllers, horse breeders, and archeologists, respectively.

Teen and post-teen students have a tongue of their own; they work hard at the youth language to maintain their membership, status, and success in the group. So the concept of languaging is in their repertory already. Building on this phenomenon, teachers can draw a parallel between the existence of a youth language and the existence of the language of each subject field.

Sometimes Students Need Help

Time after time, page after page, students have difficulty understanding. Who can best help students cope with specialized language? You, the specialist in the field. It should be you for many reasons: you have the competency; you are with the student when help is needed; you know more about your specialized language than any other person on the faculty; you want your students to learn as much as they can in your course, and you want them to continue learning after graduation.

Needless to say your goal is to be a successful teacher. One characteristic of a successful teacher is successful students. Your students have a good chance of being successful if they can deal with the language of your subject area. If they can't manage the language—write it, speak it, read it, listen to it—with understanding, it is not likely that they will be successful in your classroom.

A Matter of How-To

It really isn't a question of whether or not to help your students be successful. It's a matter of *how*. You already are doing many things day after day, semester after semester, to help them.

This book is designed to enlarge your repertory. It is divided into two parts, one for each of the questions teachers interested in teaching their subject through its language might ask:

1. What more can I do to help students manage the language of the discipline while I am teaching the content of my course?
2. What can students do to help themselves become more proficient in the language-coping skills they need for success in my course?

How to Use This Book

Part I is called *Techniques for Teaching Content through Language.* It presents techniques you might wish to add to those you already are using to develop student success. Many of the techniques deal with vocabulary since verbal and nonverbal symbols are the bases for understanding and communication. Other techniques have to do with generating understanding, specifically, getting students ready for reading assignments, improving teacher questioning strategies, and improving student questioning.

Almost all the strategies in part I were used by the author in her days as a secondary teacher, first of journalism, then of reading. They are offered as supplements to your own daily classroom behaviors and are not meant as an exhaustive coverage of vocabulary and comprehension techniques. Many other texts on the market have that as a goal.

The strategies or methods are designed to be the *process* through which content is taught. Sometimes that *process* is reading in its narrowest definition; at other times, it is reading in its most global definition, making sense of and bringing meaning to all kinds of signs and symbols. Student success is enhanced when the subject matter teacher becomes as skillful with process as she or he is knowledgeable about the subject matter.

While part I concentrates on the classroom techniques of the teacher, part II has the student as the doer. Part II, *Activities for Learning Content through Language,* suggests activities in the subject areas of

business
driver education
English, speech, and journalism
fine arts: art, music, and theatre

home economics
industrial and vocational arts
mathematics
physical education

foreign languages   science
health   social studies

The activities are designed for students to use alone, by twos and threes, in larger groups, and as a whole class. You may wish to arrange your classroom or lab or shop to provide housing for an Activities Center, or Learning Center, where students can go at your suggestion or on their own volition to practice language-coping skills in which they are weak. It can be as simple as a filing cabinet or as elaborate as a sectioned off corner of the classroom.

Will an Activities Center work? May you have the same fortune as a math teacher who built a lab similar to an activities center except on a larger scale. Students cut lunch hours and study halls to work with the activities in the math lab!

Fish Food for Thought

A proverb fits appropriately in this book: "If you give a man a fish, he will have a single meal; if you teach him how to fish, he will eat all his life." Students who learn how to cope with the language of your subject area will continue their learning for a lifetime. Students skilled in making sense of symbols, particularly printed symbols, will become adults who can solve problems and make decisions.

Techniques
for Teaching Content
through Language

PART I

Before exploring teaching techniques designed for successful student learning, it would be wise to clarify what the term *language of a subject field* means. It is not surprising to learn that the term *language* has its roots in the Anglo-French word for tongue. English is the mother tongue of Americans, the tongue in which they officially communicate and interact. There are tongues within tongues. In this country, for instance, there are English dialects and levels of usage in various geographical areas and among various subcultures.

In addition, people who group together because of a common interest develop and use a special tongue for communicating and carrying on business with one another. So it is that your specialized field has a tongue of its own, a lingo, a jargon, a special language with which its disciples and devotees communicate and work. In order to function in the field, one must be skillful with the specialized language. In addition, one must be able to cope with another language, the one which is common to all disciplines: ordinary American English.

The *language* of your field and the *vocabulary* of your field are not synonymous terms. *Language* carries with it a two-part concept. Language is indeed a body of words, a vocabulary, if you will. But it also is a scheme for the *use* of the words. *Language* also includes the way authors and speakers join words together to suit their purpose for communicating, whether that purpose is to give instructions or to inform, compare, persuade or entertain.

The Two-fold Concept of Language

In order to plan experiences through which students can learn how to cope with the language of your field,

3

you will want to take into consideration the dual implication of the word *language* and plan accordingly.

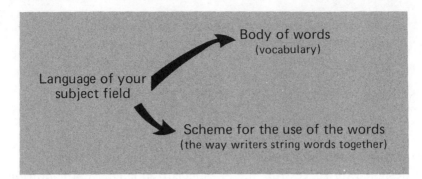

Figure 1. *The Two-fold Structure of the Concept of Language.*

Recognizing that the duality of the concept of language facilitates planning experiences in both areas you should remember that both are important in their own right, but each is only part of the whole.

Both verbal and nonverbal symbols constitute vocabulary (body of words) in various subject fields. Words constitute vocabulary, and so do abbreviations, acronyms, formulas, symbols, and signs such as %, $, #, ♭ , ♯ . The scheme used by a writer or speaker for putting words together requires *comprehending* not only groups of words, but also sentences, paragraphs, and larger pieces.

A writer's scheme for putting words together is correlated with his or her purpose: to give directions, to persuade, to classify, to inject an opinion, to state cause and effect, to summarize, to explain, to entertain. A writer also communicates through organization of a book, chapter, or article; mechanical devices; graphs; charts; tables; pictures.

Therefore if students are to be successful with the language of a subject, you will have to arrange the environment so that learners will have many experiences in both of these areas of language.

There is some basis for truth in statements about assumptive teaching: teachers can become so expert in their field that they assume others are knowledgeable also. Because of their expertise, they tend to jump from pinnacle to pinnacle in their presentations, forgetting to fill learners in on what lies in the valleys. Students tune out when they can't understand the concepts because they can't manage the words on which those ideas ride.

Probably one of the most frequently used methods for having students learn vocabulary is the word list. The teacher hands out dittoed copies of words and says something like: "You will need to know the meanings of these words if you are going to understand the new unit. Look them up in the dictionary (or the glossary), write the definition, and (sometimes) write a sentence with each word. Memorize them well because we'll have a test on Friday."

Possibly you are smiling because that happened to you when you were a student. How long did you

CHAPTER 1

Teacher Strategies for Vocabulary Development

remember the words? Until Friday, if you were lucky. What about the day after and the next week?

There are techniques for teaching vocabulary that are more compatible with learning theory.

TALK THROUGH

The process of **Talk Through** incorporates several factors that contribute to student success in vocabulary development:

1. **Talk Through** has its feet in the psychological principle of paired association, the process of connecting new ideas with old. The technique of paired association is used as a cornerstone for commercial memory courses and training in salesmanship. Pairing is a respected memory device.
2. **Talk Through** minimizes teacher input and increases student responses. Engaging the class in **Talk Through,** the teacher uses a particular type of question to try to elicit the meaning from individuals (student discovery) instead of imposing the meaning on them (teacher input).
3. **Talk Through** builds on students' strengths to shore up weaknesses. For instance, when the unknown word is related to something students already know, something in their everyday, ongoing lives, almost all students can give successful responses. The example demonstrates that all students will be able to speak out, even those who usually don't for fear of giving an incorrect answer. Students will remember the unknown word because they will remember their own participation and their classmates' contributions.

Prior to **Talk Through** the teacher identifies those *key concept* words that are apt to give students trouble. They may be new or once-learned words that have been forgotten, or slippery words, those that mean one thing in industrial arts but something different in the social sciences or theatre.

An Example of Talk Through

This sentence has been put on the blackboard (or on an overhead projector or on a dittoed sheet):

<u>Importation</u> of sugar stopped when Castro took control of the government.

Two points merit underscoring. First, it is important for the word under discussion to be in writing so students can see it as **Talk Through** proceeds. One of the objectives is to have students recognize this word when they meet it again in printed form. Second, the word should be in context, not in isolation, giving students the benefit of context clues.

So the sentence is now on the blackboard and the process of eliciting, the **Talk Through** relating to students' everyday lives, begins. The teacher *asks,* not *tells.*

"Joyce, you had a new camera at the football game Friday night. Where was it made?" Joyce responds in Japan, or Germany, perhaps.

"You told me about a present you received from some relatives, Cindy. Where did your linen hanky come from?" She responds from Ireland.

"Who's been to Tang's Imports?" Show of hands. "What did you find in the store?" The teacher takes answers from all who volunteer.

"What do we notice alike about all these products we've been discussing?" The response will be that they were made in foreign countries and brought into this country to sell to Americans.

Now the teacher makes her first input. She pulls the word from its sentence and writes

importation

and erases "im" and the "ation." To "port" she adds "are" and shows

portare

"This word means to carry, and that's what your answers implied. All the products we talked about were carried into this country—by boat or perhaps by air. What other words can you think of that have root *port* in them and have something to do with carrying?

"Who carries your bag at the airport?" Response: porter.

"What's a small version of a television set called?" Response: portable.

An alternative method to erasing the prefix and suffix would be to circle the root word.

The teacher has tried to establish meaning for the word *importation* by relating the word to students' everyday lives. Hopefully the meaning for the word as it is used in the example has been *discovered* by the students, and someone other than the brightest students in the class will be able to discuss what the word means in the context of the sentence on the blackboard. Then it is necessary for the teacher to take the discussion back to the word in the sentence for closure.

Art

How might an art teacher use **Talk Through** to discover what students already know about what might seem to be an unknown word to them? The word *aquarelle* lends itself well to **Talk Through**.

> Aquarelle describes transparent painting where the white of the paper furnishes the light.

How can the teacher help students remember that *aquarelle* means water color? By eliciting from them what they already know about

1. Aquarius—sign of the Zodiac—water bearer
2. aquaplane
3. aquarium
4. aqualung—scuba diving

When students have a mind set on the association between *aqua* and *water,* the art teacher would get closure by taking their attention back to the sentence and the word *aquarelle.*

Science

An example of the way a science teacher might use **Talk Through** and the pump-primers she might use as questions focus on the word *insulators* in this sentence:

> A house whose walls and roofs contain insulators will hold heat in and keep fuel bills lower.

She elicits responses about the function of

1. clothing
2. acoustical tile in the auditorium

3. island—and how it differs from a peninsula. (The word *insulate* comes from *insula,* the Latin word for island.)

Then back to the word *insulators* in the context of the sentence to make the relationship.

Industrial and Vocational Arts

One of his jobs in the bindery was to spot-check the quality of the <u>spines</u>.

Where in students' everyday world could the printing teacher go to help students make the association between what they already know about *spines* and *spines* as the word is used in the sentence?

1. vertebrae—and why we have them
2. spineless person—lacking courage, no backbone
3. framework of a cactus

The relationship to *spine* that holds a book upright becomes clear. In this instance, the word *spine* probably is not an unknown word to students, but its explanation in a new context is necessary.

Mathematics

Any quantity may be <u>substituted</u> for its equal.

For the sake of illustration, assume that the math teacher has already helped the students with the concept of quantity. If he was introducing the concept of *substitute,* he might wish to question students about the word used to describe a teacher who takes the class when he is absent, about one player going into the basketball game to replace another, about using sweet milk and vinegar in a recipe that calls for buttermilk.

Health

What kinds of questions might a health teacher use to elicit from students what they already know about the word *disinfection?*

Carbolic acid was used for the <u>disinfection</u> of surgical instruments.

How can the teacher use students' strengths to establish a relationship between their everyday lives and the word that means destroying germs? The teacher might ask students why chlorine is used in swimming pools; why they use a medicated spray when they have a cut; why public swimming pools require swimmers to walk through a foot bath before entering the water.

Talk Through is a technique for helping students make a relationship between what they already know and a word which might be unknown or hazy to them, or which might have multiple meanings. To present a word to a class and ask a volunteer or a bright student to give the meaning does not make this relationship. Such a technique does not encourage students to discover relationships, nor does it build on the strengths of many students. **Talk Through** links the known with the unknown.

WHO DREAMED THAT WORD UP?

Just as the **Talk Through** technique is based on the psychological principle of paired association, so is **Who Dreamed That Word Up?** In the latter exercise an unknown or new word is paired with the story, often amusing, of its origin. The teacher arranges for students to have some experience with the history of the word, banking on the story being recalled when the student meets the word in print and is able to bring meaning to it.

For example, if you did not know the word *mnemonic,* would it help if you were told this story? Mnemon was a companion of Achilles, the man with the vulnerable heel who supposedly also had a memory problem. The main reason Achilles kept Mnemon around was to be his memory. Mnemon, in fact, means mind or memory, thus our word *mnemonic.*

Hopefully you would be reminded of this story when you saw the visual stimulus *mnemonic* and would pull the story from your storehouse and be reminded that mnemonic means memory helper. This would be an appropriate word to do **Talk Through** on also: a string around your finger, a note to yourself; these are memory helpers. Amnesia combines *a,* meaning without, and *mne,* memory.

By checking the indexes of the following sources, you can easily find word histories for some of the key concept words in your discipline.

Sources of Word Histories

Asimov, Isaac. *Words from History.* Boston: Houghton Mifflin Co., 1968.

_____. *Words from the Myths.* Boston: Houghton Mifflin Co., 1961.

_____. *Words of Science.* Boston: Houghton Mifflin Co., 1959.

_____. *Words on the Map.* Boston: Houghton Mifflin, 1962.

Blumberg, Dorothy R. *Whose What?* New York: Holt, Rinehart and Winston, 1973.

Evans, Bergen. *Dictionary of Mythology.* Lincoln, Nebraska: Centennial Press, 1970.

Funk, Charles E. *A Hog on Ice.* New York: Paperback Library, 1973.

Funk, Wilfred J. *Word Origins and Their Romantic Stories.* New York: Funk and Wagnalls, 1950.

Garrison, Webb B. *Why You Say It.* New York: Abingdon Press, 1955.

Lambert, Eloise. *Our Language, the Story of the Words We Use.* New York: Lothrop, Lee and Shepard Co., 1955.

Mathews, Mitford. *American Words.* New York: World Publishing Co., 1959.

Morris, William and Mary. *Dictionary of Word and Phrase Origins.* New York: Harper & Row, vol. 1, 1962; vol. 2, 1967; vol. 3, 1971.

Norman, Barbara. *Tales of the Table.* Englewood Cliffs, New Jersey: Prentice-Hall, Inc., 1972.

O'Neill, Mary. *Words, Words, Words.* New York: Doubleday and Co., 1966.

Severn, Bill. *People Words.* New York: Ives Washburn, Inc., 1966.

_____. *Place Words.* New York: Ives Washburn, Inc., 1969.

Sorel, Nancy. *Word People.* New York: American Heritage, McGraw-Hill Co., 1970.

You might want to start accumulating histories of the key words in your subject area and use the stories as mnemonic devices to help students remember. In the following section you will find some examples of these stories.

French

Etiquette

French military orders were always posted in a public place on a piece of paper called an *etiquette.* The word means label, tag, or ticket. Capitalizing on this custom, a gardener to the French court posted etiquettes in the royal gardens to show people where to walk. Visitors obeyed the etiquettes because it was the proper thing to do. And today etiquette means the proper thing to do anywhere.

Restaurant

Would you believe *restaurant* was the name of a soup at one time? The word is a form of the French verb meaning *restore,* and the soup so named was thought to cure ailments. An owner placed the word on the front of his eating establishment to announce that the soup was served there. Today restaurant means a place where all kinds of food are served.

Business

Bankrupt

Long ago in Italy moneylenders set up benches in the marketplace at which they did business with their customers. The Italian word for bench is *banca.* If his financial venture went under, the lender literally broke his bench as a sign that he no longer was in business. The Latin word for break is *ruptura;* thus *banca* + *ruptura* equals bankrupt.

Affluent

There's a country saying, "Them what's got, gits." And the derivation of the word *affluent* lends credence to the saying. The word literally means to flow (*fluere*) toward (*ad* assimilated to *af*).

English

Desultory

In the old Roman circus days, the performer who jumped from one horse to another was called the *desultor,* meaning a person who leaps. Thus today a desultory person is one who rambles in his or her conversation, jumping from one topic to another.

Maverick

Old Sam Maverick, a Texas rancher in the 1800s, had a soft heart, so soft, in fact, that he refused to brand his cattle. Cattle rustlers dubbed the unmarked stock *mavericks.* The label has been transferred to people who are different, out of the ordinary.

Physical Education

Amateur

Students usually know that professionals get paid and *amateurs* do not, but do not know why the label *amateur* is used to describe their standing. Perhaps that's because fewer students enroll in Latin classes these days. Amo, amas, amat—I love, you love, he, she, it loves—provide the basis for *amateur,* one who participates for the love of the game itself.

Muscle

What animal does *muscle* bring to mind? The French thought the rippling of a muscle was akin to the scurrying of a mouse and borrowed the Latin word *muscalus,* meaning little mouse.

Social Studies

Conspirator

This is an interesting word especially in light of politics and government in the 1970s—the word *conspirator* is made up of the root word taken from the Latin *spirare,* meaning to breathe, and the prefix *con,* meaning together. Truly conspirators breathe together, are of one accord. Sometimes they "sing" together too.

Capital Punishment

Originally capital punishment meant death by one means only: severing the head from its body. The Latin word for head (*caput*) is the base for the term. Today the meaning of capital punishment has been broadened to include execution by any means.

Person and Place Words

Certain words are part of the specialized vocabulary of your subject area because of a person's name, others because of place of origin. Sharing your knowledge with students as part of your regular presentations will help them remember the words and their meanings. The memory device of paired association will be at work.

A tyro in the area of science or health education having trouble with the word *pasteurize* or *pasteurella,* for instance, might remember it if he connected it with Dr. Louis *Pasteur,* the French bacteriologist who discovered a process that destroys certain microorganisms.

A student in sheet metal shop might have less difficulty with the word *galvanize* if she knew about Luigi *Galvani,* the Italian physiologist.

Undoubtedly there would be fewer diners ordering "ropefort" cheese if one of their teachers had thought to explain that it was in *Roquefort,* a town in southern France, that the cheese was first made. The names of many cheeses are place words: Camembert (Normandy), Gouda (Holland), Limburger (Belgium).

Caesarean section must indeed be a strange phrase to health education students. Would it be more understandable if it were understood as a surgical operation supposedly performed at the birth of Julius *Caesar?*

An art student might be particularly adept with the *silhouette* and yet have difficulty with its spelling. He might earn high marks in both instances if he knew that the art form got its name from Etienne de *Silhouette,* a French minister of finance in the 1700s who was accused of "shady" deals.

Literature and drama students might have a better understanding of *bowdlerize* (meaning to modify parts considered vulgar) if they knew about Thomas *Bowdler* (1754–1825) who had the effrontery to publish an edition of Shakespeare without some of the bard's indelicate words.

And everyone interested in the women's liberation movement should know about Nicolas *Chauvin* whose blind and vociferous devotion to the

Napoleonic cause stamped his surname on all who unreasonably champion a cause; chauvinists, in other words.

These word origins are just a few examples found in the books given as references. If your curiosity is piqued, ask your librarian to buy several of them and start doing your homework. Dividends for students also can result from the purchase of dictionaries that devote generous space to word origins. When students pair the story behind a word and the word itself, the two are stored in the memory bank together. When the visual stimulus is met again in printed form, the pair is retrieved together. Remembering the story; students bring meaning to the word.

In the student section of this book there are some suggestions for activities in which students can involve themselves and each other in the stories behind words.

BLORDS

In addition to unknown words, or words for which students might have a different referent, another type of vocabulary that can block comprehension is one word that is manufactured from two or more words, such as an acronym or a blend, renamed blords, a portmanteau word that rhymes with cords. Students enjoy creating bl(ending) (w)ords.

Acronyms

An *acronym* is a pronounceable word formed from the beginning letters or groups of letters in words that make up a phrase. For example, scuba is a word created from the phrase, s(elf) c(ontained) u(nderwater) b(reathing) a(pparatus). Fubar represents f(ouled) u(p) b(eyond) a(ll) r(ecognition). Often newly formed organizations name themselves by first finding an appropriate acronym and then expanding it to words. How else could they fit the organization's objective so perfectly? Consider FEAST, Food Education and Service Training program. Or BIRP, Beverage Industry Recycling Program, an organization whose objective is to reclaim used bottles and cans.

Teachers who are concerned about students' comprehension will incorporate teaching the meaning of the various acronyms into their lesson plans because comprehension actually is hidden in the parts of the phrases that were dropped when the acronym was created. Note that in *sonar,* for example, it is in the letters one does not see that the principle lies: so(und) na(vigation) r(anging). Perhaps some teachers are so familiar with the meanings of acronyms in their field that they neglect the good teaching practice of letting students in on the secret. Theoretically, acronyms are mnemonic devices, memory helpers, but in practice the reverse is true if teachers do not intentionally teach their meanings.

The vocabulary of many subject areas includes acronyms. Which of these examples are used in the course you teach?

Examples of Acronyms

- Alcan Highway—Al(aska) Can(ada)
- Alcoa—Al(uminum) Co(mpany of) A(merica)
- Amerind—Amer(ican) Ind(ian)
- Gestapo—Ge(heime) Sta(ats) Po(lizei) which translates secret state police
- coth—cot(angent) h(yperbolic)
- CARE—C(ooperative for) A(merican) R(emittances to) E(verywhere)
- napalm—na(phthene) palm(itate)
- Nazi—Na(tional So) zi(alist)
- hifi—hi(gh) fi(delity)
- SALT—S(trategic) A(rms) L(imitation) T(alks)
- ASCAP—A(merican) S(ociety of) C(omposers) A(uthors and) P(ublishers)
- Rand—r(esearch) an(d) d(evelopment)
- rococo—ro(cailles) co(quilles et) co(rdeau) which translates rocks, shells, string
- sial—si(lica and) al(uminum)
- sima—si(lica and) ma(gnesium)
- Univac—Univ(ersal) A(utomatic) C(omputer)
- zip—z(one) i(mprovement) p(rogram)
- vat—v(alue) a(dded) t(axes)
- M*A*S*H*—m(obile) a(rmy) s(urgical) h(ospital)
- cyborg—cyb(ernetic) org(anism)
- denim—(serge) de Nim(es) which translates serge from Nimes (France)

- flak—Fl(ieger) a(bwehr) k(anone) which translates aircraft defense cannon
- juco—ju(nior) co(llege)
- camp—c(ompanies) a(gencies) m(arkets) p(ositions)
- amphetamine—a(lpha) m(ethyl) phe(nyl) et(hyl) amine
- amtrac—am(phibious) trac(tor)
- Euromart—Euro(pean) mar(ke)t
- Tass—T(elegrafnoye) A(genstvo) S(ovyetskovo) S(oyuza) which translates Telegraph Agency of the Soviet Union

Blends

A *blend*, or portmanteau word, is very similar to an acronym in that it represents a blend of sounds and meanings of other words. In fact, many people call it an acronym. The difference lies in the type of merger. While an acronym is made up of the first letters of several words, a blend usually is composed of the beginning portion of one word and the ending of another. Sometimes it is formed from the beginning of one word and a whole word. Both blends and acronyms can be hindrances to comprehension until their meaning is made clear from the portions of the words that have been dropped.

The most famous blend probably is *brunch,* which is a combination of br(eakfast) and (l)unch. Which of these examples are part of the language of your course?

Examples of Blends

- Calexico—Cal(ifornia) (M)exico
- contrail—con(densation) trail
- Medicaid—medic(al) aid
- smaze—sm(oke) (h)aze
- smust—sm(oke) (d)ust
- Twissors—tw(eezers) (sc)issors
- arcology—arc(hitecture) (ec)ology
- twinight—twi(light) night
- telecast—tele(vision) (broad)cast
- quasar—quas(i) (stell)ar
- albeit—al(though) it be

- riboflavin—ribo(se) flavin
- agribusiness—agri(culture) business
- aquaculture—aqua (agri)culture
- splatter—spl(ash) (sp)atter
- motel—mo(tor) (ho)tel
- twirl—tw(ist) (wh)irl
- flurry—fl(utter) (h)urry
- radwaste—rad(io active) waste

You can get assistance in identifying acronyms and blends used in the language of your discipline from several sources.

Sources of Acronyms and Blends

Crowley, Ellen T. and Robert C. Thomas, eds. *Acronyms and Initialisms Dictionary.* Detroit: Gale Research Co., 1970.

Kleiner, Richard. *Index of Initials and Acronyms.* Princeton, N.J.: Auerbach Publishing Co., 1971.

Moser, Reta C. *Space-age Acronyms.* IFI/Flenum Press, 1969.

Pugh, Eric. *A Dictionary of Acronyms and Abbreviations.* Hamden, Conn.: Archon Books, 1970.

Spillner, Paul. *World Guide to Abbreviations.* New York: Bowker, 1970.

As frequently as the media use manufactured words, it would seem advisable that all teachers of all subjects help students remove obstacles to comprehension by teaching language per se.

Students can help themselves too. Some suggestions are offered in part II, *Activities for Learning Content through Language.*

SLIPPERY WORDS

Slippery words are those that have multiple meanings. If concepts ride on the backs of words, and learning rides on the backs of concepts, it's easy to see how incorrect concepts for words can block learning. *The Random House Dictionary of the English Language,* for example, lists 178 mean-

Added financial burden is feared

Counties urge state funding of Medicaid

Arizona county officials told legislators Thursday that if they want Medicaid they should make it a state program and not look to the counties for funds.

The county officials said that they support the concept of Medicaid, which provides medical care to the poor, but that current proposals for salvaging the program pose too many questions.

They s added fir ties, brin tion for

Related story on Page B-1

still leave the counties with a sizable number of poor persons to care for.

Rep. Burton Barr, R-Phoenix, House majority leader and chairman of the daylong meeting, told the officials that they had

id questions
ry to work

edicaid and
vorked out,
aid the

Gov. Raul Castro started the meeting by pledging his support to Medicaid and urging county officials to keep an open mind.

"We need to see what we can do to preserve this legislation," he said.

Dr. A
on finan
for the
keep
progr
millio
is not
To
wou'
pro'

a legislative expert
rogram

.9
ite

, it
s to
but

Out for insurance

Juco leaders hunt state race security

By GREG LOGAN

Security problems confront Scottsdale Community College and Central Arizona College as the team leaders of their respective in the Arizona C College Athletic prepare for imp bleheaders on Saturday.

Defending AC Scottsdale hold pears to be a three-game le talent-rich Va while Central game cushion become a tw the State Divi

Robbins (3-2) have been Glendale's pitching stoppers, but freshman Gary Hillery from Agua Fria is just beginning to live up to poten in Boetto's

Panel favors Eximbank on U.S. budget

Associated Press

WASHINGTON — The House Banking Committee voted Thursday to put the Export-Import Bank back under the unified budget where Congress can scrutinize its loan decisions.

The committee voted 17 to 15 to reverse a 1971 decision which removed the Eximbank from the federal budget.

Conigliaro aiming in Bosox comeback

BOSTON (AP)—Tony Conigliaro, who made a fabulous comeback after a severe beaning in 1967, tries again today with the Boston Red Sox after being out of baseball for three years.

"Now the fun starts," Conigliaro said, looking ahead to the American League opener with the Milwaukee Brew

"My eyesight is excellent shape. I fe rarin' to g

Euromart protests uranium delay

Figure 2. *Examples of Words Manufactured by the Media.*

ings for the simple word *run.* Although *Random House* offers only 115 meanings for the word *set,* a recent newspaper article reported that over 200 meanings have now been attached to the word.

In many instances, perhaps in most, slippery words are short, simple words—words teachers easily could overlook as hindrances to comprehension.

Bookkeeping

In bookkeeping, for example, the word *gross* could easily block understanding if the student has a frame of reference different from that of the teacher. (In fact, the teacher has two legitimate meanings within the context of bookkeeping itself: gross, meaning with no deductions, as opposed to net; gross, meaning 144 items, or twelve dozen.) On hearing or seeing the word *gross,* a student automatically might think of its meaning in youth jargon, something negative as in "You wouldn't date her! She's gross!" Another student's referent might be the act of being uncouth, unrefined, without manners. Another might think of something large or massive. When none of their ideas are compatible with the meaning of the word in bookkeeping, what happens to comprehension?

Home Economics

In foods and clothing classes there are many slippery words. Consider the word *Capri.* Is it an automobile? An island? a wine? Or a pair of pants? Or consider the word *tack.* Is it a short nail? A stitch? A fastening? Stickiness? One of the many nautical meanings? Gear worn by a horse, like saddle and bridle? A course of conduct? Food, as in *hardtack?*

If teachers were psychic, they could intuit the concept(s) individual students have for words. As it is, their own expertise with vocabulary causes them to make many fallacious assumptions. Too often the terms they use are not clarified.

Slippery words build a pretty good case for teaching students how to use context clues, a means to figure out the meaning for a word from other words in the sentence or paragraph. If the goal is teaching students how to fish rather than giving them a fish, teachers will identify context clues, give guidance in their use, and allow practice time.

Another way for the teacher to handle slippery words is to call for all meanings that are known by students in the class. This system might be called a saturation, panoramic, or broad-base approach. It pays dividends to extend students' vocabulary through incidental learning. A teacher who hasn't considered the ego-building of *extension* learning says to a student, "No, that isn't what the word means in this sense," and lets it go at that.

As you call for all meanings, turn to the blackboard or a transparency on an overhead projector and record students' responses. Put the responses on spokes extending from a hub when the meanings given are not what the word means in your course. Put the appropriate response in the hub.

Suspension

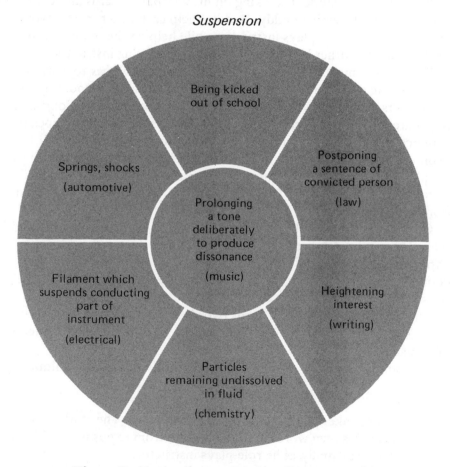

Figure 3. *Music: Suspension is a slippery word.*

BUDDY VOCABULARY CARDS

Although this is a student-oriented activity and you may think it belongs in part II of the handbook, it has a place here because of the teacher's involvement as a facilitator and as a member of one of the dyads.

Students can be quite effective in teaching each other with **Buddy Vocabulary Cards.** You will note that the technique is a variation of a card system that has been in use in classrooms for a long time. The buddy concept was borrowed from recreational swimming, the practice of pairing swimmers, each being responsible for the other's safety, as well as imitative instruction.

Instead of each student working on his vocabulary cards alone, as is the custom, he works with a buddy. Buddies help each other master troublesome words. One role-plays instructor while helping the buddy learn his words. Then the other buddy has his turn role-playing instructor.

Each buddy makes two-sided cards for words he *wishes* to learn. (See Figure 4.) He might find them in the textbook, other classroom materials, newspapers, magazines. The source really does not matter, as long as the words are related to the course. On a 3 X 5″ card he prints or types the sentence in which he found the word and underlines the word. (Note again the emphasis on words in context, not in isolation.) Next he writes the phonetic spelling. He might get it from the dictionary, from a classmate, or from the teacher. This side (side 1) of the card will be the side from which he works.

On the other side of the card (side 2), which will be seen by his buddy, the student again prints the sentence, underlines the word, adds the phonetic spelling. In addition, he writes a meaning for the word. The definition may come from the dictionary, a glossary, a knowledgeable classmate, or the teacher.

The teacher makes a set of cards (words in any area) for his own use. If there is an uneven number of students in the class, he becomes a member of a dyad.

The buddy approach to vocabulary card study has several unique features:

1. Learning takes place on both sides of the card. The student is learning his own words, and the buddy, from exposure to side 2, learns incidentally as he role-plays instructor.
2. "Dumb bunny" stigma is removed. Every student in a class (teacher,

CRAFTS

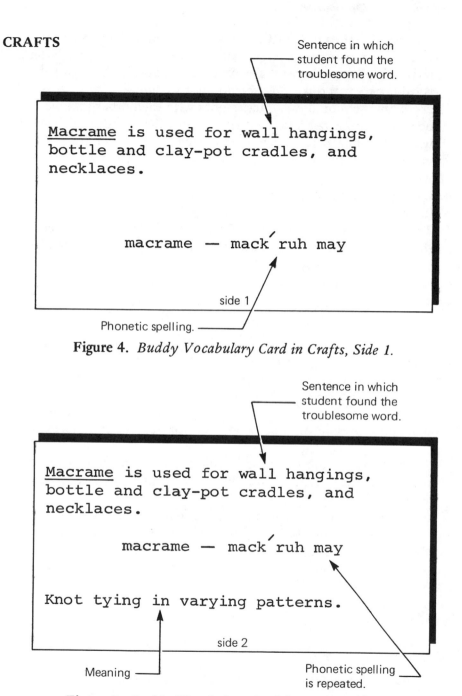

Sentence in which student found the troublesome word.

Macrame is used for wall hangings, bottle and clay-pot cradles, and necklaces.

macrame — mack′ruh may

side 1

Phonetic spelling.

Figure 4. *Buddy Vocabulary Card in Crafts, Side 1.*

Sentence in which student found the troublesome word.

Macrame is used for wall hangings, bottle and clay-pot cradles, and necklaces.

macrame — mack′ruh may

Knot tying in varying patterns.

side 2

Meaning

Phonetic spelling is repeated.

Figure 5. *Buddy Vocabulary Card in Crafts, Side 2.*

23

too) finds some words that are unknown to him. When a bright
student, for example, is paired with an average student, the latter's
self-concept gets a boost. "The smartest student in the class has
vocabulary cards too. So I guess I'm not so dumb."

3. Peers can use methods and techniques with each other that would
   be inappropriate for a teacher to use. For example, peers can get by
   with expressing exasperation that a teacher would suppress. "Come
   on, lunkhead, this is the third time in a row you've missed the same
   word."
4. Buddies learn to deal with each other as human beings as they
   interact.
5. Teacher demonstrates that vocabulary building is a lifelong activity,
   that no one is exempt from bête noires that block comprehension.

WORD PARTS: PREFIXES, ROOTS, SUFFIXES

A valuable skill for unlocking meaning for unknown words is the ability to
dissect, to examine part by part. Teachers who are concerned about
students' comprehension will incorporate teaching the meaning of prefixes, roots, and suffixes into their lesson plans. It is the *use* of word parts
that will deposit meanings in students' storage banks for retrieval as
needed; memorization is not only a poor substitute, but an unnecessary
one.

Many methods are known for improving coping with prefixes, roots,
and suffixes, and many teachers use them. The **Student Booklet** technique
may be one of the lesser known.

The **Student Booklet,** prepared by the content teacher or reading
resource teacher, contains the prefixes, roots, and suffixes important to
understanding the language of the subject. Just as every subject area has a
language of its own, every subject area has its own important prefixes,
roots, and suffixes. In the column following the word part(s) the teacher
puts the meaning(s); next, an example incorporating the part; then a
column for the student's contribution.

Student Booklet Format

Root or Affix	*Meaning*	*Example*	*Your Word*
pseudo	false	pseudoped	

The front cover of the booklet is designed to be a motivational device (see the accompanying example). Four other factors make the booklet attractive to students:

1. It is 5 1/2 inches wide and 8 1/2 inches long (1/2 of an 8 1/2 X 11″ sheet). Reason: this size allows it to fit into the textbook where it should always be kept for handy reference.
2. It is mimeographed rather than dittoed. Reason: poorly dittoed materials do more to dissuade than motivate frequent use.
3. It is printed on colored mimeograph paper. Reason: so it can be easily identified; handouts usually are on white paper.
4. You have gone to a greal deal of work in behalf of their success in your class.

Where do you start? The index of your textbook is a logical guide to the word parts to be emphasized in the **Student Booklet.** From it you choose important vocabulary words that carry the concepts around which your course is built.

An Example of the Student Booklet

A **Student Booklet** for biology class is presented as a guide for teachers of other disciplines and of other science specializations, such as botany, chemistry, and physics.

MICROGLOSSOSCIENTIVERBISECT

Translation:
A Small Glossary of Scientific Word Parts

The Language of Science contains many long, unfamiliar words, but most of these words are a combination of word parts: prefixes, roots, and suffixes. By learning the meanings of some of the common word parts, you will know the meaning of hundreds of unfamiliar words, and it will be easier to understand what you read in science.

Practice making words with the following word parts. An easy way to build your vocabulary and increase your understanding of what you read is by becoming interested in how words are put together and how they are used.

THE LANGUAGE OF SCIENCE:
Some Common Word Roots and Affixes

Root or Affix	Meaning	Example	Your Word
a–, an–	without	anaerobic	
ab–	away from	abnormal	
ad–	to, toward	adhere	
aero–	air	aerobic	
ambi–, amphi–	both	ambidextrous	
ante–	before	anterior	
anthropo–	man, human	anthropology	
anti–	against, opposite	antigen	
aqua–	water	aquatic	
astro–, aster–	star	astronomy	
auto–	self	automatic	
avi–	bird	aviary	
baro–	pressure	barometer	
bene–, bon–	good	benefit	
bi–	two, twice	biped	
bio–	life	biology	
capit, cephalo–	head	decapitate	
cardi(o)–	heart	cardiogram	
carni–, caro–	flesh	carnivorous	
chlor–	green	chloroplast	
chrom–	color	chromatin	
chrono–	time	chronology	
circum–	around	circumference	
com–, con–, co	together, with	combine	
contra–, contro–	against	contraception	
corpus	body	corpse	
cyclo–	circular	cyclotron	
cyto–	cell, hollow	cytoplasm	
dermato–, derm–	skin	epidermis	
di–, dis–	two	dissect	
dorsi–, dorso–	back	dorsal	
entomo–	insect	entomology	
epi–	upon, outer	epidermis	

Root or Affix	Meaning	Example	Your Word
erg–	work	energy	
ex–	out, from	excrete	
eu–	good	euphoria	
frater	brother	fraternal	
gen–	race, kind, born, produce	generation	
geo–	earth	geology	
germ–	sprout	germinate	
graph	write, record	graphite	
gyneco–, gyn	female	gynecology	
helio–	sun	heliograph	
hemi–	half	hemisphere	
hemo–	blood	hemoglobin	
herb	plant	herbivorous	
hetero–	mixed	heterogeneous	
hexa–	six	hexagon	
homo–	same, alike	homogeneous	
hydr(o)–	water	dehydrate	
hyper–	over, excess	hyperactive	
hypo–	under, less	hypodermic	
ichthyo–	fish	ichthyology	
in–	not	insomnia	
in–, en–	into	inbreed	
inter–	between	intercellular	
intra–	within	intramuscular	
iso–	equal	isometric	
–itis	inflammation	tonsillitis	
junct	join	junction	
kine–	movement	kinetic	
lact(o)–	milk	lactic	
–logy	science, study of	biology	
lunar	moon	lunarian	
–lysis, –lyze	break up	analysis	
macro–	large	macroscopic	
magni–	great, large	magnitude	
meta	change, beyond	metaphase	

Root or Affix	Meaning	Example	Your Word
—meter	measure	altimeter	
micro—	small	microscope	
mono—	one, single	monocyte	
morpho—	form	metamorphosis	
mortal, mort—	death	mortality	
multi—	many	multicellular	
natal	birth	postnatal	
nebul	cloudy	nebulous	
neuro—	nerve	neuron	
non—	not	nonnitrogenous	
octo—	eight	octopus	
oculo—, ophthalmo—	eye	oculist	
omni—	all	omnivorous	
ornitho—	bird	ornithology	
ortho—	straight	orthopterous	
osteo—	bone	osteopath	
patho—	disease, feeling	pathology	
pedi—, pod	foot, footed	anthropod	
per—	through	permeate	
phono—	sound, voice	phonograph	
photo—	light	photosynthesis	
physio—	organic	physiology	
poly—	many, much	polyembryony	
pos, pon	place, put	position	
post—	after	postnatal	
pre—	before	prediagnosis	
pseudo—	false	pseudopod	
psycho—	mind	psychology	
pro—	for, forward	procreate	
pteron	winged	lepidoptera	
quad	four	quadruped	
retro—	backward	retroactive	
rhodo	rose, red	rhodolite	
—scope	view, examine	microscope	
sect	part, divide	dissect	

Root or Affix	Meaning	Example	Your Word
som(a)	body	chromosome	
somn	sleep	insomnia	
son(i)–	sound	supersonic	
sphere	round, globe	spherical	
sub–	under	subconscious	
syn–	together, with	synthesis	
tele–	far, distant	telescope	
ten–	to hold	tenaculum	
thermo–	heat	thermometer	
trans–	across	transmutation	
un–	not	undeveloped	
under–	below	underactive	
vita–	life	vitamin	
–vor(e)	eat	herbivorous	
zoo–	animal	zoology	

Your own enthusiasm at the time the **Student Booklet** is given to members of the class is in itself a motivator. The following activities can be employed to impress students with the idea that knowing word parts will help them break down unknown words which may look formidable.

First, it is important that students have the concept of *meaningful word parts.* Flip cards can help establish this concept:

CYCLE	*METER*
BI	SPEEDO
TRI	THERMO
QUADRI	HYDRO
HEXA	ALTI
OCTO	BARO

Using the flip cards, draw the students into a discussion of how meaning changes with different word parts and help them visualize six and eight-wheeled vehicles and different purposes of measuring devices.

Another activity allows students to draw conclusions about the suffix *-logy.* Once it is established that the suffix means the science that deals with a certain discipline, they can see how the element retains its meaning as the root changes:

anthropology	entomology	ornithology
astrology	genealogy	osteology
biology	hemotology	pathology
cardiology	hydrology	physiology
chronology	ichthyology	psychology
cytology	microbiology	zoology

In addition, you should break down a few words, helping students piece together meanings of parts to produce a whole and referring to the same parts as they operate in the everyday world:

antiseptic: anti/septic
             an agent that stops growth of bacteria outside the body

anti against
          (antimissile, antifreeze)
septic infected with bacteria
          (septic sore throat, septic tank)

The teacher follows up the original presentation of the material in the **Student Booklet** by giving students frequent opportunities:

1. To refer to the booklet as words are encountered in lessons.
2. To make up titles for lab sheets.
3. To coin new vocabulary words for specific topics, for scientific phenomena yet to be discovered, such as *astro*psychology.
4. To write science fiction stories incorporating scientific pseudo terminology.
5. To work through student activities on prefixes, roots, and suffixes, similar to those found in part II of this book.

CHAPTER 2

Teacher Strategies for Generating Understanding

Developing strategies for helping students understand the vocabulary of a subject field is a vital teacher function. Preplanning tactics and building them into lesson plans certainly are expedients for promoting better student understanding of the language of a content area. They are better ways to assist learning, but not maximal use of potential.

Vocabulary is just one facet of language. The second aspect involves more than just a body of words; it embraces a writer's scheme for using words to accomplish his or her purpose for communicating.

In order to interact with an author readers must have skills enabling them to identify the author's scheme for stringing words together, think it through, and arrive at some conclusions. This task demands that readers go beyond just coping with words and phrases. Conceptualization of sentences, paragraphs, short and long pieces of writing is required. All of your students will need help with the task some of the time; some of them all of the time.

That some teachers do not give this help is both tragic and deplorable. It is tragic from the standpoint that some learners spend six or seven periods a day, five days a week spurning the printed word instead of learning with it; it is deplorable from the standpoint that without needed help during their school years odds are that they will continue to ignore or misuse the printed word as a resource for data-gathering and pleasure in adult years. Generally these instructors are "straight content teachers." If there are students in the room who do not have the skills for ferreting out this content, that's too bad. They can sit in the back of the room and be quiet.

Teachers who couple *process* with content build into their classroom behaviors, methods, and techniques for generating comprehension of the ways in which writers string words together. They identify techniques for coping with an author, give guidance in the use of the techniques, and allow students practice time with *process and content.*

Undoubtedly you are using the process/content approach to teaching or you would not have progressed this far into the book. You might wish to add some of the following strategies to your repertory of teaching behaviors.

BRIEFING FOR READING ASSIGNMENTS*

"Read chapter 3 tonight. We'll have a quiz tomorrow."

"For tomorrow read the next three short stories."

"We'll start class tomorrow in the lab, so read the experiment thoroughly before then."

"We're going to begin a new sport tomorrow: volleyball. I've mimeographed the rules for you, so be sure to read them."

Do teachers give reading assignments in this manner? A spot check of students would confirm that many teachers do. They teach assumptively. When they give a reading assignment, they assume students know or can figure out the key vocabulary. They assume students can determine essential concepts. They assume students can answer trivial, as well as significant, questions once they have read the assigned material. And most

---

*Adapted from Dorothy Piercey, "Briefing for Reading Assignments," *Reading Improvement 9* (1972): 10–12. Reprinted with permission.

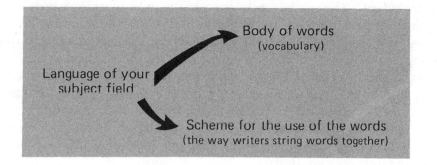

Figure 6. *The Two-Fold Structure of the Concept of Language.*

important of all, they assume students have built-in motivation for doing the reading.

It is possible, in fact probable, that upper-level teachers were not taught in education methods classes either to prepare students for reading or how to do it. However, some method of readying readers should precede every assignment if teachers are committed to successful experiences for students.

The method offered here is called **Briefing,** a concept borrowed from the military and the sales world. Briefing is done in advance, prior to an aircraft crew's taking off, prior to the sales representative's contact with prospective buyers. In both instances the briefing involves ammunition for success.

To give students ammunition for success with a reading assignment, the teacher helps them with:

1. vocabulary in the upcoming reading,
2. concepts they will meet as they read,
3. the purpose for reading, and
4. enthusiasm

Briefing Precedes Reading

Before sending them out on a reading assignment the teacher briefs the students on:

1. Vocabulary.   The teacher seeks out what may be blocking words. They may be new or once-learned words that have been forgotten. **Talk Through** is a technique for helping students learn vocabulary words during **Briefing** so that learners will know them when they meet them in the reading assignment. **Talk Through,** explained step by step in *Teacher Strategies for Vocabulary Development,* calls for the teacher to do some homework. The objective is to relate unknown words to what students already know so they can capitalize on the association. Homework involves making notes on student knowledge and experiences that can be tied to the unknown vocabulary.

2. Concepts.   Just as the teacher selects important vocabulary words in the upcoming reading, he identifies those concepts intended to be conveyed from the writer to the reader. When the teacher gets into the habit of talking through unknown words, he will see value in using the same procedure for helping students understand concepts. He can talk concepts through just as he does unknown or slippery words.

3. Purpose-setting.   Questioning is the key to purpose-setting. The teacher sets up questions, and, armed with those questions, the student reads for a purpose—to find answers.

The idea of giving questions to students in advance is sometimes disturbing to teachers and students alike, but in both instances, the reaction is only conditioning at work. Questions are that "stuff" of which tests are made. Questions and testing have been partners for so long that it takes a change in mind-set to be comfortable with the concept of giving, on the part of the teacher, and receiving, on the part of the students, questions in advance.

Questions aren't meant to be kept in locked drawers; they belong out in the open to be used for a very important function: giving the student a purpose for which to read. "Read chapter 3 tonight" is no purpose for reading unless that purpose is to please teacher, a worthless raison d'être.

It makes sense for the teacher to formulate questions. After all, it is he who knows his own objectives; it is he who, by reason of his expertise in the subject area, knows the few important concepts hidden in the wordiness of many authors; it is he who knows the importance of the process of learning, as opposed to the product of learning.

How many questions are needed to set purpose? Certainly not as many as authors put at the end of their chapters. It is the contention of this writer that authors do not intend teachers to hold students accountable for twenty to twenty-five questions; they intend teachers to *select* from that number. Unfortunately, some teachers even ask students to write out the answers to all of the questions. The number of questions is relative to the teacher's objective. One might be enough for a short piece of poetry.

What kinds of questions should be used as guides to students' reading? In most instances, the teacher should draw from all levels of comprehension—literal, interpretive, critical, creative—and formulate some questions at each level.

If the teacher asks only literal-level questions, then students are confined to literal thinking as they read. This type of question is the easiest to formulate and the easiest to evaluate, and too many teachers fall into the literal trap. Answers are either right or wrong: 1492, not 1493, is the year Columbus discovered America; Louis Pasteur is the father of vaccines, not Louis Armstrong; three teaspoons, not two, are the equivalent of a tablespoon. Some literal-level questions, and therefore answers, should be included because they are the base on which to build interpretive, critical, and creative questions, and therefore answers. Literal-level questions guide the reader to what the author said.

To lift the level of comprehension, the teacher also suggests questions that get at the how and why of things, questions that cause the student to read between the lines, to ferret out what the author has implied rather than stated. If the how and why are stated in the text, how and why questions are literal level. If the how and why must be pieced together, reasoned through, and synthesized, this type of question is interpretive.

The teacher lifts the level of comprehension again when he or she includes a question(s) in the critical area, a question that causes students to evaluate against a standard and make a judgment. Values come into play at the critical level. The key for students to learn before they make a judgment is that judgments are based on data (literal level) and evidence, not on whim. This important key, if internalized, will be used to their advantage for a lifetime.

The highest level of comprehension in the model discussed here is the creative position, the top of the hierarchy. Creative questions allow students to operate in the affective as well as the cognitive domain. They require the student to put himself into the situation in order to apply, relate, predict, and offer a better solution to a problem.

4. Enthusiasm. A fourth, and exceedingly important, factor involved in **Briefing** is the teacher's enthusiasm, the degree of which will come through to students via voice and facial expressions. If the teacher is interested, eager, and impressed with what is to be learned in the reading assignment, this mind-set comes through to the students. If he or she is bored, matter-of-fact, or listless during the **Briefing**, this mind-set will come through too.

Briefing Is Teaching

Briefing is teaching. In fact, the dictionary says that to brief is to prepare in advance by instructing or advising. Like all good teaching, briefing can't be done in a minute or two or even three. It might take twenty to twenty-five minutes to brief for a difficult assignment. And those minutes might well be the best teaching the teacher has done all day. Pay dirt for the teacher includes the demonstration of better comprehension and increased participation. Pay dirt for the students includes self-satisfaction and a feeling of success.

In summary, students have a better than even chance of comprehending reading assignments if teachers prepare them by:

1. Talking through troublesome vocabulary words (see **Talk Through**),
2. Talking through concepts,
3. Setting a purpose by giving students questions in advance (no. 3 requires teachers to bone up on their questioning skills), and
4. Setting the pace with enthusiasm and eagerness.

QUESTIONING*

Teachers are not only obliged to improve their own questioning skills, but they should also be committed to passing on the skills to their charges. It is understandable why questioning skills are not students' strong points. As a rule, school is a place where teachers ask the questions and students try to give the right answers.

*Adapted from a speech by Dorothy Piercey, "Questioning Strategies in Reading," at the Fourth Annual Conference, Western College Reading Association, Los Angeles, April 3, 1971; printed in *Proceedings* 4 (1971): 107–12.

But once the student is out of school, who's to ask the questions? Having been nurtured on even the improved questioning of teachers which motivates him to think at deeper levels, will he be able to continue thinking deeply when no one asks him questions, when no one provides the stimulus to which he is supposed to respond? School occupies only from 10 to 23 or 24 percent of a person's life. Without anyone to ask him questions for the remaining 70 to 80 percent of his life span which constitutes adulthood, do the higher thinking processes that the teacher-questioner tried to stimulate begin to debilitate, grow flabby and weak? Can a student become a sponge soaking up what any typewriter-beater turns out? Does teacher improvement in the skill of questioning make questioners of students? If so, how? by osmosis? by contagion? by imitation? Probably not any way.

Direct Training Needed

Surely the training in questioning strategies stops short if it stops with the teacher. By passing on the expertise of questioning, the how and the why of the skill, students will be let in on the secret too. If the teacher identifies the art of questioning as a learning technique, guides students in its use, and arranges the environment so they can practice it, the school might be changed from a place where students are taught to answer to a place where students also learn to question, both as they listen and as they read; they may learn to question in order to investigate, to reason, to make decisions, to solve problems.

Three, four, and five year olds are quite good at questioning. By the age of five they are well on their way to being pros. They are walking question marks. What happens to their curiosity, their growing facility to question? How is it that after a few semesters in school, children perceive that to ask a question is to stand nakedly ignorant before the rest of the class, indeed the rest of the world?

To reteach students the art of questioning is to reverse the educational practice:

Students = Answerers
Teachers = Questioners

To reteach is to help students become adults who will spend the rest of their lives questioning as they read. Having competency in questioning gives readers greater management over the printed word designed to exert influence. Because students have had years of conditioning in becoming answerers instead of questioners, their retraining might not be easy. It can be done by working on the learning principle that

> **When a skill is identified,**
> > **given guidance, and**
> > **provided practice time,**
> **growth takes place.**

The *first* job then is to identify for students the skill of questioning as a way of understanding a writer, as a way of pinpointing a writer's purpose, as a way of synthesizing what a writer says into ideas and concepts, as a way of evaluating an author's ideas, as a way of making judgments, as a way of formulating alternate solutions to problems posed in print. Good readers search among a writer's words to find what he is thinking and/or what he wishes the reader to think. Good readers search with questions.

Dialogue with a Book

Share this dialogue between a book and a reader* with students to get the idea of questioning across.

Book: Won't you please ask me a question?

Man: Why do you ask?

Book: Because I can only ask you to ask me questions and can only answer the questions you ask.

Man: Why don't you just tell me what you have to say?

Book: I can't. I have nothing to tell you except answers to your questions.

Man: Haven't you the same thing to say to every reader, all put down in black and white?

Book: No! I never say the same thing twice. Black letters on white paper are nothing in themselves. You can only read meaning, and so much of that is in you. You never ask the same ques-

---

*By Helen Rand Miller, from Helen Rand Miller and John J. DeBoer, *Creative Reading* (Seymour, Indiana: Graessle-Mercer Co., 1951), pp. 12–13. Reprinted with permission of Graessle-Mercer Co.

tion twice because you are living and that means changing all the time. Your experiences and your interests grow if you are alive.

Man: I'll read you from cover to cover; I'll read every word. I won't miss a thing. I'll pass an examination on you!

Book: Oh, vain, stupid, foolish, little man, to say that you will get out of me all that is in me. You can't. There is nothing in me except as you bring me to life in your living mind, imagination, and heart.

Man: So you don't live except as you live with living people?

Book: That's right. Nothing does. You don't yourself.

Man: But how can I ask you questions before I know what you have to say?

Book: Use your brain. Think of what I might be able to tell you. I didn't say that you had to ask all your questions before you began to read. Let's have a little cooperation. Ask me one question at a time and look for my answer. Keep on asking questions as you read. Think ahead as you look ahead when you drive your car. What happens when you don't know where you are driving? It's your responsibility to ask the questions that will let me be at my best in answering you.

Man: I don't always want to work when I read. Sometimes I just want to enjoy my reading. I'd like to relax while you entertain me.

Book: And I want you to enjoy yourself whether you are working or just enjoying yourself. You'll have more fun if you are a bit companionable. It won't tire you to go along with a character and ask, "Does he love me? Will he come?"

Man: So I must play along with the characters in a story I'm reading for pleasure.

Book: Of course, if you are to share their pleasure. If you don't do your part, you let me down.

Man: And what if you don't answer the questions I want answered?

Book: Then I let you down. Don't waste your time and wear me out unless I have what you want.

Man: Don't I have to read you to find out whether you have what I want?

> *Book:*   No, not if you know how to have a good look at me.
> *Man:*   So, I must learn to ask questions?
> *Book:*   Yes, everything depends upon that.

The *second* job is to demonstrate for students how questioning is done, in order to derive maximum learning—much as a golf pro demonstrates body movements for effecting the best drive.

The *third* step is to arrange the environment so students can practice the skill of questioning. This third step raises something of a problem for teachers. The ultimate objective is to help students reach the point where they question writers as they read. Questioning writers is a somewhat difficult and complex concept because writers usually are people the reader does not know, and the reader has to interact from a distance. Therefore students should begin their practice by questioning themselves. The plan is to telescope questioning skills from self to peers and other people known by the student, then to writers, unknown persons whose ideas the student can know only through the printed word, whether the author wrote the words last night for this morning's newspaper or wrote them centuries ago.

The plan is to introduce the skill of questioning by asking students to apply questioning strategies to the present that revolves around them— much as fledgling reporters are trained to observe, to deal in evidence, to weigh sources, to describe, to report, to interpret, to spot assumptions, to evaluate against a standard, to make judgments, to predict, and to work with parts to see if they fit into a jigsaw of events. Some suggested categories of questions are presented in the model. The labels certainly are not sacred cows. Their use is for the purpose of holding concepts still long enough for students to take a look at them. They, or other categories the teacher might create, are directly teachable.

> **At Stage I the student initiates his practice by questioning himself, first using the sample questions offered and then by creating his own questions in each of the categories.**
>
> **When he achieves some skill in questioning himself, he moves to Stage II and practices questioning his peers, acquaintances, and other people he knows, again creating additional questions in each of the categories.**
>
> **When he acquires some facility at this level, he is ready to apply his skill by questioning writers and others outside his sphere of personal cognizance.**

*Telescoping Questioning from Self, to Knowns, to Unknowns**

Categories of Questions	STAGE I	STAGE II	STAGE III
	Sample Questions for Yourself	Sample Questions for Peers, Other Knowns	Sample Questions for Writers, Other Unknowns
DESCRIPTIVE	What is it like? What kind of a situation is it? What do I see? Smell?	In Stage II student shifts emphasis from "I" to "you" and practices questioning in the various categories with peers and other knowns in his life.	STUDENT AUTHOR
COMPARATIVE	How are two or more things different or alike?		By Stage III the student's practice in questioning himself, peers and other knowns has established the concept that while reading he questions an author in like manner.
HISTORICAL	How did things get the way they are? What's behind what I see?	For example, in the experimental-methodological category, questions would be "How could *you* test your guess? How could *you* explain this to someone else?"	
CAUSAL	What is the reason for such a thing? Why? What is the result? Why do I believe this or that is true? Why does this make sense to me?		

*This schema is an adaptation and extension of the work of Dr. S.N. Cummings, Arizona State University, and is used with her permission.

Telescoping Questioning from Self, to Knowns, to Unknowns—continued

	STAGE I	STAGE II	STAGE III
EXPERIMENTAL-METHODOLOGICAL	How could I test my guess? How could I find out? How could I do this? How could I explain this to someone else?		For example, in the causal category, questions would be "What is the reason *the author* gives for such a thing? Why does *the author* believe this or that is true?"
PREDICTIVE	What will it be like ten years from now for me?		
EVALUATIVE	What is good, better, best? What do I like about it? What do I dislike about it? What yardstick am I using?	STUDENT PEER	
APPLICATIVE-CREATIVE	How is this relevant to my situation? How can this be changed to fit my situation? How would I have done this?		

The third level is the reward, both for the student and for teachers committed to helping students become lifelong questioners of the printed word.

MAIN IDEA

Improvement in the art of questioning the ideas in an author's work enhances comprehension skills since answers to self-imposed questions serve to lay before the reader both the manner of stringing words together and the writer's purpose for doing so.

One comprehension skill which may need additional teaching and learning is the ability to separate the main idea from supporting details. It is not surprising that students have difficulty with this skill, considering evidence that reports the inefficiency of many adults.

Part of the difficulty of coping with a main idea lies in the fuzziness of the concept itself, perhaps induced by the label *main idea.* Some textbooks and workbooks explain the term *main* by equally fuzzy words like *important* or *principal,* both relative concepts. A student-directed question often used is "What did the author say?" Well, the author said a lot of things, and often the student trying to answer the question is in limbo.

What makes sense to students often unblocks impasses that prevent learning. What students can see operating in their everyday world can be used as a bridge into the school world. Two groups of people who are masters at capsulizing main ideas are telegram senders, who are short on funds, and newspaper headline writers, who are short on space. Role-playing these experts' tasks can be a technique for improving recognition and identification of main ideas.

When introducing the telegraph activity, the teacher should try to use the actual form used in telegraph offices. A local agent probably would supply one for each student when told what they were to be used for. An alternative would be to ditto copies even though facsimiles are not as effective as the actual form. The teacher announces the current rate per word and students write a telegram communicating the main idea of a paragraph, article, chapter, or book.

Limited by space and motivated to catch readers' attention, headline writers are adept at serving main ideas in a nutshell. With practice students become more adept at it too. After the teacher demonstrates how newspaper writers concisely summarize a story into a headline, students try their hand at it, using newspaper stories they have brought from home from which the teacher has detached headlines. A local editor probably would be willing to spend a period with students discussing how he or she goes about writing headlines. The next step is to write headlines, limited to a specified word count. incorporating the main idea of a paragraph, article, chapter, or book.

Both of these activities help get across the concept of main idea. They make sense to students; they are behaviors pursued by real people; they are nontextbook-oriented.

MAIN IDEA IN FICTION

Getting the main idea from a novel seems to be the most difficult of all reading tasks for some students, perhaps because there are so many words and pages. To reduce a large work to a sentence of twenty-five or thirty words seems a ponderous task. How often have you asked a student for the main idea of a book only to hear a long and involved explanation of the story plot?

Students with whom the following teaching technique was used nicknamed it the "mental itch" or "Las Vegas" approach. The first tag grew from a suggestion they learned to ask themselves as they read a novel: "What mental itch did the author have to scratch? What did he believe so strongly that it drove him to the typewriter to share it with others?" The "Las Vegas" label is self-explanatory in this mini-lecture used by the author with upper-level students.

Mini-lecture on Getting the Main Idea in Fiction
(Visuals Are Transparencies)

Maybe we can help turn the light on for those of you who are having trouble with finding the main idea and help make the light shine a little brighter for those of you who already are having some success with it.

This is a skill you need right now. You'll need it most particularly after your school days are over, when there are no more weekly tests and semester finals. When you are no longer a student, you will read almost everything for its main idea.

Picture a man sitting at a typewriter. His hands are poised above the keyboard. He has an idea, a message he wants to share, a mental itch he has to scratch.

He has to have a vehicle to get that idea from his head to yours. ESP is not yet a public commodity. Science has devised no way to put a metal cap on his head and one on yours and have electrical sparks fly through the air transmitting from one brain to another.

As he sits there his idea is without form to you. Until he clothes it, you won't be able to receive it. (Remember the Invisible Man? He was present but you couldn't see him unless there were clothes and bandages hanging on his invisibility.)

In order to transport his idea to you he must clothe it. He must use a vehicle of transportation. He clothes his idea in *words.*

(Teacher: Show transparency B here.)

You are able to receive his words through one of your senses—your eyes. His idea is perceivable by you because he has wrapped it in words.

(Show transparency C here.)

Now another process—and this one is your responsibility. You must strip the words off and return the message to its original state: to an idea. Then you can reach over and shake hands with the author. You

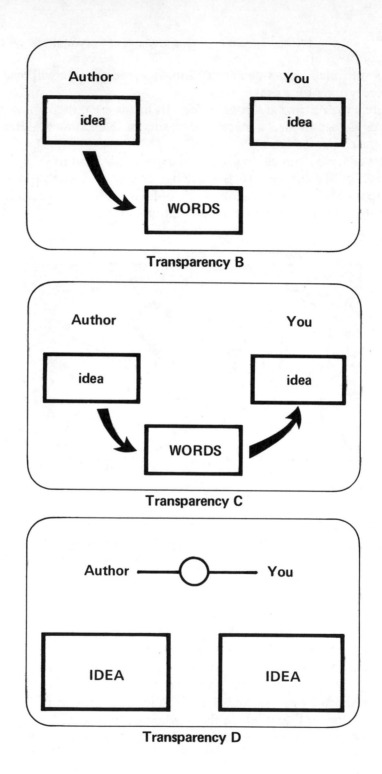

now have his point of view. You are one with him. You've gotten his message, his main idea.

(Show transparency D here.)

An author could put his main idea in a sentence or two. And if this were the way it happens, you would have no trouble getting his message.

But another problem exists for the author, and therefore for you. Although he might be able to express his idea in a few words, he can't peddle it that way. Who would publish an article of one sentence? Who would come to a play with only one line? Who would buy a book having one sentence and 200 blank pages?

Therefore the author adds supporting details to his main idea:

1. Background material
2. Examples to prove his point
3. Arguments
4. Plot
5. Comparisons and contrasts
6. Perhaps persuasive statements

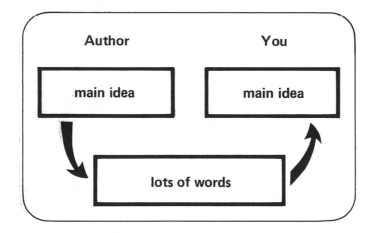

You must peel back lots of words to his main idea. You must strip off the words and get back to his original message, the mental itch that sent him to the typewriter.

So an author has a problem of finding the right clothes in which to dress his main idea.

Your problem is to strip back the words until you end up with the same idea with which he started.

After this introduction students practice stripping back words to arrive at the author's main idea or theme.

SUMMARY

Part I has focused on teacher behaviors for helping students cope with the language of the various subject areas in the school curriculum. It has shared some selected techniques through which the teacher can help students be successful in learning language skills as they learn content. Additional methods may be found in two companion volumes to this book, *Improving Reading in Every Class: A Sourcebook for Teachers,* by Ellen Lamar Thomas and H. Alan Robinson (Boston: Allyn and Bacon, 1972) and *Teaching Reading and Study Strategies: The Content Areas,* by H. Alan Robinson (Boston: Allyn and Bacon, 1975).

Activities
for Learning Content
through Language

PART II

Learning theory postulates that in order for growth in a skill to take place, three factors are important:

1. The skill should be identified.
2. Guidance should be given in developing the skill.
3. Practice time should be provided for the learner.

Identification of skills and guidance in their use are basic to the underlying philosophy of this book. The first two premises of the learning theory call upon you to let the students in on the secret. For example, share with students the concept that the skill of identifying a main idea belongs to the thinking skill of organizing. Not only is it an important and useful skill in school tasks, but also one whose mastery is advantageous for a lifetime. To demonstrate that thesis, show students how the skill works in their everyday lives. A simple example and one often used is the headline of a news article, which

indeed is its main idea. When students get the point, shift to textbook material and demonstrate main ideas in that milieu. Using materials from students' everyday world prepares the ground. If your students can operate successfully with main idea in their everyday world, with your additional guidance, they can repeat the success with your subject matter.

Part II, *Activities for Learning Content through Language*, focuses on the third factor, practice. It offers student-oriented activities for practicing skills important to learning in various content areas.

Purpose of the Activities

Because students learn at different rates there are invariably those, even in a homogenously grouped class, who do not catch on or get the point as rapidly as others. The teacher finds that he or she must attend to the learning of the majority in the class, and thereby chooses to leave some students behind rather than leave a large number in a state of limbo.

Students who need additional time to absorb concepts and/or to become adept at skills can be guided to activities designed to provide practice. Students who need a variety of avenues through which skills and concepts are developed can be guided to activities to fill that need.

Nature of the Activities

The activities in part II are valid, alternative ways to learn language-coping skills and content. They provide practice and variety. They are home-made. They are practical. In most instances, they use materials and formats totally unlike textbook offerings—newspapers, magazines, bill-boards, telephone books, cereal boxes, bumper stickers, games—but they accomplish the same goal. More important, unlike textbooks and work-books, the materials are representative of students' daily life. Some are designed for a student to use alone, others for small groups, some even for the entire class. The latter are useful to you as you demonstrate skills in students' everyday world, factor two of the learning theory.

The couple of hundred ideas in this book added to those you already use are just a beginning. Every time you look at a piece of print, whether it is a motto on the back of a delivery truck or a sign on a backpack trail, hopefully you will ask yourself two questions: 1) What kind of a skill can I develop with it? 2) How do I set up the activity? Hopefully you'll think of new trappings for old ideas. Hardly any idea is created from scratch. Sometimes it is impossible to remember sources for ideas. We meet an idea; it idles on the mind for varying lengths of time. It is resurrected, merged with other ideas, even synthesized, and enters the mainstream of usefulness. Should any of the ideas developed in part II be kissing cousins or the brain children of others, no appropriation was intended.

More and more texts on teaching reading in the content areas are hitting the market; publishers are becoming increasingly aware of the value of merging the teaching of process and content. You will want to examine them with an eye to adding to your repertory. In some, class-room teachers share ideas that have worked for them.

Wherever your ideas come from, work them up into interesting, viable learning materials that help your students excel in process as they accu-mulate data and ideas important to the subject area.

You will not want to overlook the talent within your classroom. Activity-designing is infectious. Not only are students able to implement the activities suggested in part II, but they have the creativity to design their own exercises and would cherish being invited to do so. Look to them also to help you construct the activities proposed in this text.

Structure of the Activities

All of the activities in this section have been designed around this format: subject area, grade level, objective of activity, student preparation, teacher preparation, and procedure. The *grade level* stated may be deceptive. Some of the junior high activities can be beneficial to middle grade students, and some of the more advanced activities will appeal to junior college students. You know your students; therefore you can judge if an activity will be a good fit for them.

As a rule, the stated *objective* is the main objective. For example, the stated objective might be application of the thinking skill of drawing conclusions. Other skills, prerequisite to drawing conclusions, such as gathering data, organizing data, and evaluating data, are implied rather than stated.

Student preparation means that the teacher has brought the students to the point where they are ready to practice skills. The teacher has identified skills and given guidance in their use.

Teacher preparation refers to the steps the instructor goes through to ready the activity for students' use, and the *procedure* section covers the step-by-step operation of the exercise.

Housing the Activities

Where classroom space is limited, activities certainly can be kept in a cupboard or in filing drawers. For greater accessibility and acceptability, however, a corner of the classroom could be redesigned as an activities center where students can go of their own volition or at the suggestion of the teacher, singly or in small groups, while others in the classroom are at a different learning task. Before and after-school accessibility is important.

A Trustworthy Learning Theory

Growth in a skill, in this instance, language-coping skills, takes place when the teacher

1. Identifies the skill,
2. Demonstrates how it operates, and
3. Provides practice time.

If you are starting the book here, you are coming in on the middle of the act. Part I is the curtain raiser; it builds up to the use of the business section.

CHAPTER 3

Business

Once there was a breed of man who made his own arrows, killed his own meat, clothed his own loins. But one day a wanderer strolled by with a better flint, a tastier piece of meat, a prettier loincloth. A trade was on—and business was off and running. Greener grass and better mousetraps have given business its second wind, its third, ad infinitum. It is the story of goods—and services—and money as the medium of exchange.

Business is so complex and pervasive that it entangles all but a small percentage of the adult population today. In school, students read and learn the story of business and prepare for their own entanglement in it.

For some the language of business will be difficult, so half the activities in this section have vocabulary as their target. In addition, there are activities designed to generate understanding, specifically, analyzing, comparing, drawing conclusions, and problem solving. The latter is by no means a complete list of skills that are the properties of successful learning in business education. Others are scattered throughout the sections for other disciplines.

Everyday materials demonstrated in this section include graffiti, advertising, tic-tac-toe, bingo, cross-clue puzzle, and newspaper clippings.

▶SUBJECT AREA

Bookkeeping

GRADE LEVEL

10–12

NAME OF ACTIVITY

Memory Mural

OBJECTIVE OF ACTIVITY

This activity hypothesizes that if students involve themselves with the origin of business and bookkeeping terms not only their interest but also their operational procedures will be solvent, loosely translated as flowing freely.

STUDENT PREPARATION

The student has been introduced to business and bookkeeping terms in class instruction and the textbook.

TEACHER PREPARATION

Get permission from the principal for a graffiti-like mural to be painted on the classroom wall. Provide paint and brushes. Have word origin books available (for which a bibliography is given in part I of this book; examples used here are based on Funk and Garrison books, see page 11). Prepare a ditto similar to the example. If school rules prohibit painting a wall, obtain butcher paper to cover the wall. Prepare students psychologically for creating a memory-helper mural.

PROCEDURE

Given the teacher's ditto, the students are to find the origin of words used in bookkeeping and business and paint a mural of words and drawings that are visible reminders of the meanings of terms during class discussions, tests, and bookkeeping operations.

NOTE

The teacher will want to paint the wall a neutral color again or remove the butcher paper so that each new bookkeeping class can make its own mural.

Here is an example of a ditto for this activity.

Memory Mural

The walls in our classroom are rather unimaginative and can be put to better use. How about a mural that will tell the origin of the words we use in business and bookkeeping—a mural complete with your own drawings and sayings? I'll provide the paint and brushes; you provide the imagination and talent.

Many of the words we use in bookkeeping have interesting origins. Knowing where the words came from will help you remember them and might increase your interest in bookkeeping procedures. Terms on this list have origins that lend themselves to art work. The two examples give an idea or two about beginning the mural. Claim a word and get started. Follow these steps:

1. Look for your term in one of the word history books in the classroom.
2. Write notes to yourself about the origin of the term.
3. Think about how you can show on the mural
   a. the term itself,
   b. a saying that includes the meaning of the term, and
   c. a drawing that will help you and your classmates remember it.
4. Stake a claim on an area of the mural and go to work.
5. Don't forget to paint your name or initials at the bottom of your work.

Examples:

ledger: The term dates back to the early church when the monks handwrote books of prayer. Such a book had to remain in the church; it had to lie where it was placed. From the old word for "to lie" came its term lidger, later changed to ledger.

How one student might handle the word ledger on the mural: After printing the term on the wall, he might demonstrate its origin by drawing an open book chained to some kind of a stand since the book was never permitted to be removed. The saying might be: Book of accounts must lie in safe place.

Another student might draw an open book as the torso of a reclining body and add legs, arms and head.

discount: Literally "from the count" or "not in the count." Early merchants set aside a portion of merchandise being purchased and then counted the rest on which they computed the cost to the customer. What was not counted was free, like the thirteenth cookie in a baker's dozen. Instead of merchandise not counted, the term now applies to a portion of the price not counted.

One student's drawing might show a baker shoving aside one cookie from thirteen. To another student might come the idea of showing a hardware man picking up an extra handful of nails to add to those he had already weighed and priced. Another student might show a produce man adding an ear of corn to a dozen.

GET THE IDEA? Then you are ready to go to work. If you need me, I'll be here to help before school, during my planning period, and after school. Here are some other words for the mural and some clues:

- retail: Had something to do with splitting logs.
- commission: Came from early days of royalty.
- account: What else—but counting?
- money: Check a goddess named Juno Moneta.
- bill: Would you believe "bubble?"
- calculator: Had something to do with pebbles.
- capital: What's it have in common with head?
- chattel: The source of steaks isn't a bad guess.
- charge: Carrying a load.
- company: Couple it with bread.
- finance: The end?
- garnishee: Let that be a warning to you.
- stocks: The word has a connection with tree trunks.
- bonds: They're binders.

- liabilities: They're binders too.
- mortgage: Something to do with death.
- salary: Please pass the salt.
- cash: Box makes sense.
- credit: "I believe for every drop of rain that falls . . ."
- reimburse: Rhymes with purse.
- securities: Not a care in the world.
- deposit: Out of sight, out of mind.
- debit: I owe, you owe, he, she, it owes.
- fiscal: Get a basket.
- salvage: Had something in common with the king's wine taster.

SUBJECT AREA

Bookkeeping

GRADE LEVEL

10–12

NAME OF ACTIVITY

Adaptation of the Fundamental Equation

OBJECTIVE OF ACTIVITY

To help students analyze each business transaction in light of its relationship to the fundamental equation:

$$\text{Assets} = \text{Liabilities} + \text{Proprietorship}$$

STUDENT PREPARATION

The student knows the common terms of bookkeeping.

TEACHER PREPARATION

Make cards with symbols to show the transactional effect on each element of the equation. Make another set of cards with proprietorship remarks. Build a wooden easel that has hooks to support the cards so they can be placed in position to hold the transactional narrative, the parts of the equation affected by the transaction, and the proprietorship remarks.

PROCEDURE

The student is given a card of the narrative of a business transaction. Then he places a card with the symbol plus (+), minus (−), or nothing (0) on the hooks of the equation to evaluate the transaction in terms of a fundamental bookkeeping equation. In addition, he displays an appropriate card containing proprietorship remarks if the transaction changes the proprietor's equity. The student receives two points for fitting the transaction into the equation and one

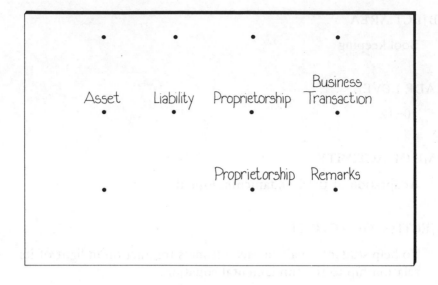

point for analyzing the proprietor changes. He may compete against himself or against a partner. The teacher may wish to monitor the activity, or it may be monitored by a student with one or more students participating.

The objective is to determine how all possible business transactions fit into the equation and specifically how owner's equity or proprietorship is affected by using + and − signs along with proprietorship notations.

These are examples of Business Transaction cards.

The owner invested cash, $2,000, and equipment, $300, in the business.

2. Purchased a truck for $3,400, paying $1,000 cash and giving a note payable for the remainder.
3. Purchased supplies for cash, $70.
4. Recorded sales on account and sent invoices to customers, $1,920.
5. Paid premiums on property and casualty insurance, $296.
6. Received cash for job completed, $120.
7. Purchased additional equipment on account, $150.
8. Purchased supplies on account, $260.
9. Paid creditors on account, $240.
10. Received an invoice for truck expenses, to be paid in November, $41.
11. Received cash for job completed, $140. This sale had not been recorded previously.
12. Paid rent for period of October 16 to end of month, $75.
13. Received cash from customers on account, $1,400.
14. Paid wages of employees, $410.
15. Withdrew cash for personal use, $300.
16. Paid miscellaneous expenses, $33.
17. Paid wages of employees, $430.
18. Estimated depreciation on the equipment to be $25.
19. Determined by taking an inventory that the cost of supplies used was $5.

These are examples of Proprietorship Remarks cards.

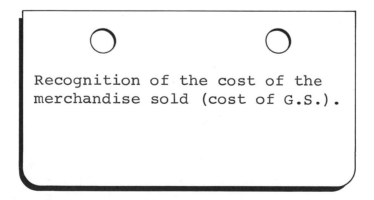

Recognition of the cost of the merchandise sold (cost of G.S.).

2. Consumption of assets for proprietor's personal use.
3. Consumption of assets without beneficial effect (loss).

4. Consumption of assets which produce beneficial effects upon the sales transaction (expense).
5. Revenue transaction (exchange of merchandise for cash or some other asset).
6. Use of cash asset to pay a debt.
7. Purchase of an asset making a down payment and remainder on a long-term contract.
8. Exchange of assets having equal value.
9. Purchase of asset on credit.
10. Original investment by owner to start business.

SUBJECT AREA

Distributive Education

GRADE LEVEL

10–12

NAME OF ACTIVITY

You Be the Judge

OBJECTIVE OF ACTIVITY

Many distributive education students work in retail establishments that sell nationally advertised merchandise. These experiments, set down for students step by step, are designed to illustrate the fine art of advertising. They are instruments for developing several skills:

1. To test claims.
2. To follow written directions.
3. To gather data.
4. To record data accurately.
5. To compare and analyze data.
6. To draw conclusions on the basis of data.
7. To prepare a visual record of data.
8. To make the student investigators and their peers sensitive to the claims of advertisers.

STUDENT PREPARATION

None prior to receiving assignments.

TEACHER PREPARATION

Clip ads from magazines, particularly ads for well-known products, that make claims. Laminate the ads for durability. Prepare a set of step-by-step directions (see example) for carrying out an experiment to test each claim made by a manufacturer. To draw school-wide attention to the activity, arrange with the principal to have the experiments conducted in a well-trafficked area of the school grounds, preferably during the lunch hour.

PROCEDURE

The laminated ads and step-by-step directions are assigned randomly to pairs of students several days prior to the day of the experiments so students can assemble the materials needed. One student of each pair conducts the experiment; the other records the data. The students follow the directions and culminate their experiments by (1) preparing a graph (their choice) of the data gathered, and (2) writing a short report for class presentation. As a final activity, a committee from the class writes a news story for the school newspaper to announce the results to the student body and the faculty.

NOTE

The instructor may wish to alert the local newspaper and television station on the experiments.

Example of Step-by-step Directions

Niblets and Corn on the Cob

Step 1: Take note of the claim made in the ad. (Note to readers: the Niblets corn ad used in the example tells its readers that Niblets is just like corn on the cob. Niblets is a registered trademark of Green Giant Company.)

Step 2: Purchase a can of Niblets and a couple of ears of corn.

Step 3: Cook the corn and cut it off the cob and place both the Niblets and the fresh corn in identical containers.

Step 4: Choose twelve people who say they have tasted both canned and fresh corn.

Step 5: Write the names of the tasters on your experiment sheet.

Step 6: Serve the products to the tasters.

Step 7: Ask the tasters which is the canned and which is the fresh corn.

Step 8: Write responses next to their names.

Step 9: Draw conclusions on the claim of the ad after all twelve tasters have made their choices.

Step 10: Draw a graph (your choice) depicting visually the results of the experiment.

Step 11: Prepare a short report to the class, including the claim of the ad, the responses of the tasters, and the graph. Send a copy to the Green Giant Company.

SUBJECT AREA

Distributive Education

GRADE LEVEL

10–12

NAME OF ACTIVITY

Balance Sheet

OBJECTIVE OF ACTIVITY

Sometimes students are surprised to learn that there is more to distributive education than across-the-counter sales. Many of the concepts of retail merchandising may be rather formidable to them. This activity is designed to acquaint students with key terms of the balance sheet.

STUDENT PREPARATION

The student has met the vocabulary of the balance sheet in his or her reading of the text and during classroom instruction.

TEACHER PREPARATION

On a piece of graph paper enter the letters of the key words backwards (to increase concentration) in scattered positions. Fill in remaining squares with assorted letters. At the bottom of the sheet, give definitions of the terms. (See example.) Ditto copies for the entire class.

PROCEDURE

The students follow directions by placing a box around the terms that match the descriptions. This activity is a good "class-starter" while the teacher is taking roll and attending to individual students.

NOTE

Students might like to make term teasers for their peers to solve. An appropriate time is the day new units or key concepts are introduced in class. The creator of the teaser profits from manipulating terms and definitions, and peers profit by unraveling them.

INSTRUCTIONS

This word teaser is simple to make, and students seem to enjoy unraveling key concept terms with this technique.

Use as many spaces as necessary to enter the terms that are important for students to know in order to proceed with their bookkeeping operations. Type definitions at the bottom of page. Then fill in blank spaces in the teaser with random letters.

	T			S							
		E	T								T
			E							L	I
		S	H					I			D
	S			S			A				E
A					E	B					R
					I	C					C
				L			N				
			I					A			
		T	I	B	E	D			L		
		I								A	
	E										B
S											

Examples of Terms

- Things owned by a business that can be converted to cash.
- Debts owed by a business.
- Statement of assets, liabilities, and capital.
- Recorded item of debt.
- Entry of payment.

SUBJECT AREA

General Business

GRADE LEVEL

10–12

NAME OF ACTIVITY

Tic-Tac-Toe

OBJECTIVE OF ACTIVITY

This old children's game serves as a motivation for learning important concepts and terminology, for paraphrasing, and for speaking before peers.

STUDENT PREPARATION

The student has read the textbook unit that serves as a basis for the questions and answers and has received classroom instruction on the unit.

TEACHER PREPARATION

Prepare questions and answers covering new vocabulary and concepts presented in the unit. Type each question and its answer on a 3 X 5″ card. The questions and answers in the examples develop the concept of a bank as a service institution. They foster the understanding of money matters and the role a bank plays in everyday economics.

PROCEDURE

The players consist of two contestants, a moderator, and nine panel members. The rest of the class is divided into two rooting groups for the contestants and shares in the prize. The moderator reads the questions, rules on the correctness of the answers, and places the Xs and Os on the tic-tac-toe graph on the chalk board. The contestants take turns picking a panel member to answer the moderator's question. The contestant must then agree or disagree with the panel member's answer. If he agrees and the answer is correct, he receives an X in the spot in the graph that corresponds to the position in which the panel member is seated. If a contestant agrees and the answer is incorrect, he receives an O. Panel members sit in three rows of three:

$$
\begin{array}{ccc}
1 & 2 & 3 \\
4 & 5 & 6 \\
7 & 8 & 9
\end{array}
$$

The first contestant to complete a row horizontally, vertically, or diagonally wins the game and shares the prize with his rooters.

Examples of Tic-Tac-Toe questions and answers:

1. Q: Is a bank a corporation?
   A: Yes. It must obtain a charter before it can do business.
2. Q: What is a bank?
   A: A business enterprise that deals in money and credit.
3. Q: What three services must a commercial bank provide?
   A: It accepts and has an obligation to keep safe money which has been deposited. It transfers money paid by check. It makes loans to persons, businesses, and governments.
4. Q: What is a charter?
   A: A grant that gives permission to begin a corporation. It is given by a government.
5. Q: What is a deposit?
   A: Money left with a bank for safekeeping.
6. Q: What is a depositor?
   A: A person who puts money into a bank.
7. Q: What is a withdrawal?
   A: It occurs when money is taken out, or withdrawn, from a bank.
8. Q: What is an account?
   A: A bank's record of a customer's deposits and withdrawals.
9. Q: What is a savings account?
   A: A bank account on which interest is paid.
10. Q: May a bank require notice from the customer before funds can be withdrawn from a savings account?

A: Yes. The bank has a legal right to require thirty to sixty days' notice before money can be withdrawn from a savings account.

11. Q: What are demand deposits?
    A: A deposit that can be withdrawn by the customer at any time without prior notice.

12. Q: What is FDIC?
    A: The Federal Deposit Insurance Corporation. FDIC insures each account's deposits up to a certain amount.

13. Q: What is currency?
    A: Money.

14. Q: What is the difference between a state bank and a national bank?
    A: The charter for a state bank is obtained from the government of the state in which it is located. The federal government charters a national bank.

15. Q: What does a federal reserve bank do?
    A: It is a bank's bank, that is, it does for national and state banks what those banks do for their customers.

16. Q: What is a trust service?
    A: The bank manages investments for a client.

17. Q: What is interest?
    A: Money paid to depositors for use of their money.

18. Q: What makes a safe deposit box safe?
    A: It usually is in the vault, and it can be opened only with the renter's key plus the bank's key.

SUBJECT AREA

Shorthand

GRADE LEVEL

11–12

NAME OF ACTIVITY

Shorthand Bingo

OBJECTIVE OF ACTIVITY

To help students cope with the brief forms of shorthand.

STUDENT PREPARATION

The student has had instruction and guidance, as well as practice in learning brief forms.

TEACHER PREPARATION

When students know the forms well enough to enjoy an alternate practice route, make forty bingo cards using the brief forms of the system being taught. In order to accommodate the various positions of shorthand forms on the forty cards, make approximately 130 to 150 guide cards for the caller. (See examples.) If candy corn is used to cover symbols, even the losers get prizes.

PROCEDURE

As the caller calls out the outlines, each student looks for the brief form on his card and covers it with a piece of candy corn. The teacher may do the calling or assign a student to do it in order to be free for personal help to the players. The student who covers five spaces in a row horizontally, vertically, or diagonally wins providing the caller verifies accuracy. Additional interest is added if types of games are varied, for instance, four corners, black-out in which all squares must be covered, or B row, I row, N row, G row, or O row.

Examples of guide cards* for the caller (1 3/4 × 1/2″):

B	I	N	G	O
their, their	great	suggest	over	street
B	I	N	G	O
am	than	morning	state	and
B	I	N	G	O
in, not	them	must	speak	between

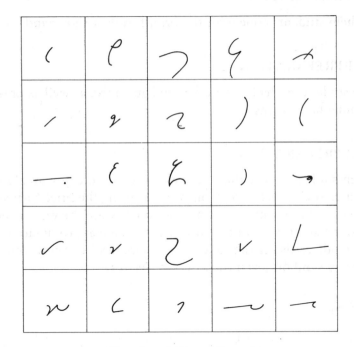

Shorthand Bingo Board.

*The Gregg Shorthand outlines contained herein are used with the permission of the Gregg and Community College Division of the McGraw-Hill Book Company, copyright owners and proprietors of Gregg Shorthand.

put	about	govern	probable	quantity
it, at	yesterday	company	have	be, by
morning	speak	object	for	request
ordinary	state	envelope	short	gentlemen
street	upon	wish	Mr.	must

Shorthand Bingo Board Key.

▶SUBJECT AREA

Shorthand

GRADE LEVEL

11–12

NAME OF ACTIVITY

Shorthand Cross-Clue Puzzle

OBJECTIVE OF ACTIVITY

To facilitate learning shorthand symbols through context clues.

STUDENT PREPARATION

None

TEACHER PREPARATION

Compose several paragraphs to use as the base for the cross-clue puzzle (see example)* or copy a passage from a shorthand text. Make sure that the passages contain context clues, so students can get a hint from the words surrounding the blank. For beginners, the passage should be a composite of words and symbols, as in the example shown. (As shorthand students become more proficient, write the entire passage in symbol form.) Prepare the puzzle form and the key.

PROCEDURE

The teacher may want the whole class to work on the puzzle or may assign the puzzle to those students who could profit from having an alternate route for practice. Students can check their accuracy with the key.

---

*The Gregg Shorthand outlines contained herein are used with the permission of the Gregg and Community College Division of the McGraw-Hill Book Company, copyright owners and proprietors of Gregg Shorthand.

Notice to Employees

With the enclosed __(9D)__ the company sends you __(21A)__ very best wishes for a happy holiday __(5D)__ .

In __(6A)__ to sending our greetings, we would __(19D)__ to share with you __(4A)__ plans for the __(18D)__ year. Curtailment of __(11D)__ in the __(16A)__ quarter __(1D)__ upon us a curtailment of expenses. All employees are asked __(8D)__ save __(7D)__ ordinary expenses "at work" as you __(3D)__ "at __(12A)__ "_ __(20A)__ lights, __(17D)__ , air conditioning. While paid holidays will remain the same in __(22A)__ new year, the following will be shelved until __(15D)__ returns to normal: one coffee __(15A)__ per day, summer __(2D)__ , Christmas __(2A)__ , and unfortunately, the Christmas __(10A)__ . Despite the curtailments, let's try to __(13D)__ next year a __(14D)__ New Year.

Shorthand Cross-Clue Puzzle.

Shorthand Cross-Clue Puzzle Key.

SUBJECT AREA

Typing

GRADE LEVEL

9–12

NAME OF ACTIVITY

Setting Newspaper Type

OBJECTIVE OF ACTIVITY

To add variety to practice materials.

STUDENT PREPARATION

None

Phase I

TEACHER PREPARATION

Clip articles from newspapers that might be of interest to adolescents. Laminate them for durability or mount them on cardboard and place in a box. (See examples.)

PROCEDURE

As a break in the routine from practice exercises in the typing book, students type the newspaper articles.

Phase II

TEACHER PREPARATION

Clip ads from the classified section of the newspaper that require lines to be centered. Laminate or paste them on cardboard and store them in a box. (See examples.)

PROCEDURE

Students practice centering and justifying lines in a manner used by a newspaper typesetter.

Examples of Classified Ads.

Sports Editor
VERNE BOATNER

No escape
from women

SOMETIMES, it seems, the safest place in the world is the men's locker room, surrounded by jocks. Even if they didn't like what you've written about them!

There I was, minding my own business, wandering through a supermarket, picking up the few items I can afford without floating a loan, when this big mama walks up. For the benefit of the Liberation Front, she WAS a big mama, standing about 5-9, weighing around 160, with three kids busily chunking goodies into her cart.

Big Mama: You're Verne Boatner, aren't you?

Little Verne: Uh, ah, I suppose I am, heh! heh!

BM: Well, I want to know why you don't give women equal coverage on your sports pages?

LV: Uh, I wasn't aware they'd started fielding football and hockey teams yet but there are so many new leagues forming I may have overlooked it in all the jumble.

BM: Veeery funny! You male chauvinists are all alike. You think the only sports activity going on around here involves men.

LV: Well, ma'am, I'd love to be able to run stories on all women's sports

but there's a matter of space. Believe it or not, there are thousands of men involved in sports who seldom see the light of print So it isn't just women. We are able to touch only a few things of great interest.

BM: Well, if you'd just throw out all those stories about the Suns and whatever they call that stupid hockey team, you'd have plenty of space for women's sports.

LV: Just what in particular is it that you'd like to see in the paper?

BM: Girls' softball. My daughter plays on a softball team and there are hundreds of them in Phoenix. But you never see a thing in the paper about them. How come?

LV: We run stories on women's softball. How old is your daughter?

BM: Eight, but what's that got to do with it?

LV: We don't run stories on any sports below the high school level, boys or girls, so you see . . .

BM: That's the silliest rule I ever heard of. If you'd just come out and watch them . . .

LV: I'd love to talk to you further on this subject, ma'am, but my ice cream is melting.

And with that, I beat a hasty retreat.

Wedding cake to top record

TULLAMORE, Ireland (AP) — Kathleen Hanley plans to have a record 15-foot wedding cake, but the big problem will be getting it across the Irish Sea.

Miss Hanley, 21, and her 27-year-old fiance James Daly are getting married in Rhyl, Wales, but the 30-tier, 300-pound, $500 wedding cake is being baked by Bridie Dunn, a Tullamore confectioner.

Mrs. Dunne has just about finished the cake and a local trucking firm has undertaken the task of getting it safely to Rhyl on the north coast of Wales in time for the Nov. 11 ceremony.

The trucker said he's praying for calm seas on the ferry crossing to Liverpool. From there he will drive to Rhyl.

Miss Hanley got the idea for the cake while visiting her uncle, John Hanley, who's footing the bill.

"We wanted to give everyone a wedding to remember and it looks as if we are going to succeed," she told reporters.

Miss Hanley said she believed her wedding guests would only consume the 60-pound bottom tier. The rest will be distributed to hospitals.

The latest Guinness Book of Records says the largest wedding cake ever made was 10 feet high and had 27 tiers. It was for Kathy Alwin, who was married in London on Aug. 18, 1973.

Guinness says of all cakes ever baked, the biggest stood 26 feet, weighed 25,000 pounds and was cut at the British Columbia Centennial on July 20, 1971.

Examples of Newspaper Articles of Interest to Adolescents.

CHAPTER 4

Driver Education

If you are starting the book here, you are coming in on the middle of the act. Part I is the curtain riser; it builds up to the use of the driver education section.

"Driver education almost invariably is the best taught subject in any secondary school. The students vie for admission, they study and practice faithfully, and the success rate is phenomenally high." This is the belief of Harry Sartain, who also stated that "driver education courses from their beginnings have usually utilized the known principles of the psychology of learning. Instead of remote, uninteresting goals, their objectives have been to develop specific competencies which the students know to be useful. Instead of purposeless readings and busy work, their assigned reading and practice experiences have contributed directly to the attainment of those competencies."*

Driver education students are highly motivated. Sometimes,

*Harry W. Sartain, "Content Reading—They'll Like It," *Journal of Reading 17* (1973): 47-51.

however, students' motivation exceeds the skills necessary to handle the assignments and experiences that deal with the printed word. In these instances, the driver education instructor needs to build practice time into teaching/learning experiences as necessary to shore up weak reading skills.

The sample practice activities in this book are motivating for, like the experiences Sartain talks about, they contribute to developing specific reading competencies such as categorizing and classifying, interpreting, map reading, following directions, and recognizing propaganda, as well as becoming adept with driver education vocabulary.

Everyday materials demonstrated in this section include a driver license manual, road symbols, state maps, auto brochures, and a motorcycle riders' guide book. Check other sections for additional everyday materials and techniques.

SUBJECT AREA

Driver Education

GRADE LEVEL

9–10

NAME OF ACTIVITY

Drive

OBJECTIVE OF ACTIVITY

To reinforce the specialized vocabulary connected with driving an automobile.

STUDENT PREPARATION

The student has been introduced to the forty to fifty terms used in the activity and has studied them in the text.

TEACHER PREPARATION

Prepare three DRIVE cards, each containing twenty-five squares, as in a bingo game, on ditto masters. Two of the cards should be completely different, and the third card contains words from the other two. (One example is given.) Provide definition cards, such as:

1.   V
     area in which driver
     may not pass another car   (no passing zone)

2.   V
     person killed in
     accident on the road   (highway casualty)

3.   E
     driving dangerously close
     to rear of another vehicle   (tailgating)

Make paper squares to be used for markers from construction paper.

PROCEDURE

Teacher calls the definition, and students place a marker on the word if it is on their card. The student who covers five squares in a row horizontally, vertically, or diagonally signals by calling out DRIVE. If his answers are correct, he receives ten points. The player with highest points after a time limit wins. After several rounds students should trade cards so they will have practice with all the vocabulary words.

D	R	I	V	E
acceleration	choke	muffler	liability	cylinder
defroster	U turn	overpass	rear end collision	tailgating
optional equipment	piston	**FREE**	highway	exhaust
cruising speed	fan belt	intersection	no passing zone	emergency brake
coasting	combustion chamber	antifreeze	lubricate	connecting rod

Example DRIVE Card.

Driver Education

GRADE LEVEL

9–10

NAME OF ACTIVITY

Throwing the Case

OBJECTIVE OF ACTIVITY

The activity has several objectives:

1. It permits students to self-check their knowledge of information which, when acted upon, promotes pleasure and safety in driving an automobile.
2. It fosters categorization of data. (A factor that promotes retention is cluster memory, or remembering groups of things that all have something in common. When driving an automobile, cluster memory permits the driver quick access to many alternatives.)

STUDENT PREPARATION

When the student believes he has studied factors involved in driving an automobile well enough to check himself on accuracy, he uses this activity.

TEACHER PREPARATION

1. Design the case and hang it on the classroom wall. The case is made of 1/4″ plywood or other durable material. It is 34″ wide, 19″ long, and 4″ deep, accommodating 45 pigeonholes, 3 1/2″ square divided by 1/4″ strips of plywood. Make the case durable and strong so that it can be used for varying and different activities.
2. Select categories, for example, Unfavorable Driving Conditions,

and on 3 × 5″ cards type various kinds of adverse conditions. On the reverse side of the card type the name of the category, in this instance, Unfavorable Driving Conditions. Make cards for as many categories as are discussed in the driver education text or in teacher-made materials that have been distributed in class. (Several examples are given.)

3. Print the names of the categories on slips of cardboard that will slide into a holder affixed to the 1/4″ plywood strip above the pigeonholes. The cards are stored in the lower pigeonholes, which are labeled with the slips of cardboard in their appropriate holders.

PROCEDURE

When a student is ready to check her knowledge, experiences, and thinking processes on three or four of the categories, she pulls the cards she wishes from the lower pigeonholes and moves the category labels to upper pigeonholes. After putting all cards in one stack and shuffling them well, she "throws the case." In other words, she tosses each card into the section in which she thinks it categorically belongs. When she finishes throwing the case, she removes the cards and self-checks her accuracy by referring to the backs of the cards that bear the labels of the categories.

Here are some examples of categories and cards.*

Unfavorable Weather Conditions (label)

Cards:

1. Steamed-up windows.
2. Dusk-twilight visibility.
3. Driving east at sunrise or west at sunset.
4. Low visibility.
5. Rain.

*The examples are based on information from *Let's Drive Right,* 5th ed., written by Maxwell Halsey, Richard Kaywood, and Richard A. Meyerhoff for Scott, Foresman and Company, Glenview, Illinois 60025.

6. Fog.
7. Snow.
8. Slick curves, upgrades, and downgrades.
9. Wet pavements.
10. Wet leaves on roadway.
11. Frosted pavements.
12. Night driving.
13. Blowing dust or sand.
14. Standing water on road surface.
15. Ice and snow on windshield.

Car Systems (label)

Cards:

1. Power is produced in the cylinder of the engine.
2. A spark from the spark plug ignites an explosive mixture of air and gasoline vapor.
3. The crankshaft turns the driveshaft when the piston moves up and down.
4. Electricity goes through the starter, the battery, the coil, and the distributor to get to a spark plug.
5. Pressure on the accelerator controls the amount of fuel fed to the cylinders.
6. Oil reduces friction, helps carry away heat, and keeps the engine cool.
7. Radiator fan, water pump, and thermostat join with oil to keep car engines cool.
8. First gear is superior to second and third gear in giving a gearshift car greater force.
9. Engine, clutch, transmission, driveshaft, and differential are in an automobile's power train.
10. Shock absorbers and springs contribute to comfort, keep the car in balance and easy for the driver to handle.
11. If brake fluid leaks out of a brake line, the other two wheels will still get fluid from the working side of the dual master cylinder.

Emergencies (label)

Cards:

1. Knowing why some actions are better than others will help a driver make good, quick decisions and will help prevent panic, which leads to wrong decisions.
2. Try to lift a stuck pedal with toe or try tapping it a couple of times with toe if accelerator is stuck.
3. If brakes fail, pump brake rapidly to build up pressure, or apply parking brake slowly, or shift to lower gear.
4. If headlights go out suddenly, slow down and flash brake lights.
5. If car catches fire, pull off the road and get people out and away from it.
6. Head for right shoulder in your lane if another car is coming at you in your lane.
7. A rear-end collision might start a fire in your car. Get out quickly after any collision.
8. If wheels drop off the pavement, do not apply brakes. Keep speed low, but don't jerk wheels back.
9. Results of braking violently might be skidding, loss of steering, and being hit from the rear.
10. The worst crashes occur on good roads, in good conditions.
11. Turn on emergency flashers if you are changing a flat tire.
12. A car with windows and doors closed will float from three to ten minutes.
13. Roll down a window rather than try to force door open if you're caught in a submerging auto.
14. Emergency situations are always unexpected.

SUBJECT AREA

Driver Education

GRADE LEVEL

9–10

NAME OF ACTIVITY

Domino Vocabulary

OBJECTIVE OF ACTIVITY

To reinforce vocabulary studied.

STUDENT PREPARATION

The student has studied the vocabulary words in the unit.

TEACHER PREPARATION

Cut domino-like rectangles from cardboard. At one end of each piece of cardboard, type or print a definition for a vocabulary word. At the other end print a vocabulary word, but not the one that matches the definition. (See examples.) Make the key.

PROCEDURE

Two or more players may participate in Domino Vocabulary. All the pieces of cardboard are turned face down except one, which is placed face up in the center of the table. Each player in turn turns over a domino, checks to see if either end matches an end of the exposed domino(es). He joins the domino to its match if possible. If he has no match, he places it in front of him. A player may either draw or use from the dominoes he has accumulated from previous turns. For each successful match, the player writes the vocabulary word on his score sheet. The winner has the largest number of matches. Disputes are settled with the teacher's key.

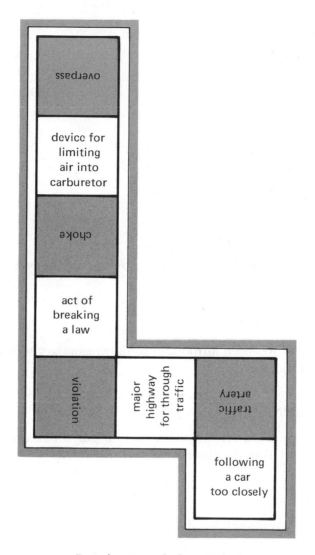

Domino Vocabulary Board.

▶SUBJECT AREA

Driver Education

GRADE LEVEL

9–10

NAME OF ACTIVITY

Where Did that Word Come From?

OBJECTIVE OF ACTIVITY

To enhance retention of vocabulary by associating words with their unusual origins.

STUDENT PREPARATION

The student has been introduced to the vocabulary terms in classroom instruction.

TEACHER PREPARATION

Have several word origin books available (for which a bibliography is given in part I) in the classroom or school library.

PROCEDURE

Using the vocabulary words provided by the teacher, the student finds a history for each word and categorizes it on a sheet similar to the one shown. In addition, he uriefly writes why the particular term is used.

Here are some examples of terms used in driver education that have unusual origins:

- Caprice—like a goat, frisky, lively
- jeep—from Army's official title of the vehicle, General Purpose, or G.P.

- macadam—invented by man named J. L. McAdam, a Scottish engineer
- turnpike—word for barrier set across highway until traveler paid a toll
- Eldorado—fabulously wealthy, like the city sought by the early Spanish explorers in South America
- coupe—shortened coach, big enough for two
- LUV—acronym for lightweight utility vehicle

PERSON, PLACE, THING WORDS IN DRIVER EDUCATION

Person Words	Place Words	Thing Words
macadam—named for inventor, J. L. McAdam		

▶SUBJECT AREA

Driver Education

GRADE LEVEL

9–10

NAME OF ACTIVITY

Road Symbols

OBJECTIVE OF ACTIVITY

Many states are changing their highway signs from written regulations to totally nonverbal symbols. The objective of this activity is to assist driver education students in becoming familiar with the new traffic control devices.

STUDENT PREPARATION

The student is familiar with the signs stating verbal regulations and has studied the abstract equivalents.

TEACHER PREPARATION

Clip both the old and the new signs from a brochure provided by the state highway department. Paste them on 3 X 5'' cards.

ROAD/STREET SIGNS
ARE CHANGING TO SYMBOLS

OLD   NEW   OLD   NEW

SCHOOL CROSSING   SLIPPERY WHEN WET

PROCEDURE

After shuffling the cards, Player A deals five cards to Player B and to himself and stacks the rest face down between them. Player B begins by asking for a card to match one in her hand. She continues as long as A can supply the card requested and places the matched pairs in front of her. Then Player B draws one card from the pile. At her turn Player A repeats the process. The player putting down the most pairs is declared winner when no more cards remain unmatched.

SUBJECT AREA

Driver Education

GRADE LEVEL

9–10

NAME OF ACTIVITY

Touring the State of _____

OBJECTIVE OF ACTIVITY

To reinforce map reading skills, to give practice in following directions, and to familiarize students with the location of counties,
cities, rivers, national monuments in the state where they live.

STUDENT PREPARATION

The student has been introduced to road maps.

TEACHER PREPARATION

Obtain a road map issued by the State Highway Department for
each student in the class. Prepare a dittoed sheet of instructions,
indicating the location of city of departure and providing clues for
the trip. (See example.)

PROCEDURE

Using the map provided, students (individually or in pairs) find the
starting point designated. They use each clue in sequence to arrive at
the correct point or feature on the map. The trip may be a short or
long one, depending on the number of clues. Just as solitary road
trips are boring, so is this simulated one. But two students traveling
together not only keep each other company but provide assistance
to each other along the way.

Here are some examples of clues based on a map of Arizona:

Touring Arizona

This road map of the state of Arizona has several features you will need to use so that you can follow the clues:

- At the lower left hand corner is a scale of miles.
- Directly above the scale is a symbol indicating North, South, East, and West.
- At the left and right edges of the map are capital letters: A, B, C, through L. At the top and bottom edges of the map are numerals: 1, 2, 3, through 9.

We're gassed up and ready to go!

1. At I-1 we will begin our tour. This town on the banks of the Colorado River was the site of the prison that held some of the most dangerous desperados of the early West. The name of the town is _____.
2. Our first destination is 183 miles northeast. Approximately 35 miles from our starting point, we pass a military installation, called _____. Using the capital letters and numerals, we locate it at _____. At the end of our 183 miles, we enter the capital of Arizona, _____.
3. Turning southeast, we are heading for the second largest city in Arizona by way of Interstate _____. En route we'll take some side trips. South of Sacaton, we exit from the freeway on State Road 287 to well-preserved ruins of a four-story dwelling used by ancient peoples. It is called _____.
4. To get back on the freeway, we'll retrace our steps so we can visit a town (H-5) where the San Francisco Giants have their winter training camp. The camp is located near _____.

Key:

1. Yuma
2. Yuma Proving Ground
   I-2
   Phoenix
3. 10
   Casa Grande Ruins National Monument
4. Casa Grande

SUBJECT AREA

Driver Education

GRADE LEVEL

9–10

NAME OF ACTIVITY

Wading through Inferences

OBJECTIVE OF ACTIVITY

To help students who are prospective car buyers to identify techniques of persuasion.

STUDENT PREPARATION

None

TEACHER PREPARATION

Visit automobile agencies and collect brochures automobile dealers use as advertising pieces. For each brochure write a set of questions designed to evaluate students' ability to distinguish between "selling" and "telling."
For example:

1. List five facts and five non-facts in this brochure.
2. What kinds of words does the manufacture use to tempt you to buy his product? Usually they are adjectives. List ten tempting words used in this brochure.
3. Which of two factors is emphasized more—comfort or performance? Give evidence of your answer.
4. Does the brochure include facts you want to know? Miles per gallon? Parts guarantee? Price? Down payment? Financing? Optional features for which you pay extra? Horsepower? Improvements over last year's model? What conclusion can you draw about the manufacturer's objective in printing the brochure?

5. This brochure features (well-known personality). What is the manufacturer's purpose in quoting this person? Do you believe the person was paid for the use of his or her picture, name, and quotes?
6. Does the brochure discuss safety features built into the automobile? How many do you have to pay extra for?

PROCEDURE

The student notes answers to the questions that have been attached to the auto manufacturer's brochure. After he shares his data with the class, he makes a commitment on whether or not he has been influenced to buy the car. He also gives his reasons for his decision. Members of the class then may pose questions within the standards of behavior previously decided on by the class.

▶SUBJECT AREA

Driver Education

GRADE LEVEL

9–10

NAME OF ACTIVITY

Motorcycle Game

OBJECTIVE OF ACTIVITY

To stimulate reading and learning the literature on safe rules of motorcycling.

STUDENT PREPARATION

Before beginning the game, the student has studied the motorcycle riders handbook or guidebook issued by the Motor Vehicle Division of the _____ Highway Department.
                        (State)

TEACHER PREPARATION

Obtain copies of the guidebook so every student has his own. Purchase an inexpensive deck of Playing Cards in a box rather than a package. Write fifty-four questions and answers (fifty-two cards plus two jokers) based on the guide book. (See examples.) With transparent tape attach question to design side of each card and answer to face side. Provide Rules of the Game (see Procedure) on a piece of cardboard that will fit in the cards' box.

PROCEDURE

From two to four students may play the game following the study of the manual or guidebook. The shuffled cards are placed in a stack with the question side up. After determining which student will begin the game, the player draws a card from the *bottom* of the deck. If she answers the question to the satisfaction of the other players, she turns the card to see if she has given the correct answer. If the answer is correct, she keeps the card in front of her for scoring later. If she answers incorrectly or cannot answer, she places the card on the top of the deck, and the play goes to the next student.

When all cards have been used, points are totaled as follows:

2–9— 5 points

10, J, Q, K—10 points

Ace—25 points

The winner has the highest score.

Examples of questions and answers:

Spades

A Q: If the speed of a motorcycle is 50 mph, how far in back of the car ahead should it be?
   A: 200 feet back (40 feet for each 10 mph). p. 11.
2 Q: How much is the fee that must accompany the application for a license?
   A: The fee is $2.50. p. 4.
3 Q: How many times may an applicant try to pass the exam?
   A: Three times. p. 4.
4 Q: What percentage of people in automobile accidents receive injuries?
   A: Thirty percent. p. 5.
5 Q: Under what circumstances may a driver ride on private land?
   A: Only with permission. p. 11.
6 Q: Explain the meaning of riding sidesaddle.
   A: To have both legs on one side of the seat.
7 Q: State two ways a motorcyclist can help prevent fires.
   A: Do not smoke while riding. Be sure motorcycle muffler is equipped with an approved spark arrestor for trail riding. p. 12.
8 Q: What is the regulation about handlebars?
   A: Handlebars or grips cannot be raised more than 15 inches higher than the level of the seat. p. 4.
9 (The nine of spades is a direction card.) Forgot helmet. Lose one turn while you go back after it.

10 Q: Explain the use of the brakes while making a turn.
    A: Always use your brakes before rounding a turn, not while making the turn. p. 7.

J Q: State two things that could happen if a motorcyclist rides between two lanes.
    A: 1. One of the cars could swerve or make an unsignaled turn.
       2. Cycle rider may be hit by a long rearview mirror. p. 8.

Q Q: What is the courteous way to drive if horses are present?
    A: When meeting riders on horseback, stop cycle and motor. Allow them to pass. When overtaking, wait until they stand aside and proceed slowly. p. 12.

K Q: Give the three rules for passing.
    A: 1. Pass on left side.
       2. Do not pass on hill or curve.
       3. Never ride between two lanes of cars. p. 8.

Hearts

A Q: Give four reasons why it is best to travel to the left of the center of the lane.
    A: 1. You avoid the oily strip in the center.
       2. You can be seen by the driver of the vehicle ahead.
       3. You have a better view of the road ahead.
       4. Riding to the right of the center may put you in the blind spot of the driver ahead. p. 9.

2 Q: Where is a good place to practice when learning to drive a cycle?
    A: It's best to practice in an empty parking lot. p. 5.

3 Q: How long does the applicant have to pass the exam from the date of application?
    A: Six months. p. 4.

4 Q: What might cause a bike to lose traction and spill in a turn?
    A: Applying the brake. p. 7.

5 Q: The rearview mirror must provide a view for what distance?
    A: For a distance of 200 feet. p. 4.

6 Q: Explain the use of the feet and knees on dirt trails.
    A: Rest your feet on the footrests and knees against the tank pads for balance. p. 11.

7 (The seven of hearts is a direction card.) Add 25 points for keeping up your school grades after buying your bike.

8 Q: What should be used to control speed on climbs and descents?

A: Utilize the transmission to control your speed on climbs and descents. p. 11.

9 (The nine of hearts is a direction card.) Add 25 points for helping clean the picnic area after the motorcycle meet.

10 (The ten of hearts is a direction card.) Deduct 25 points for careless driving.

J (The jack of hearts is a direction card.) Bike broke down. Sit out two turns for repairs.

Q Q: Name three things the cycle must be equipped with for the operator.

A: Rearview mirror, seat, and footrests. p. 2.

K Q: What percentage of people involved in accidents on two-wheeled vehicles receive injuries?

A: Eighty percent. p. 4.

Diamonds

A Q: State the five leading causes of motorcycle accidents.

A: 1. Driving too fast.
 2. Failing to yield right of way.
 3. Inattention.
 4. Driving after drinking alcohol or consuming drugs.
 5. Following too closely. p. 12.

2 Q: Name two things that a rider must wear on his head.

A: Helmet and glasses. p. 2.

3 Q: What is necessary for noise prevention?

A: Every motorcycle shall be equipped with a muffler to prevent excessive noise. p. 4.

4 Q: Which is the most powerful brake?

A: The front brake. p. 7.

5 Q: What might happen if the brakes are applied while in the turn?

A: The cycle may lose traction and spill. p. 7.

6 Q: How should the feet be used during a turn?

A: Keep feet on footrests to maintain control and balance and protect your legs. p. 8.

7 (The seven of diamonds is a direction card.) Bonus for safe driving. Add 30 points.

8 Q: What percent of accidents involve damage to the head?

A: Forty-five percent. p. 4.

9 (The nine of diamonds is a direction card.) Traveling too close. Deduct 20 points.

10 Q: Explain defensive driving.

A: Protecting yourself from another vehicle by constant alertness. p. 3.

J Q: Explain the motion of the body in a turn.

A: Lean into the turn with your body. p. 8.

Q Q: Explain a safe way for beginners to practice operating the controls.

A: Practice on a stand with the engine off, then with the cycle moving slowly. p. 5.

K Q: Name five things that must be in good working order in order to take the skill test.

A: Horn, headlight, tail light, stop light, and muffler. p. 4.

Clubs

A Q: State five things that a passenger should be instructed to do.

A: 1. Hold handrail.
   2. Keep feet on rest.
   3. Avoid tensing body.
   4. Lean in same direction as operator.
   5. Avoid hot muffler. p. 9.

2 Q: Avoid traveling in the _____ spot of another vehicle.

A: Blind. p. 10.

3 Q: What is the best plan if there are doubts about a trail?

A: Get off and walk until you reach safe ground. p. 11.

4 Q: Name the location in which most motorcycle accidents occur.

A: Intersections. p. 9.

5 Q: Name three things the cycle must be equipped with for a passenger.

A: Seats, footrests, and handrails. p. 2.

6 Q: How old must an applicant be for a cycle license?

A: Sixteen years of age or older. p. 1.

7 Q: Explain how to cross bridges with metal gratings.

A: Drive in a gentle zigzag motion. p. 10.

8 Q: What is a blind spot?

A: An area behind a car not visible to the driver when he looks in the rearview mirror. p. 10.

9 (The nine of clubs is a direction card.) You are asked to go for a free ride. Add 50 points to your score.

10 (The ten of clubs is a direction card.) Take an extra turn for passing the skill test on the first try.

J Q: Explain the best way to cross railroad tracks.

A: Cross at 90 degree angle to avoid skidding or catching your wheels. p. 10.

Q Q: When may a driver omit wearing glasses, goggles or face shield?

A: When the motorcycle is equipped with a protective windshield. p. 2.

K (The king of clubs is a direction card.) You have been fined for traveling at excessive speeds. Deduct 25 points.

Jokers

(Direction card.) Deduct 60 points for property destruction.
(Direction card.) Add 45 points for insisting that your girlfriend wear shoes when riding with you.

Driver Education

GRADE LEVEL

9–10

NAME OF ACTIVITY

Motorcycle Crossword

OBJECTIVE OF ACTIVITY

To help students learn state equipment specifications and license requirements for operating a motorcycle.

STUDENT PREPARATION

The student has read the motorcycle manual issued in his state.

Motorcycle Crossword Format.

TEACHER PREPARATION

Prepare a crossword puzzle using information contained in the state-issued motorcycle manual. (See example.) Mimeograph it so that it may be used as a whole class activity, as well as an individual exercise. Prepare the key to the puzzle.

PROCEDURE

The student works the puzzle from memory if possible and refers to the manual for information he or she does not know.

Across

3. Disengages engine from transmission.
6. When turning you must _____ in the direction you turn.
8. First brake device to apply.
9. Illegal to perform on hill.
10. Tests required for license are written and _____ tests.
14. Eye protectors.
15. Permissible side to pass on.
16. Front brake device.
17. Safety device on each side of frame.
19. Protection for head.
20. Applicant's minimum age.
24. Hazardous road condition.
25. Used to deflect wind.
26. Support for the back.
27. Maximum penalty points permitted.

Down

1. Term for footrests.
2. Warning device.
3. Special case for equipment.
4. Used to accelerate.
5. Required for passenger.
7. Deadens noise of motor.
9. Rear braking device.

11. _____ mirror.
12. System to ignite fuel mixture.
13. Manner of driving to protect self and others.
17. Number of feet required between forward vehicle and cycle.
18. Connects hub to rim of wheel.
19. Two _____ feet requirement for horn audibility.
21. Steering bar of cycle.
22. Cycle seat.
23. Change gears.

KEY:

Across	*Down*
3. Clutch	1. Pegs
6. Lean	2. Horn
8. Rear	3. Carrier
9. Pass.	4. Throttle
10. Road	5. Handrail
14. Goggles	7. Muffler
15. Left	9. Pedal
16. Lever	11. Rearview
17. Footrest	12. Ignition
19. Helmet	13. Defensive
20. Sixteen	17. Forty
24. Wet	18. Spoke
25. Windshield	19. Hundred
26. Backrest	21. Handle
27. Eight	22. Saddle
	23. Shift

CHAPTER 5

English, Speech, and Journalism

If you are starting the book here, you are coming in on the middle of the act. Part I is the curtain raiser; it builds up to the use of the English, speech, and journalism section.

Every time we use words we do so as senders or receivers. When we transmit, we write or speak words. As receivers, we read or listen to words. It is language arts teachers, in the main, who accept the responsibility for strengthening students' skills in transmitting and receiving, the teachers of language and literature, of speech, of journalism—the word lovers.

People who are in love with words infect others with the excitement and gaming involved. Word-lovers—and English, speech, and journalism teachers usually are—enjoy manipulating, creating, merging, playing with, juggling words wherever they find them, and they do find them far and near. One word-loving author was moved to entitle his textbook *English Everywhere.*

Everywhere an English teacher looks are materials to help infect students with a love of the language of their country—in the subway, in a supermarket, on billboards, in a restaurant, on a street marker. Some suggestions are made in this section; other activities are at the tip of your imagination.

Some of the skills reinforced in the activities for speech students include identifying strategies of propaganda and persuasion, distinguishing between fact and opinion, and extending the use of synonyms. Some of the techniques demonstrated include poker, jokes, and newspaper clippings.

Journalism teachers, many of them former or current newspaper writers, bring to the classroom their own skills in producing a newspaper and perhaps even more importantly, their love of the newspaper. Journalism classrooms constantly look like a paper recylcing depot. Students learn newspapers by studying newspapers, all kinds—big ones, little ones, good ones, poor ones, dailies, weeklies, local papers, and those from all over the country. Journalism requires a great deal of reading prowess from its devotees; some of them are dealt with in this section. But the section for journalism students and teachers is really sixteen sections long, the whole book, since all of the activities are learning experiences for journalism tyros.

ENGLISH

Activity I for Multi-Board

▶SUBJECT AREA

English

GRADE LEVEL

7–9

NAME OF ACTIVITY

Is That a Fact?

OBJECTIVE OF ACTIVITY

To encourage students to discriminate between fact and assumption and to follow directions.

STUDENT PREPARATION

The student has been instructed in the differences between what is acceptable data and assumptions related to that data.

TEACHER PREPARATION

Construct the game board (see illustration), called a Multi-Board because it houses four different activities:

· Is That a Fact?
· Facts and Opinions
· Grammar Quiz Whiz
· Block Buster Descriptions

Each of the four circuits is drawn with a different colored ink, and game cards for each activity are color-coded to match the particular circuit.

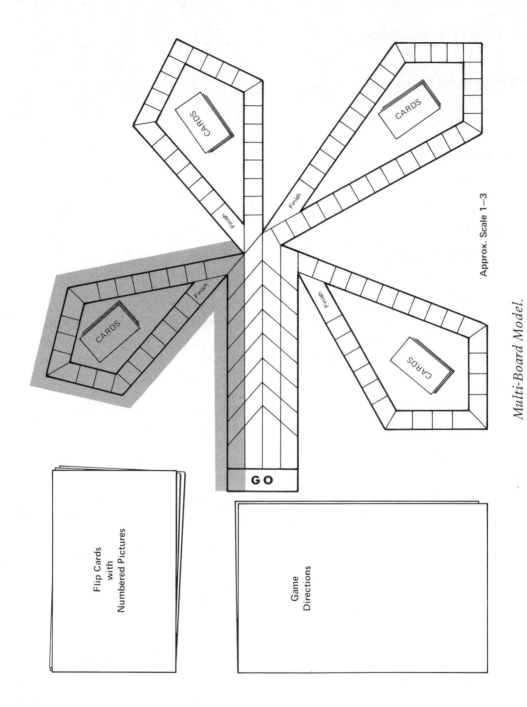

GO

CARDS

CARDS

CARDS

CARDS

Finish

Finish

Finish

Finish

Flip Cards
with
Numbered Pictures

Game
Directions

Approx. Scale 1–3

Multi-Board Model.

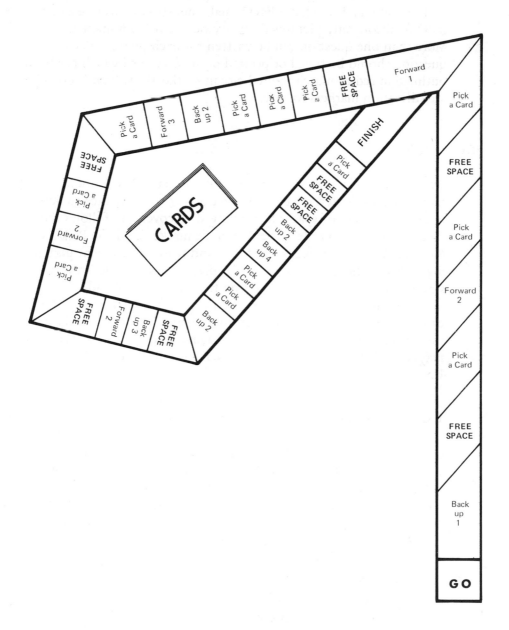

Detailed View of a Multi-Board Segment.

115

For Activity I, Is That a Fact?, make question cards (see examples) to accompany pictures that have been cut from magazines. More than one question can be written for each picture. Each question should be typed or printed on its own card which has been outlined in red to match the red circuit of the Multi-Board. Provide identification markers for players.

PROCEDURE

Two or more players can be involved in Is That a Fact? Students move around the red circuit. The first player rolls the dice to determine the number of spaces he is allowed to cover and follows the direction written on the space. When his marker lands on Pick a Card, another player picks a red card and reads a statement pertaining to one of the given pictures. The player must decide if the statement is a fact or an assumption from the picture and tell why he made the decision. If his answer tallies with the answer on the card, he moves his marker forward one space. If it is not, he hears the correct answer and his marker remains. In either event, the next player has his turn. The player to reach the end first is titled UNDUPABLE.

Examples of card queries for Activity I of Multi-Board:

1. Look at picture 6. This man is relaxed and happy to have a birthday party with his family. Fact or assumption? (Assumption. It was a publicity stunt to make him look human.)
2. Look at picture 13. Five people decided they needed a bath. Fact or assumption? (Assumption. Motivation cannot be determined from the photograph.)
3. Look at picture 17. A general is reviewing six soldiers. Fact or assumption? (Fact. Four stars on a soldier show he's a general. Soldiers can be counted.)
4. Look at picture 20. A boy and a woman are staring into the camera. Fact or assumption? (Fact. Observable in the camera.)
5. Look at picture 14. This man is fishing for garbage. (Assumption. He was fishing for fish.)

6. Look at picture 19. A boy is standing on one foot. Fact or assumption? (Fact. Visually verifiable.)
7. Look at picture 19. The boy is jumping into the fire. Fact or assumption? (Assumption. Can't be proven from the photograph.)
8. Look at picture 18. Round tanks are on railcars. Fact or assumption? (Fact. Visually verifiable.)
9. Look at picture 18. These are tank cars of gasoline being stored until prices rise. Fact or assumption? (Assumption. The contents can't be seen.)
10. Look at picture 9. This man just rescued a puppy from an avalanche. Fact or assumption? (Assumption. Pictures can't show what came before.)
11. Look at picture 8. This is a picture of a mother and child. Fact or assumption? (Assumption. Picture doesn't show the relationship.)
12. Look at picture 8. There is a woman and a child in the picture. Fact or assumption? (Fact. Observable.)
13. Look at picture 6. Mother and two children are on their way to grandmother's. Fact or assumption? (Assumption. Picture doesn't show relationship or destination.)
14. Look at picture 6. One girl is holding flowers. Fact or assumption? (Fact. Observable.)
15. Look at picture 11. Two men are carrying out a body. Fact or assumption? (Assumption. What they are carrying can't be determined from the picture.)
16. Look at picture 10. One man is torturing another man. Fact or assumption? (Assumption. The picture was staged.)
17. Look at picture 7. The woman is smoking. Fact or assumption? (Assumption. The picture only shows that she is holding a cigarette.)
18. Look at picture 7. The woman likes cigarettes. Fact or assumption? (Assumption. Motivation for holding cigarette is not observable.)
19. Look at picture 3. Three women have their faces covered. Fact or assumption? (Fact. Observable.)
20. Look at picture 4. Protesters are angry about the cost of living. Fact or assumption? (Assumption. Motivation for actions can't be seen.)

Activity II for Multi-Board

▶SUBJECT AREA

English

GRADE LEVEL

7–10

NAME OF ACTIVITY

Facts and Opinions

OBJECTIVE OF ACTIVITY

To promote students' ability to discriminate between fact and opinion and to follow directions.

STUDENT PREPARATION

The student has had instruction in what constitutes factual data.

TEACHER PREPARATION

The orange circuit of the Multi-Board is used for this activity. Write fact/opinion cards (see examples), outlining the cards in orange to match the orange-colored circuit on the board.

PROCEDURE

Two or more students may participate in the orange circuit activity. The first player rolls the dice and moves his marker the number of spaces indicated, following the directions written on the space. When a player's marker lands on Pick a Card, another student in the game picks an orange card and reads it to the player, who must decide if the statement read is fact or opinion and give his rationale. If he answers correctly, he moves to the next space without rolling the dice. If he responds incorrectly, his marker remains on the space

until his next turn. The player completing the circuit wins the title
SHARP SKEPTIC.

Examples of cards for Activity II of Multi-Board:

1. America is not as good as it used to be. Fact or opinion? (Opinion. Not measurable.)
2. Auto deaths decreased in the first six months of this year, according to a study commissioned by HEW. Fact or opinion? (Can be accepted as fact on the authority of the agency.)
3. Morality in the United States is on the decline. Fact or opinion? (Opinion. Morality can't be measured, sometimes not even agreed upon.)
4. Sudso was developed in the laboratory of a famous university. It's got to be good. Fact or opinion? (Opinion for two reasons: (a) development at a university does not necessarily make it good; (b) statement can't be checked because the university is not named.)
5. The attacks of the enemy failed to gain ground because of our troop's courage. Fact or opinion? (Opinion. Courage is not measurable; other factors could have entered in.)
6. Agricultural production rose last year, according to Agricultural Secretary John Doe. Fact or opinion? (Can be accepted as fact, relying on agriculture department having statistics to back up the statement.)
7. Women are poor in mathematics and are too emotional. Fact or opinion? (Opinion. No statistical data to support statement.)
8. The *Times* called the book "the most important book of the century." Fact or opinion? (Fact. It can be shown that the *Times* supported this opinion.)
9. You can't trust a politician. Fact or opinion? (Opinion. Generalization.)
10. Poverty is caused by laziness. Fact or opinion? (Opinion. Laziness is not measurable.)
11. Housing starts for December were down from the previous year. Fact or opinion? (Fact. Supportable with statistical data.)
12. Beefyburgers can give you a lift in the middle of the day. Fact or opinion? (Opinion. Lift is a relative term and is not measurable.)

13. Beefyburgers supply protein to the body. Fact or opinion? (Fact. Verifiable. Nutritionists can measure protein.)

14. Concern is being expressed by the Director of the Wildlife Preservation over the decrease of birds in the sanctuary. Fact or opinion? (Fact. Director would be knowledgeable on this point.)

15. Mary said that high heels are hard to walk in. Fact or opinion? (Opinion. High heels may be hard for Mary to walk in, but she can't speak for all who wear high heels.)

Activity III for Multi-Board

▶SUBJECT AREA

English

GRADE LEVEL

7–9

NAME OF ACTIVITY

Grammar Whiz Quiz

OBJECTIVE OF ACTIVITY

To enable students to apply grammatical skills and to follow directions.

STUDENT PREPARATION

The student has had some work in the grammar unit.

TEACHER PREPARATION

The green circuit of the Multi-Board is used for this activity. Make up the query cards (see examples), outlining each card in green ink to match the green circuit of the game board.

PROCEDURE

Two or more students may play the green circuit. The first player rolls the dice and moves his marker along the green track of the board the number of spaces indicated by the dice throw. He follows the directions on space. When the direction says to pick a card, he selects a card, reads it aloud and makes a response. He shows the back of the card to another player to verify his accuracy. If the player has answered correctly, he moves his marker one space forward and waits for his next turn. If he answers incorrectly, he retains the card and tries to answer the same question when it is his turn again. If correct, he moves forward one space. The player who completes the green circuit first is named GRAMMAR WHIZ.

Examples of cards for Activity III of Multi-Board:

1. Her purple <u>feet</u> smelled like grapes. What is the underlined word called? (noun/subject of sentence)*
2. He dumped his toys <u>into the river.</u> What part of speech is the underlined phrase? (prepositional phrase/adverbial phrase)
3. Name four prepositions. (into, over, under, around, through, to, above; any others)
4. <u>Running naked through the briars</u> is dumb. What do we call the underlined phrase? (gerund phrase/subject phrase)
5. Gerund phrases are usually _____. (nouns)
6. Gerunds are formed by adding _____ to the end of a verb. (ing)
7. Unscramble this sentence. fingers his ate messy Martin fish with. (Messy Martin ate fish with his fingers. Martin ate messy fish with his fingers. Martin ate fish with his messy fingers.)
8. Correct the verb in this sentence. Billy don't swim well; he sinks like a ton of lead. (*doesn't* instead of *don't*)
9. Don't play with the gorillas. What is the subject of the sentence? (The subject is not stated. It is "you" understood.)
10. Jim jumped over a dead cow, or tried to. What tense? (past)
11. Mary made mud pies, <u>and</u> she threw them at the wall. What part of speech is the underlined word? (conjunction)
12. <u>Zonkers</u>! That's a large canary! What part of speech is the underlined word? (interjection)
13. They <u>goes</u> fishing when the creek is running. Correct the sentence. (go)
14. The <u>beautiful</u> movie star Nora Desmond is making a comeback. What part of speech is the underlined word? (adjective modifier)
15. Bob eat his cereal with a knife. Correct the sentence. (eats/ate)
16. There ain't nothin' I'm too proud to do. How would you say this to impress your teacher? (*isn't anything* instead of *ain't nothin'*)

*Answers appear on the back of the card.

17. What are the three main tenses of English? (past, present, and future)
18. The boys paddled <u>furiously</u> to escape the falls. What does the underlined word modify? (paddled)
19. Her mother forced her <u>to go</u> to church. What part of speech is the underlined phrase? (infinitive)
20. How can you recognize an infinitive phrase? (An infinitive phrase begins with <u>to</u> and ends with a verb.)

Activity IV for Multi-Board

▶SUBJECT AREA

English

GRADE LEVEL

7–12

NAME OF ACTIVITY

Block Buster Descriptions

OBJECTIVE OF ACTIVITY

To foster students' use of subjective adjectives beyond their speaking vocabulary and to promote use of the dictionary and the ability to follow directions.

STUDENT PREPARATION

The student has had training in systematic use of the dictionary.

TEACHER PREPARATION

The purple circuit of the Multi-Board is used for this activity. Clip attractive pictures from magazines that depict situations which lend themselves to out-of-the-ordinary descriptors. Make a card(s) to accompany each picture and select three words from which students are to choose one. Choose words in such a manner that only one can be an appropriate descriptor. The cards should be outlined in purple to match the purple track of the Multi-Board.

PROCEDURE

Two or more players roll dice and move markers accordingly on the purple circuit. When a player's marker stops on a Pick-a-Card space, he selects a card, chooses the apropriate picture, reads the card aloud and shows the picture to other players, and makes a response. He shows the back of the card to other players to verify his accuracy. If the player has answered correctly, he moves the marker ahead one space. If incorrect, he is not allowed to see the answer but looks up the various words in the dictionary so he can answer correctly on the next round. Then he can move ahead one space. First player to finish is a VOCABULARY BRAIN.

Examples of cards for Activity IV of Multi-Board:

1. Look at picture 1. What word best describes it? a) pristine b) mundane c) undulating (pristine)*
2. Look at picture 9. Is he a) desiccated b) robust c) insidious? (robust)
3. Look at picture 2. Are they a) diaphanous b) lackadaisical c) vivacious? (lackadaisical)
4. Look at picture 13. Are they a) effervescent b) loquacious c) congenital? (effervescent)
5. Look at picture 6. Are they a) derelict b) vicarious c) demure? (demure)
6. Look at picture 20. Is the scene a) communal b) philanthropic c) disheartening? (disheartening)
7. Look at picture 8. Is this scene a) maternalistic b) paternalistic c) preternatural? (maternalistic)
8. Look at picture 21. Are these men a) exuberant b) sedate c) phlegmatic? (sedate)
9. Look at picture 4. Are these men a) exuberant b) disinterested c) unperturbed? (exuberant)
10. Look at picture 17. Are these men a) conscripted b) undisciplined c) unruly? (conscripted)
11. Look at picture 17. Are these men a) ebullient b) sanguine c) regimented? (regimented)
12. Look at picture 19. Is the picture a) idyllic b) bucolic c) volatile? (volatile)
13. Look at picture 1. Is it a) catalytic b) primeval c) gregarious? (primeval)
14. Look at picture 5. Is the girl a) irascible b) sensual c) repulsed? (sensual)
15. Look at picture 5. Is the girl a) enamored b) profane c) flavescent? (enamored)

*The correct response is on the back of the card.

16. Look at picture 16. Is the picture a) belligerent b) malignant c) domestic? (domestic)
17. Look at picture 10. Is the portrayal a) diabolic b) benign c) tumescent? (diabolic)
18. Look at picture 7. Is the picture a) pastoral b) urban c) garrulous? (pastoral)
19. Look at picture 12. Are these men a) unmitigated b) lethargic c) industrious? (industrious)
20. Look at picture 3. Are these women a) flagrant b) immodest c) coy? (coy)

►SUBJECT AREA

English

GRADE LEVEL

7–9

NAME OF ACTIVITY

Dictionary Clues

OBJECTIVE OF ACTIVITY

To introduce variety into learning sessions with the dictionary.

STUDENT PREPARATION

The student has had instruction in basic dictionary skills.

TEACHER PREPARATION

This activity is housed in a file folder. Contents include clues which give a message when unraveled. Make sets of clue cards similar to the four examples given. (The example clues are geared to *Webster's New Collegiate Dictionary*, eighth edition, 1975. Clues should be written for the dictionary available in each classroom.) Place each answer card in a separate envelope; it serves as the student's self-check. Also include a set of directions to the student in the file folder.

PROCEDURE

The student selects a clue card and follows the directions. As he finds the answers to the clues, he writes them in sequence. When he completes the clue card, his individual answers total to a message. He checks his accuracy with the answer card. This activity works well with two participants also. Each uses his own dictionary to follow up the clue and is a doublecheck for the other student as the two progress.

Examples of clue cards:

Clue Card A

1. It is the word following "goober."
2. It is the plural of the word which is the last entry in the left column on page 1350.
3. It is the word that is directly before "area."
4. It is the word on pages 1352–53 that has four meanings, one of which is "of value."
5. It is the word on page 754 that is a synonym for "great."
6. It is the word that is "used as a function word to indicate connection or addition" and is across from "anemometric."
7. It is the fifth word down from the guide word, "coryza."
8. It is the word on page 672 that is a synonym for "small."

Clue Card B

1. It is the word on page 56, right column, that means "unusually fitted or qualified."
2. This word has "Worcestershire sauce" on top of it.
3. It is the word on page 526 that takes up almost half a column of space.
4. It is the seventh entry under the guide word, "powder monkey."
5. You'll find it under TNT.
6. The last word in this sentence is the sixth entry after "us."

Clue Card C

1. It is the last entry of the left column on page 1208.
2. It is the only word on page 846 that has seven meanings.
3. It comes right after the letters that stand for Internal Revenue Service.
4. It is the shortest whole word on page 1208.
5. It is in the left column across from "tonsil."
6. It rhymes with love and it closes the left column on page 796.
7. It is the same as the first and fourth word in this message.
8. It is the word in the right column that rhymes with "kind."

Clue Card D

1. It is the last word in the column under the guide word, "that."
2. It is the word on page 317 that is an antonym for "sameness."
3. This word is between "bettor" and "betwixt."
4. It is the same as the first word in this message.
5. This word on page 997 is a synonym for "correct."
6. This word has "Worcestershire sauce" on top of it.
7. This word on page 43, left column, rhymes with "land."
8. This word follows "thaw."
9. It is the word that is just before "alms."
10. It follows "rigging" and has a homonym, "write."
11. It is the word that is five words after "woozy."
12. This word is the first syllable of the word "Israeli."
13. It is the same as the first word in this message.
14. It is the third last word after the guide word, "dictograph."
15. This word is pronounced "bi-ʹtwēn" and is five words after "better."
16. In the right column, on page 665, this word usually accompanies "thunder."
17. It is a three-letter word that precedes "andalusite."
18. It is the shortest word in the right column on page 1208.
19. It leads the words in right column on page 665.
20. It is the shortest word in the right column, page 144, that rhymes with "hug."

SUBJECT AREA

English

GRADE LEVEL

7–9

NAME OF ACTIVITY

Syllable Spin

OBJECTIVE OF ACTIVITY

While students' speaking vocabularies are sometimes more colorful than teachers find acceptable, they usually overwork nondescript words such as run, pretty, fat. This activity is designed to add synonyms for overused words to students' vocabularies and to promote use of dictionary and thesaurus.

STUDENT PREPARATION

None.

TEACHER PREPARATION

Type simple, everyday words on 3 X 5″ cards and place them in an envelope. Examples:

talk	love	hold	walk	set
money	thin	fat	red	say
road	help	fight	pretty	see
sad	run	try	bit	nosy
rain	start	want	chair	pan

Make a spinner with designations of 1, 2, and 3.

Syllable Spinner.

PROCEDURE

Two or more players can take part in the activity. In his turn each student draws a card from the deck. He names the word he has drawn and uses the spinner to determine how many syllables are to be contained in the synonym he gives. If he spins a two and correctly gives a two-syllable synonym, he has two points on his score. If player is unable to provide the word, the next player has an opportunity to give a word and collects the two points. Students may consult a dictionary on thesaurus for the amount of time set by the teacher.

SUBJECT AREA

English

GRADE LEVEL

7–9

NAME OF ACTIVITY

Critters

OBJECTIVE OF ACTIVITY

This activity has four objectives:

1. To build vocabulary through writing.
2. To emphasize noun-adjective relationship.
3. To stimulate imaginative anecdotes.
4. To encourage use of the dictionary and other reference materials.

STUDENT PREPARATION

None.

TEACHER PREPARATION

Select adjectives outside students' speaking vocabulary but likely to
be encountered in reading. For example:

melancholy	enormous
aggressive	ingenious
exuberant	ramshackled
assiduous	adroit
gargantuan	amicable
shrewd	indolent
expeditious	staunch
tenacious	diminutive
ravenous	garrulous
docile	remorseful

Put the words on slips of paper or cards and house them in an envelope. In a second envelope put cards bearing the names of critters, such as

coyote	porcupine
mastiff	wolverine
bushmaster	tapir
ptarmigan	dingo
albatross	malamute
alpaca	bison
pachyderm	capuchin
grebe	cheetah

Have dictionaries that use many illustrations and encyclopedias available. Put the materials together with a set of directions in a file folder.

PROCEDURE

The student draws one card from the critter envelope and five cards from the adjective envelope. Using the critter as his central character, he creates a fifty-word anecdote incorporating the five descriptors.

VARIATION

The adjectives and names of critters can be dittoed for use with an entire class. In this case, each student would choose his own critter and five descriptors.

SUBJECT AREA

English

GRADE LEVEL

7–12

NAME OF ACTIVITY

Alternate Routes for Finger Walking

OBJECTIVE OF ACTIVITY

"Let Your Fingers Do the Walking through the Yellow Pages" is a familiar slogan to students. According to a study made by Audits and Surveys Company of New York City, 51 percent of the references to the Yellow Pages were made without a name in mind. The principal objective of this activity is to encourage students to seek alternate names for services and products (synonyms). Additionally, reinforcement will be given alphabetizing, classifying, and dictionary skills.

STUDENT PREPARATION

None.

TEACHER PREPARATION

Obtain a copy of a telephone directory for each student in the class. (Some companies will give obsolete directories away after new books have been delivered.) Prepare the activity on a ditto (example given) that has been divided into four columns: Situation; Service or Product Needed; Found Under; Name and Phone Number of Supplier. Have dictionaries and a thesaurus available.

PROCEDURE

Individually, in pairs, or in small groups, students do their finger walking. When they have completed the task, the teacher leads class members in creating their own activity patterned after the one used.

Alternate Routes for Finger Walking*

The truth about directory assistance?

This year,
millions of your telephone dollars will be spent
for operators to look up over 37 million
telephone numbers already listed in the directory.

If you want to end this waste,
please look in the book first.

INSTRUCTIONS

Help keep costs down on telephone service by knowing how to get information from the *Yellow Pages.* In this activity, you may need to think of other headings under which services and products are listed. A couple of examples should help you get started.

Situation	Service/product needed	Found under	Name/phone number of supplier
Winter's coming and you don't want your car to freeze up.	anti-freeze	Service Stations	Rudy's Texaco Service 249-2304
Your fish are out of food.	fish food	Tropical Fish	The Tropical Reef 947-6344
You want to build a wooden coffee table.			
Your mother got a job and told you to get the names of centers			

*Telephone Advertisements and Excerpts Reprinted With Permission of Mountain Bell.

where she could leave your baby sister during the day.			
You're going to court and you need some legal help.			
You want to fly to see your grandmother.			
You would like some information on taking flying lessons.			
You have a prescription to get filled.			
Your dad asked you to find out where he could get a hitch for your RV (recreational vehicle).			

SUBJECT AREA

English

GRADE LEVEL

7–9

NAME OF ACTIVITY

Abbrev.

OBJECTIVE OF ACTIVITY

To provide individual experience in decoding abbreviations.

STUDENT PREPARATION

The student has had previous introduction to abbreviation usage.

TEACHER PREPARATION

Prepare the activity in a file folder, including abbreviation cards, category envelopes, answers, abbreviated messages, and directions for individual use. (See example for construction, suggested abbreviations, and suggested abbreviated messages.)

PROCEDURE

The student sorts abbreviation cards by categories into envelopes. When he is finished, he raises the bottom panel to check his answers. After working with single abbreviations, he decodes abbreviations in sentences. The decoded response is on the back of the card for self-checking.

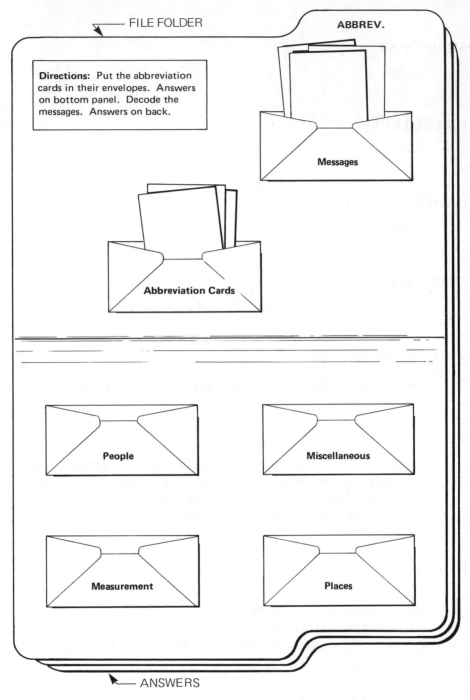

File Folder Format for Abbreviations Activity.

Possible abbreviations for cards:

Capt.	P. O. Box	gm.
Mrs.	WW II	i.e.
Sgt.	Ave.	Alta.
PhD.	Assoc.	WPA
Ms.	3-br.	Wed.
Mr.	USA	yr.
Dr.	LA	p.m.
PTA	e.g.	apt.
etc.	mo.	gr.
St.	lb.	jr.
misc.	mm.	Inc.

(Note: Sources for acronyms and abbreviations are listed in Part I of this book.)

Examples of abbreviated messages:

Dr. & Mrs. Wm. Jones will arr. on T.W.A. Thur. aft. Mar. 16th. They are prepd. to devote Fri. p.m. for loc. an apt. near the E. St. Sch. They have 2 ch. so will req. at least 3 bdms. Please asst. them.

Mr. Wms. is the new instr. for the bus. dept. He will be assg'd. the comb'd. cl. of bus. and pers. typg. He rec'd. many bks. of int. at the conv. and is prepg. a lect. to pres. at our 1st conf. in the spr.

SUBJECT AREA

English

GRADE LEVEL

9–12

NAME OF ACTIVITY

Feelings about Words

OBJECTIVE OF ACTIVITY

To enable students to discover the tie between words themselves and feelings about words.

STUDENT PREPARATION

None

TEACHER PREPARATION

After studying biographical data on well-known persons, prepare a list of descriptors that apply to each. (See examples.)

PROCEDURE

Students study the descriptors, list by list, and react to each piece of data by checkmarking columns labeled: Positive Feeling, Negative Feeling, or No Feeling Either Way. After they complete the list, the teacher leads students in a discussion of connotation with questions designed to climax in the teacher's announcement that each group of characteristics describes properties of *one* well-known person. The ultimate conclusion at which the class should arrive is that feelings about words vary in degree, depending on the amount of knowledge and experience the viewer of the word has. An obvious conclusion students might arrive at is that since each person has varying knowledge and experiences, each person's view of another will differ.

Example of ditto:

Feelings about Words*

DIRECTIONS

Words have no feelings in themselves, but they do take on negative or positive meanings when they are used by human beings. Words that are positive to some people are negative to others, depending on the experiences in peoples' backgrounds. So there is no right or wrong in this activity. Look at each word, decide how you feel about it and checkmark the column that represents your feeling.

	Positive Feeling	Negative Feeling	No Feeling Either Way
1. Big leaguer			
2. Record breaker			
3. Orphan			
4. Hall of Fame			
5. Yankee			
6. College dropout			
7. Dutch			
8. Painter			
9. Miller's helper			
10. Overnight success			
11. Polish			
12. Governess			
13. Bicycle rider			
14. Nobel Prize winner			
15. College professor			
16. Physicist			
17. Pulitzer Prize winner			
18. Goatkeeper			
19. Guitarist			
20. Biographer			

*Descriptors based on information in *Great Lives, Great Deeds* © 1964 The Reader's Digest Association, Inc.

21. Bootblack			
22. Poet			
23. Hobo			
24. Southerner			
25. Slave			
26. Coal miner			
27. Janitor			
28. College founder			
29. Disciplinarian			
30. Hall of Fame			

Teacher's Key: 1–5   George Herman (the Babe) Ruth
                      6–10   Rembrandt van Rijn
                      11–16   Madame Curie
                      17–23   Carl Sandburg
                      24–30   Booker T. Washington

VARIATION

Use biographical data on persons in students' everyday life: sports figures, musicians, radio, TV, and movie stars.

SUBJECT AREA

English

GRADE LEVEL

7–12

NAME OF ACTIVITY

Accent Changes → Meaning Changes

OBJECTIVE OF ACTIVITY

To emphasize the importance of syllable stress in changing the meaning of a heteronym.

STUDENT PREPARATION

None.

TEACHER PREPARATION

Discuss heteronyms, words that have different sounds and different meanings but the same spelling. Begin with the simple ones—lead, lead; wind, wind—proceeding to those heteronyms that have more than one syllable. Put on the board or on a transparency:

- The Reader's Digest'
- Good Conduct' Medal
- The object' of his affections
- relay' race
- ex-convict'
- present' participle
- Pro'ceed with Caution

Help students to deduce that the accent marks are misplaced. Then present students a dittoed sheet having several heteronyms. (See example.)

PROCEDURE

Students rewrite the heteronym, placing the accent mark, then write a phrase appropriate for the accent they have chosen. Example for digest: di'gest, The Reader's Digest. The students add other heteronyms of more than one syllable to the list and proceed according to directions.

Accent Changes → Meaning Changes

DIRECTIONS

In column I, write the heteronym with an accent; in column II, write a phrase containing the word as you have accented it. Add your own heteronyms of more than one syllable and follow the same instructions.

Heteronym	Column I	Column II
1. invalid	in'valid	flowers for the invalid
2. defect		
3. abstract		
4. advocate		
5. digest		
6. primer		
7. attribute		
8. buffet		
9. upset		
10. minute		
11. contract		
12. contest		
13. converse		
14. proceed		
15. object		
16. conduct		
17. relay		
18. upgrade		
19. address		

20. compact
21. complex
22. compound
23. compress
24. conflict
25. content
26. desert
27. discount
28.
29.
30.
31.
32.
33.
34.
35.

▶SUBJECT AREA

English

GRADE LEVEL

7–8

NAME OF ACTIVITY

Top 40 Metaphors and Similes

OBJECTIVE OF ACTIVITY

To help students recognize and understand similes and metaphors through the use of everyday resources; in this example, use of radio, records, and tapes.

STUDENT PREPARATION

The student has some knowledge of similes and metaphors.

TEACHER PREPARATION

None.

PROCEDURE

This activity involves something which almost all students enjoy doing, listening to popular music. For the period of one week, students listen to music on the radio or on their own records and tapes and identify and list as many metaphors and similes as they can find. On the appointed day each student reads his list to class members, who decide on the accuracy of choices.

VARIATION

Have students watch for and list metaphors and similes used in television commercials.

SUBJECT AREA

English

GRADE LEVEL

9–10

NAME OF ACTIVITY

Setting Set-up

OBJECTIVE OF ACTIVITY

To help students become familiar with the trappings of setting in a short story, to increase their skill in manipulating particular words and phrases to accomplish the appropriate setting for their own composition, and to promote visualizing.

STUDENT PREPARATION

Students must know what setting is and have some idea how it functions in a story or composition.

TEACHER PREPARATION

None.

PROCEDURE

The class is divided into two groups, and a leader is chosen for each group. When the groups assemble, the leader explains procedure. Each team is to create eight or ten settings that might be found in a short story or novel. The leader acts as recorder. Then each group creates ten details for each of the eight or ten settings. Each detail should be only a word or short phrase. The details are listed with their setting. An example would be the following:

Setting—primary school classroom
Details—tiny desks and chairs
        primers
        coloring books and crayons
        bathroom at back of room
        alphabet on the blackboard
        sink
        bulletin boards
        reading corner
        primary typewriter

When the lists are compiled, each group takes turns reading one list of details to the other. The opposing group must name the setting. The team receives one point if the setting is named on first try. For each successive attempt, one point is added. The group with the most points loses.

As a culminating activity, each member of the class chooses one setting-detail card and writes a short, short story.

SUBJECT AREA

English

GRADE LEVEL

7–12

NAME OF ACTIVITY

Checkers

OBJECTIVE OF ACTIVITY

To reinforce identification of style, tone, and mood as hallmarks of particular works and authors.

STUDENT PREPARATION

None.

TEACHER PREPARATION

Prepare poster board in the design of a checkerboard or obtain a commercial board. Select excerpts from poetry and prose that are strong examples of style, tone, and mood. Type the excerpts on 3 X 5″ cards.

PROCEDURE

Three students are involved in this activity. One acts as scorekeeper as the other two play. The opponents play checkers in the accepted manner, except as the pieces move onto the opponent's side of the board, the player must identify an excerpt by work and author before he may move his man. The scorekeeper has the answers and confirms accuracy or error of response. If the answer is incorrect, the player may not move his checker, and the opponent has his turn. All rules of checkers apply plus the additional rule concerning the literary excerpts.

SUBJECT AREA

English

GRADE LEVEL

10–12

NAME OF ACTIVITY

Extendi-Character

OBJECTIVE OF ACTIVITY

To promote identification of particular qualities of characters in short stories and to extend imaginative thinking.

STUDENT PREPARATION

The student has read a variety of short stories with various characters and has had classroom instruction in characterization.

TEACHER PREPARATION

It is often difficult for students to get a clear picture of a particular character in a novel or short story. If students are asked to extend the scope of their awareness of the character through imagination, they get extended insights. Compose many fictitious circumstances into which students can project characters they have met in the short stories.

For example:

A telegram has announced the forthcoming arrival of out-of-town relatives whom your character dislikes. What will he do to cope with the situation?

Your character's daughter introduces the family to a stranger with whom she eloped. Write the dialogue that follows.

Your character has been stopped by a police officer who said he ran a red light. What kinds of statements will he make to the police officer?

Rain has spoiled this afternoon's golf game. How will your character spend the afternoon?

The doctor has said your character has developed emphysema and must stop smoking. How will he cope with the news?

Your character has met a person who has offered to double her money. What will your character do?

Your character has decided to arrange a very special evening. What will he plan?

Your character has sat down next to a very attractive person on the bus. How will she react?

While reading the newspaper, your character sees quite a few ads for contemporary clothes. What is his opinion of them?

PROCEDURE

The students match up the situation created by the teacher with one of the characters they have read about in the short stories. They compose two or three paragraphs in answer to the question.

SUBJECT AREA

English

GRADE LEVEL

9–12

NAME OF ACTIVITY

Clued In

OBJECTIVE OF ACTIVITY

The activity requires the student to extract bits and pieces from his reading references and to apply them in a new way. The skill is a forerunner of the ability to sort facts from the student's referent and to find a common element among these facts to produce new learning.

STUDENT PREPARATION

None.

TEACHER PREPARATION

From the reading background of the class extract some common elements, that is, characters, theme, author, or any other factors significant to the selections. The selections should be varied and may be from plays, poetry, and novels, as well as philosophies. Write verses giving clues on dittoed sheets. Place each clue verse in an envelope and mark the envelopes, beginning with no. 1. The clues here are samples.

PROCEDURE

The groups receive several envelopes, marked in sequence, beginning with no. 1. Each envelope contains a clue or problem. When that problem is solved and the correct answer is written on it, each group is entitled to open envelope no. 2. The answer to no. 1 must be known before no. 2 can be tackled, no. 2 solved before opening envelope no. 3, no. 3 before no. 4. This is a race between groups. If the problem cannot be solved, the teacher gives the answer to the group on request and tallies a two-minute penalty. Since this is a timed race, it is conceivable that the winning group may, in fact, be the last to finish, if it had not had to ask for an answer and thus be penalized. In a forty minute-period, five minutes would be allowed for each clue.

Examples of clues:

1.

This poet wrote a "Love Song,"
but not set to music.
To him April was cruel.
Now, can you guess, "Who is it?"

He turned the mulberry bush into a
prickly pear.
And his hollow scarecrow had no hair.
The author of these thoughts shares
The same name as a nineteenth-century writer
of some fame.

2.

If things are going according to plan,
You've discovered you're not a Superman.
The pseudonym adopted by Mary Ann
Is also the first name of this man.
He and Nietzsche had the same plan, and
He expressed it in "_____."

3.

Now this man, the George in clue # two.
Wrote a play with a title of only one word.
Change an a *to* e *for a French book*
Of which you may have heard.

Since this is a toughie and might not be fair,
Unscramble these letters, and the same answer
Is there. a d d i a n C

4.

Now unscramble these for the French author's name:
    r e l t a i o V
The first three letters of this man's name
Suggest the title of an English author's play.
It's the author's name you're after.
His play had a crow, a vulture and a fly,
*And the star of this play was **very very** sly.*

5.

Now this playwright who wrote of Mosca and Voltore
Had the same name as an Englishman who wrote a dictionary.
This famous man thought literary clubs were the rage,
And Boswell recorded their meeting, page by page.

6.

Our man in clue six has the same first name,
As a writer across the ocean, of late nineteenth-century fame.
A reporter, a novelist, a lecturer, and a ham,
Can you give the pseudonym of this famous Sam?

Answers to clues:

1. T. S. Elliot and George Elliot
2. Mary Ann Evans and *Man and Superman*, G. B. Shaw
3. *Candida, Candide*
4. Voltaire, Ben Johnson, *Volpone*
5. Ben Johnson, Samuel Johnson
6. Samuel Johnson, Mark Twain (S. L. Clemens)

▶SUBJECT AREA

English

GRADE LEVEL

7–9

NAME OF ACTIVITY

Grammarace

OBJECTIVE OF ACTIVITY

To help students become thoroughly acquainted with the roles words play in grammar.

STUDENT PREPARATION

The student has learned the parts of speech and their function in sentences.

TEACHER PREPARATION

Prepare a raceway with three tracks. Mark off squares and print the name of a part of speech in each square. Several cards should be made with one letter on each. Supply markers.

PROCEDURE

Three students play Grammarace at a time. They choose markers and line up on the starting line of the race track. One by one they move to the first square which gives a part of speech. Drawing a card, each player must give an example of that part of speech beginning with the letter on the card. If the answer is correct, the player moves his marker forward the number of squares as there are letters in the word given.

Example:
    VERB   (player draws R) radiate = 7 spaces forward
              (player draws W) wander = 6 spaces forward
Winning player reaches the finishing line first.

SUBJECT AREA

English

GRADE LEVEL

7–9

NAME OF ACTIVITY

Four-Letter Words

OBJECTIVE OF ACTIVITY

To improve students' spelling and dictionary skills.

STUDENT PREPARATION

None.

TEACHER PREPARATION

Prepare cards of sixteen or twenty-five squares with one letter per square. Approximately 40 percent of the letters should be vowels. Place the letters randomly on a card.

B	A	Y	M	E
I	N	L	O	R
G	E	C	P	U
A	D	H	E	K
F	S	I	L	W

PROCEDURE

Students begin at any letter and move one square at a time in any direction to form words. Words must contain at least four letters.

Players score two points for each four-letter word and one point for each letter over four. (In the example given, the student began with the letter D on the lower left side and found the word DEAD. In the upper right corner, the student found MORE and POUR.)

VARIATION

By increasing the number of squares (thirty-six, forty-nine, or more) the limitation of using a letter only once per game could be added with the game ending when no more words could be formed.

SUBJECT AREA

English

GRADE LEVEL

7–9

NAME OF ACTIVITY

Building Words

OBJECTIVE OF ACTIVITY

To enhance vocabulary building, to increase spelling accuracy, and to encourage use of the dictionary.

STUDENT PREPARATION

Each student marks off a sheet of paper into a square containing twenty-five small squares.

TEACHER PREPARATION

None.

PROCEDURE

One student begins by calling out a letter. All players write this letter in any one of the twenty-five small squares. This continues until twenty-four squares have been filled. Each player fills in the last square with any letter he chooses. The object of the game is to form as many complete words as possible. A dictionary may be used. Any word that can be read up, down, across, or diagonally counts. Each letter of a word counts one point. The student with the most points wins.

Example of scoring:

P O S B Y	patch	by	am
A L H U H	pat	eye	it
T R A C E	tap	trace	sue
C M T Y V	hate	race	plays
H I E N S	ate	ace	lay
	hat	cart	cub
	at	art (twice)	he

69 points

▶SUBJECT AREA

English

GRADE LEVEL

7–9

NAME OF ACTIVITY

Birds of a Feather . . .

OBJECTIVE OF ACTIVITY

To help students associate novels with their authors and main characters.

STUDENT PREPARATION

None.

TEACHER PREPARATION

Make four cards per novel, putting the title of the novel on one card, the author on another, and a main character on each of the remaining two.

For example:

Huckleberry Finn	*Robinson Crusoe*
Samuel Clemens	Daniel Defoe
Huck Finn	Friday
Jim	Robinson Crusoe

As many sets can be made as desired, but a minimum should be two sets of four cards each for the number of participants; for instance, if four people are to play, there should be at least eight novel sets.

PROCEDURE

The dealer shuffles the cards and distributes the entire deck. Remembering that the object of the activity is to collect all four cards pertaining to one novel, all players pass one card to the left simultaneously. The passing continues until one player accumulates two complete novel sets. The winner describes each of the characters in the novel with a one-liner. Losers make fours cards for a novel so the deck will be constantly renewed.

SPEECH

Speech

GRADE LEVEL

9–12

NAME OF ACTIVITY

Fallacy Poker

OBJECTIVE OF ACTIVITY

This activity on detecting fallacies in speeches also has as its objectives helping students:

1. To identify strategies of propaganda and persuasion.
2. To distinguish between fact and opinion.
3. To evaluate by a standard and make judgments.
4. To interpret connotative language.

STUDENT PREPARATION

The student is somewhat familiar with and able to recognize common fallacies: hasty generalizations, false analogies, irrelevant conclusions, false authority, loaded words, and stereotyping.

TEACHER PREPARATION

On cards the size of playing cards type statements that contain fallacies of various types. Include some statements that do not contain fallacies. At the lower right hand corner type a number from 1 through 52 and prepare a key identifying the types of fallacies to these numbers.

For example:
Card: I've been in that store twice and couldn't find a thing I wanted. They have terrible merchandise.

Key: On no. 19 of the key is the identity of the fallacy: hasty generalization.

Purchase or make poker chips.

PROCEDURE

Four to five students play Fallacy Poker. They follow the conventional rules of poker, using the chips to ante and raise the pot. Players try for the best hand. If the round, for example, is draw poker, the player looks at his five cards, identifies the fallacies, groups the cards according to the fallacy, discards non-matches, and draws a like number of cards from the stack to try to match those cards he kept in his hand. (One deviation from conventional poker would be the type of winning hands. Because there are no suits on the homemade card deck, there will be no flushes, straights, and the like.) In order to win the round, a player must identify the types of fallacies in his hand. For example, if he claims four of a kind, he must name the fallacy which all four cards exemplify. He may be challenged by the other players, and the dispute is settled by a non-player who looks at the key. If two players have tie hands, for example, both have full houses (three examples of one fallacy and two of another), and if they both correctly identify their fallacies, the two students split the pot. The student with the most chips at the end of the activity period is the winner.

SUBJECT AREA

Speech

GRÁDE LEVEL

9–12

NAME OF ACTIVITY

Get the Point?

OBJECTIVE OF ACTIVITY

To make an analogy between the point of a joke and the main idea of a one-minute speech.

Phase I

STUDENT PREPARATION

Each student thinks of a joke to tell his classmates.

TEACHER PREPARATION

None.

PROCEDURE

Each student tells his joke prepared for the assignment. After each presentation, the class decides on the point of the joke. The joke teller verifies his classmates' accuracy.

Phase II

STUDENT PREPARATION

None.

Bankruptcy filings up by 20 pct.

The number of bankruptcy filings in Phoenix this year is nearly 20 per cent greater than last year and apparently will exceed the number of bankruptcies filed in the recession year of 1970.

As of Wednesday there had been 2,067 bankruptcy petitions of all types filed for the year, compared with 1,723 through November 1973. By the end of November 1970, there were 2,008 filings.

Prior to 1974, annual bankruptcy filings hadn't reached 2,000 since 1970. There were 2,199 petitions filed that year, according to Ken Grant, chief deputy federal court clerk.

Grant thinks the number of filings this year will "easily surpass" the 1970 figure. He said employes at Motorola Inc. who were recently laid off are starting to file bankruptcy petitions.

In the first six months of 1974 there were 1,025 bankruptcy petitions filed here, compared with 1,092 in the same period of 1970.

Virginia Fritz, chief bankruptcy clerk in Phoenix, said 42 of the 2,067 cases filed this year were filed on behalf of businesses. The rest were filed by individuals. She said eight of the businesses filing petitions have declared assets in excess of $50,000.

Federal Bankruptcy Judge Vincent D. Maggiore says the figure for the number of businesses filing bankruptcy could be misleading.

"We have a lot of small businesses in Arizona," he said. "Many owners of such businesses file bankruptcy petitions as individuals because of personal debts they incurred in guaranteeing their businesses. So the figure of 2,067 bankruptcies probably indicates many business failures."

Maggiore says that unless the federal government can deal effectively with the current economic problems plaguing the country, there could be as many as 3,000 individual bankruptcy filings and as many as 100 business filings in Phoenix in 1975.

"I don't want to sound like a prophet of doom," he said, "but I think we'll be feeling a greater impact from the current recession around the first of the year. The recession actually started with the gasoline shortage last year. There's usually a lag of six months to a year before the pronounced effects of a slowdown are felt."

According to Maggiore, the current economic problems are caused primarily by a lack of money for financing and capitalizing businesses. He said even large companies are affected because of the higher cost of materials and supplies and the unavailability of loans.

'Unless something happens so that more money is put back into the market, some big, important businesses may go under," he added.

Maggiore feels the government should move quickly to put more money into the economy to salvage as many businesses as possible and to insure enough jobs in the future.

He conceded, however, that the government could be attempting to find a way to spur the economy without further aggravating inflation.

Maggiore said the local high unemployment rate may be reflected in the increased bankruptcies. Unemployment in Maricopa County in October was at 6.8 per cent, the highest since February 1961, when it was at 7.2 per cent.

He said many people from other states are filing bankruptcies here. Some who move here seeking employment are unable to find jobs, and they then become bankrupt, he explained. A person who has been in Arizona the greater part of six months, or three months and a day, can file a bankruptcy petition here.

A large number of construction workers have filed bankruptcy petitions in Phoenix, according to Maggiore. He said mainly small, marginal businesses are filing petitions.

Maggiore said a company "can use the Bankruptcy Court as a respite to avoid being forced out of business if it has a business that is salvageable." Procedures for reorganization, or an arrangement to pay creditors, can provide relief for a financially troubled firm.

He said many companies may be trying to avoid bankruptcy by selling assets, and because of this, some of them will file petitions when it is too late for them to be salvaged.

News Story for "Get the Point?"

TEACHER PREPARATION

Clip enough straight news stories so each member of class will have his or her own. Straight news stories are factual accounts (see "Bankruptcy filings . . ."). The article should be relatively lengthy because the student must be able to glean enough information from it to write a one-minute informative speech. In thirty-five to fifty words write the main idea of each article on a transparency.

PROCEDURE

After studying the clipping, the student writes a one-minute informative speech based on the story and presents it to the class. After each speech, the class decides on the main idea just as it decided on the point of the joke in phase I. When a decision is made, the main idea is checked against the teacher's version on the transparency. Any difference is discussed.

Phase III

STUDENT PREPARATION

None.

TEACHER PREPARATION

Clip editorials, feature stories, and by-lined columns from the newspaper so each member of the class will have one. This type of newspaper account is based on fact, but usually has some subjective element in it (see "Bite of poisonous . . ."). The article should be long enough that the student has adequate data and ideas on which to base a one-minute talk. In thirty-five to forty words write the main idea of each clipping on a transparency.

PROCEDURE

After studying his clipping, each student writes a one-minute speech, incorporating the same point of view or angle as that of the editorial writer, feature writer, or columnist. When a student finishes his presentation, the class decides on the main idea. The class consensus is checked against the teacher's version on the transparency.

Used in kids' game

Bite of poisonous berry nearly causes boy's death

By ROBERT L. THOMAS

For the past several weeks the kids who go to Lookout Mountain School have been playing a game with death.

It was an innocent child's game and no one involved had any idea of its lethal properties.

The game was to take a white seed from a bright orange berry and "sting" another child by sneaking up and rubbing the seed across the other's bare arm or face.

The kids called the seeds "burn berries" because they stung when they touched the skin, even to the point of raising tiny blisters.

The sting wasn't too painful and many boys, to show their toughness and bravery, would pinch the seed and rub it on their own skin. But last week the true nature of the "burn berries" was revealed.

And it almost cost the life of a child. Mark Halpert, 9, a fourth grader at Lookout Mountain, was riding the school bus and like the other boys he had a supply of burn berries.

The common way for a child to remove the seed from its brown pod and orange berry was to grind it underfoot. On the bus Mark was unable to do this so he did the next best thing and bit the pod with his teeth.

In doing so he nipped off a tiny portion of the seed, perhaps a quarter of it, and accidently swallowed it.

Several hours later, in school, Mark wasn't feeling well. He went to the school nurse with nausea. Then he began to sweat heavily.

Luckily—and it probably saved his life—Mark's mother happened to be at school that day helping out as a classroom aide.

"I thought he was just coming down with the flu," she recalled. "But I decided to take him home and call my pediatrician if he felt worse.

"In the car he really got bad. By the time I got him home he was screaming with pain and perspiring very heavily," she said.

"Then his skin began to turn yellow and his lips turned blue. He vomited repeatedly and every time he did the poison from the berry in his stomach would come up and burn his throat and he'd scream in agony.

"I didn't know what to do," she continued. "I reached into his pocket for his lunch money and out rolled these berries.

"I don't know why, but as soon as I saw them I suspected they were the cause.

"Mark, I asked him, 'Did you eat some of these berries?'

" 'Only a little piece, Mom.' he said."

The boy was taken to the hospital and placed in the intensive care section. Doctors knew he was critically ill, but they didn't know what poison he had consumed nor from what berry.

"But I had the berries," said Mrs. Halpert. "We called every poison control center we could think of and described the berry and Mark's symptoms. No one knew what it was.

"By this time Mark was extremely ill. Doctors said his stomach was ulcerated and they were worried about a circulatory collapse from internal bleeding," she said.

"Then, when we'd just about given up hope, my doctor found a description of the bean or berry in a book called 'The Sinister Garden,' a book of poisonous trees, bushes, plants and seeds," Mrs. Halpert said.

"The Indians called the tree 'the suicide plant' and Indians in South America used the seed to poison their blow gun darts.

"We call it the mountain laurel. There is no antidote for its poison," she said.

The doctor, Pediatrician Don Langston, said the mountain laurel tree is common throughout Phoenix.

"After this I began to question my children about these 'burn berries,' " said Dr. Langston. "Sure enough, they knew about them too and the kids in the neighborhood had played with them. And my kids go to a school 20 miles from Lookout Mountain," added the doctor.

"That particular day," said Mrs. Halpert, "was our 10th wedding anniversary and my husband and I were sitting outside of the intensive care room staring at each other and wondering how this could happen to us."

Mark survived the night and snapped back the next day and was allowed to go home. Doctors said his life was undoubtedly saved by the fact he had only eaten a very small part of the seed.

Mrs. Halpert said she tracked down Mark's playmates and learned where they were getting the berry.

"It was from a laurel tree at a home close to ours," she said. "I went over to the house and told the man about the dangers of the seed, but I don't think I got across to him. I'm sure he thinks I was exaggerating.

"But I'm not. That little white nut is deadly. I did the same thing the kids did and the doctors at the hospital did too — rub the seed on our skin. And it really stings or burns. Swallow it and it burns your stomach."

Dr. Ella Forman, principal at Lookout Mountain School, said the brush with death strongly impressed the students and faculty.

"Right after this happened we had a talk with all the students and we told them about this terribly l e t h a l bean," said Mrs. Forman.

"We confiscated all the beans we found and we have since set up a project on poison control for education of the students," she said.

Mrs. Halpert, a Cub Scout leader, said she has been conducting a neighborhood campaign as well.

"I thank God my son is all right and is here to help me point out to his friends the dangers of this berry. I want to explain to their parents about the mountain laurel tree.

"I am so surprised that adults are so unaware of the dangers that are right in their own gardens," he said.

Feature Story for "Get the Point?"

Speech

GRADE LEVEL

9–12

NAME OF ACTIVITY

Says How?

OBJECTIVE OF ACTIVITY

To have student study the use of synonyms for the word *say,* in this example, by reading the alternatives used by headline writers.

STUDENT PREPARATION

None prior to assignment.

TEACHER PREPARATION

Newspaper headline writers are possibly unequaled in their use of alternatives for the word *say.* Their objective in behalf of variety demands that they search out and employ verbs that not only replace *say* but also describe the intent of the speaker who is being quoted. Give students three or four models (see examples) and assign them to clip verbs in headlines that are equivalents for the overworked word *say.*

PROCEDURE

Students clip twenty to twenty-five synonyms for *say* from newspaper headlines and paste them on an 8 1/2 × 11" sheet of paper (see example). On the ditto provided by the teacher they write each of the verbs and describe the manner in which the word represents *say.* For example, if the word *assails* is found, the student would write: "Says abusingly or in a ridiculing manner." Students refer to dictionaries for appropriate descriptive words.

NOTE

> Television and radio newscasters also are masters in varying their use
> of verbs that are equivalents of the word *say*. Variety can be added
> to this activity by having students study newscasters' choices.

Example of ditto prepared by teacher:

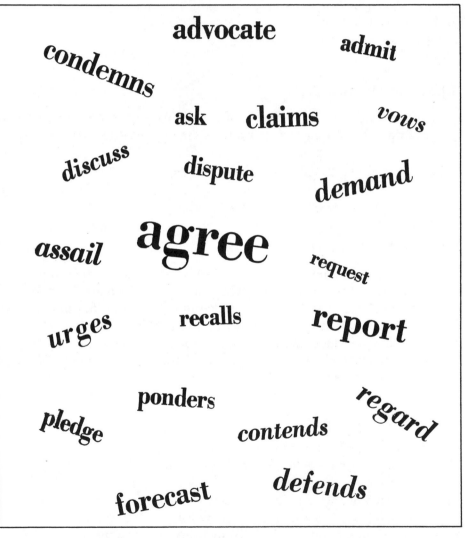

Newspaper Headlines for "Says How?"

Says How?

After you paste the words meaning *say* from newspaper headlines, write each on this sheet. In the space provided describe the manner in which the verb represents *say*. Three examples are given to get you started.

Word	Says How?
1. assails	says abusingly or in a ridiculing manner
2. consents	says in agreement
3. confesses	says he is guilty
4.	
5.	
6.	
7.	
8.	
9.	
10.	
11.	
12.	

SUBJECT AREA

Speech

GRADE LEVEL

9–12

NAME OF ACTIVITY

Erosion of English Language

OBJECTIVE OF ACTIVITY

This activity assists students

1. To interpret the written and/or spoken word from the focus of coinage and misuse of standard English.
2. To create erosive words; to use them in conversations with peers; and to predict general acceptance/rejection of their coined words.

Phase I

STUDENT PREPARATION

Students listen to entertainers such as Howard Cosell, Norm Crosby, Carroll O'Connor in the role of Archie Bunker, and Rocky Graziano, and make notes on nonstandard word and/or grammar usage. In addition, students scan newspaper headlines making notes on coined words. (See examples.)

TEACHER PREPARATION

None.

PROCEDURE

Students share their findings with classmates to further stimulate class discussion on erosion of the English language.

Awesome power of Arab petrodollars grows

U.S. prefers 'stagflation' to characterize economy

Will jawboning stave off wage, price controls?

News Examples of Eroded Language.

Phase II

STUDENT PREPARATION

Each student coins or creates a new word. (The assignment should be given two to three weeks in advance of the rest of the activity so the student has ample time to think about, play with, and mull over words and meanings.)

TEACHER PREPARATION

None.

PROCEDURE

In turn students present their new words, explain their meanings, and demonstrate use of the coined word in three sentences. Comments from the class follow.

For one week each student deliberately injects his word into conversations with peers, family, and other contacts. He keeps a daily log on responses made to his use of the word. At the end of the trial week, he presents a three-minute speech on the results of his experiment, ending with his prediction on the acceptance of his word into general usage or its rejection.

SUBJECT AREA

Speech

GRADE LEVEL

10–12

NAME OF ACTIVITY

Impromptu

OBJECTIVE OF ACTIVITY

A reporter will have devised questions in advance of an interview, but the person being interviewed responds extemporaneously. Studying impromptu verbal behavior in printed reports of interviews helps students sharpen these thinking skills:

1. To interpret meaning from responses to unknown questions.
2. To analyze.
3. To evaluate and make judgments.

STUDENT PREPARATION

Each student clips one interview story (see example) from a newspaper or magazine, mounts it on cardboard and submits it to the teacher.

TEACHER PREPARATION

Make a set of questions that will apply to all of the interview stories, reinforcing concepts studied during the unit on impromptu speeches.

Examples:

1. Analyze the interviewee's responses for sentence types: complete sentences, partial sentences, and one-word responses.
2. How is his grammar?

3. What evidence of evasion do you detect?
4. What evidence of openness?
5. Identify instances of double-talk.
6. Evaluate the logic of his answers.

PROCEDURE

Each member of the class receives an interview story and a set of questions. The teacher has assigned students to work in pairs. Each

People Reading More, Better

"Reading," says Dr. Dorothy Piercey, "is the tool for opening the whole world."

Dr. Piercey, education and reading professor at Arizona State University, says that not only are people reading more, but they're reading better than ever before.

"More attention is being paid when a child has reading problems in school," says Dr. Piercey. "Now poor readers have reading specialists to help them."

It's a good thing, too. Because regardless of television, she says, we live in a very print-oriented world.

"Book publishers will tell you their sales are up year after year — at least, they were before the paper shortage," she says. "People want to experience the world, but you can't experience everything directly. In fact, it isn't safe to do so." So people read books, magazines and newspapers instead.

To help their children become better readers, parents should teach them "love of language," says Dr. Piercey. "It's a logical step from oral language to reading and writing. How well a person reads depends a great deal on his verbal facility and his own experiences."

Experiences are very important, she adds, and parents should keep opening new horizons for their children as much as their economic situation will allow. "The more experience a person has to bring to the printed page," says Dr. Piercey, "the more he will get from it."

An adolescent will read what he wants to read no matter what parents or teachers tell him, she says. "But parents can help their youngsters develop good judgment by offering as wide a choice of reading material as possible in the home."

More and more adults who do not read well are interested in improving their reading skills, says Dr. Piercey. "Our adult basic education and community school classes attest to this. People are eager to learn to be better readers."

Patronizing public libraries and subscribing to special interest magazines are two good ways to exercise "reading muscles," she says, but those who lack basic reading skills should seek professional help by enrolling in adult education classes.

"It isn't a do-it-yourself project," says Dr. Piercey. "You need a good foundation to build on. And when parents are avid readers, chances are their children will be, too."

An Interview Story for Student Evaluation.

member of the dyad works through his questions independently and then switches interview story with his partner. When both have completed questions for the two interviews, they check their answers for similarities and differences and make judgments on the disagreements.

As a follow-up, half the members of the class prepare interview questions for partners to be chosen from the remaining half. Using the same questions, students determine their expertise in extemporaneous verbal behavior.

JOURNALISM

▶SUBJECT AREA

Journalism

GRADE LEVEL

10–12

NAME OF ACTIVITY

Inverted Pyramid

OBJECTIVE OF ACTIVITY

To help students cope with the language of newspapers by using context clues in sentences.

STUDENT PREPARATION

The student has been introduced to the concept of the straight news story and its component parts.

TEACHER PREPARATION

Compose several paragraphs to use as the base for the context clue puzzle (see example). Build the puzzle in the shape of an inverted pyramid to represent the format for writing a news story and duplicate copies of it. Prepare a master key. (See models.)

PROCEDURE

This activity can be used as a whole class activity or stored in the learning center to be used by students having difficulty with the terminology and component parts of a straight news story. The student reads the copy and supplies the missing word after looking at the context clues around the word and then writes the word in the puzzle. Students check their accuracy with the key.

Inverted Pyramid

A straight __(22A)__ story is built in the __(2D)__ of an

inverted __(4D)__, that is, the most important __(3D)__ is given

__(5D)__ the beginning of the story __(16A)__ the least important

at the __(20A)__ of the story. The news writer tells the __(11A)__,

what, when, where, why, and sometimes __(12A)__ of the story in

the __(23A)__. The lead __(1A)__ considered the __(9A)__ 35–50

__(13D)__ of the story. The __(14D)__ of the information

__(15A)__ given in descending order of __(3A)__.

There __(24D)__ several reasons for the inverted pyramid style of

a news story. Among them __(17A)__ the practice __(18A)__

printers to discard __(10D)__ bottom paragraph of the story

__(21A)__ the type will not __(19D)__ in the allotted space. A

reporter doesn't __(6D)__ to have vital information going

__(7A)__ the scrap metal __(8A)__.

Context Clue Puzzle.

Context Clue Puzzle Key.

180

Journalism

GRADE LEVEL

7–9

NAME OF ACTIVITY

Pied Newspaper Sections

OBJECTIVE OF ACTIVITY

To improve locational skills.

STUDENT PREPARATION

None.

TEACHER PREPARATION

Scramble the letters in each word in the index of the daily newspaper. The Sunday edition is recommended because the index usually has more entries than the daily edition. Prepare a ditto with the scrambled terms, allowing space for students to write the correct spelling. Scrambled terms may include:

ygolortsa	(astrology)
dirbge	(bridge)
ocmsci	(comics)
dorwsscro	(crossword)
ybba raed	(Dear Abby)
tideslairo	(editorials)
snoipoin	(opinions)
ancfinial	(financial)
seirautibo	(obituaries)
postsr	(sports)
tersthea	(theaters)

V.T.-oidar	(T.V.-radio)
deificsals	(classified)
theraew	(weather)

PROCEDURE

Given the list of pied words, students unscramble and write the correct spelling. Then they cut out the words in the newspaper's index and staple them to the appropriate sections of the newspaper.

SUBJECT AREA

Journalism

GRADE LEVEL

10–12

NAME OF ACTIVITY

Short, Shorter, Shortest

OBJECTIVE OF ACTIVITY

Headline writers face the task of capsulizing information to fit it into minimum space. Beginning journalism students find headline writing itself challenging, and the difficulty is compounded by their need to choose short words. The objective of this activity is to select short synonyms for verbs in headlines.

STUDENT PREPARATION

The student has had instruction in headline writing.

TEACHER PREPARATION

Clip headlines using short verbs for which there are several synonyms. Paste each headline on a piece of cardboard. Type four or five synonyms for the verb that are considerably longer on small pieces of cardboard. For example, *hid* is the verb used in the headline; longer synonyms for hid are concealed, screened, secreted, masked, suppressed. (See examples.) Tape each of the synonyms stack-fashion over the word in the headline. Have dictionaries and thesauruses available.

PROCEDURE

This is an individual activity stored in the learning center to be used by students having difficulty writing headlines to fit the available space. The student reads the headline, including the top synonym on the stack. His task is to think of the verb the professional headline writer used. The student jots down his guess. He looks at the second synonym and either changes his guess or confirms it. When he is sure that the word he has jotted is the word used by the headline writer, he checks his accuracy by lifting all the synonym cards.

Examples of short verbs in headlines and longer synonyms:

The synonyms on small pieces of cardboard are taped over the word *end* in the headline:

finish
terminate
discontinue
conclude

China and U.S. end talks

Synonyms for gets:

acquires
obtains
receives
inherits

Ethiopia gets royal fortune, envoy reports

Synonyms for hid:

concealed
screened
secreted
masked
suppressed

Soviets hid shortage of sugar, reports say

Synonyms for OKs:

approves
ratifies
endorses
confirms
sanctions

**Senate OKs
woman for
housing post**

SUBJECT AREA

Journalism

GRADE LEVEL

10–12

NAME OF ACTIVITY

Paraphrasing Leads

OBJECTIVE OF ACTIVITY

To facilitate ease in paraphrasing and in headline writing.

STUDENT PREPARATION

The student has had classroom instruction in headline writing and is ready to write his own.

TEACHER PREPARATION

Clip 40 to 50 straight news stories and paste the headlines and the bodies of the stories on separate pieces of cardboard. Code the heads and stories (1,1; 2,2; 3,3; to 20 or 25). Place 20 to 25 in one envelope and 20 to 25 in another.

PROCEDURE

Two teams of two each participate in this activity simultaneously. Each team divides its headlines and stories into separate stacks. One team member scans the first paragraph of an article, capsulizes the information into headline form, and passes it to a teammate. The other member of the team tries to locate the correct headline in his stack and places the article, his team member's headline, and the newspaper's headline out of reach. (The team does not know if it has completed the task successfully until all stories have been matched to heads.) The team with the most matches wins. If both teams match all correctly, the one which finishes first wins. Teams switch envelopes and team members switch roles in the next match.

SUBJECT AREA

Journalism

GRADE LEVEL

10–12

NAME OF ACTIVITY

Decoding and Encoding Cartoons

OBJECTIVE OF ACTIVITY

To aid students in translating the inferences made by cartoonists (decoding) and in depicting news stories visually (encoding).

STUDENT PREPARATION

None.

Phase I

TEACHER PREPARATION

Clip cartoons (see example) from newspapers on subjects or concepts for which there also have been news stories. (The news stories usually precede the appearance of cartoons by one to three or four days.) Clip the stories on which the cartoonist has based his sketch (see example). Laminate, paste on cardboard, or prepare the clippings in such a way that they will withstand handling. Mix the sketches and news stories.

PROCEDURE

This activity is geared for individual students whose skills in reading cartoons need reinforcing. The student separates the cartoons and the stories into two stacks, examines each cartoon, reads through the stories, and finds the story on which the cartoon was based. As a culminating activity, the student answers this question for each

An Editorial Cartoon and Related News Story.

Unemployment rises to 6.5 pct. for 13-year high

Associated Press

WASHINGTON — Nearly 6 million American job seekers were out of work last month as the unemployment rate jumped to 6.5 per cent, its highest level in 13 years, the government reported Friday.

The November increase in the jobless rate, from October's 6 per cent, prompted the White House to acknowledge the economy is deteriorating more rapidly than anticipated.

With Christmas approaching, more Americans are out of work than at any other time since 1940, when the nation was coming out of the Great Depression and gearing up for World War II. At that time there were about 8.1 million unemployed, or 14.6 per cent of that era's smaller labor force.

The Labor Department reported that 462,000 more workers joined the unemployment rolls last month, bringing the total without jobs to a seasonally adjusted 5,975,000. That was 1.9 million more than in November 1973. Nearly half of that 12-month increase was made up of workers who lost their last jobs.

Thousands of additional layoffs have been reported in the automobile and other key industries since the government collected the November employment figures. The layoffs are expected to push the December unemployment rate to nearly 7 per cent.

White House press secretary Ron Nessen said the 6.5 per cent unemployment rate is "a source of great concern" to President Ford. Nessen said the economic situation is under review and hinted the administration would seek new antirecession legislation.

Nessen acknowledged that unemployment had increased faster than expected since Ford unveiled his economic program Oct. 8, but gave no indication of what new steps might be taken.

Although the main goal of the administration's economic policy is to control inflation, Ford's economic advisers said earlier this week they were preparing a new list of options, including tax cuts if needed next year, to pump up the economy.

Speaking on behalf of Ford, Nessen urged quick congressional passage of administration proposals to authorize an additional 83,000 public service jobs and to give the unemployed an added 13 weeks of benefits.

Had Congress acted by now, these proposals automatically would have

Continued on Page A-14

cartoon-story pair: Keeping in mind that cartoons *over*present facets of news, did the cartoonist, in your opinion, visually portray the news story accurately? Give reasons for your answer.

Phase II

TEACHER PREPARATION

Clip news stories that lend themselves to cartooning and paste them on cardboard for durability. (See examples.)

Bargain hunters reflect hard times

By CONNIE KOENENN

A possible bright side to our cloudy economy, we have been told, is that it may return Americans to such old-fashioned virtues as practicing thrift and prudence.

Such a reversal is not easy for a public which has long marched to the advertising drumbeat of credit-card consumerism. But there are signs that an about-face is taking place on a spotty basis and one of the spots is the second-hand clothing shop.

Here we find some positive economic indicators.

"I'm getting more shoppers than ever, and just as many clothes," reported Betty Klotz, owner of Encore Boutique at 2913 N. 24th St. "I think people are really shopping around these days for bargains."

Promoted by the slogan "Join the Recycling Trend," her shop operates in the traditional manner, accepting used clothing on consignment ("I don't take junk," she emphasized) and selling it at prices considerably lower than its original retail value.

There are dozens of such shops in the Valley. A scattershot survey last week disclosed that, although a few are suffering business reversals ("Nobody's buying anything — not even bargains," lamented one owner), most report normal-to-increased volume.

They do notice that customers are shopping with greater care. "Women are not spending money on just anything. They're shopping for things they really need," said Peg Apodaca.

In her Scottsdale shop, Tracy's Hideaway, she serves coffee and wine to customers in a boutique setting of paisley-print wallpaper and pine furniture. "I've sold clothes to multimillion-aires in here," she said. "Lots of my customers are women who could afford to shop anywhere."

She has noticed that women aren't bringing in as many clothes as in previous seasons. This "tendency to hold on to more things" was echoed by others.

"Buyers I don't need; it's consigners I need," said Betty Ginsburg, owner of Fashions Anonymous at 1628 E. Osborn Rd. "I notice a little reluctance to let go of things now, especially current fashions," she said.

The informal setting of such shops, as customers browse through racks looking for designers' labels or practical pants suits, also serves as a sounding board for public sentiment.

Mary and Bill Hughes own the Nearly New Store at 2615 W. Glendale which has a department-store array of clothing and household items.

"Business is very good," said Mrs. Hughes. "The main change we've noticed is in the way people are dealing with us."

The Hughes buy everything for cash rather than consignment. Customers want more for the items they bring in, and want to pay less for the things they buy, said Mrs. Hughes: "We get caught in the penny-pinch."

"For a time there," she added, "when the economic news was particularly bad, there seemed to be an abnormal quiet about people. Now that seems to have changed. The attitude is more 'To heck with it — we're going to live.'"

In Youngtown, at Act II Boutique, all the news is good. Mrs. Sonya Mulroney opened the shop, in a friendly shopping center at 12031 Arizona Ave., on Jan. 2.

"I thought it would build slowly, but in six weeks I had my money back which is unusual," said Mrs. Mulroney who ran a similar shop in Washington before moving here.

"I'm really excited about how this little thing took off the ground," said Mrs. Mulroney. "I thought about doubling my space, business was so good, but I decided not to rush it."

Located near Sun City, she gets a lot of winter visitors, she said. "Everybody is talking about the economy, and how dresses that used to cost $36 now are $75."

She's not sure whether her success is due to the economy in general or a change in attitude about buying second-hand clothes. "It's become a new fad, almost a reverse status-symbol," she said.

This might indicate the sort of return to common sense consumerism the nation is being urged to adopt. If so, like any change, it also claims its victims.

News Stories for Cartoon Backgrounds.

Buyers called cheated by auto safety features

Associated Press

DETROIT — General Motors said car buyers won't get their money's worth from many new government-ordered safety and emission features and warned the added costs for such equipment could double by 1978.

The firm said the cost to consumers for current safety and clean air committments is an average $615 per car.

That cost could climb to $1,225 if the strictest proposals being discussed for 1978 are implemented, GM claimed.

"As a nation, we have come to the point in regulatory requirements where we can no longer consider each regulation in isolation from its effects on fuel economy and the economy," GM told the Senate Government Operations Committee in a statement released Friday.

The auto giant called for a complete review of federal laws and regulations that it feels "disproportionately affect car costs and energy use by adding equipment which does not pay its own way' in value to the consumer."

GM was testifying in support of a three-year moratorium on additional design or engineering standards that would add weight or cost to future models.

The firm proposed that a joint review by government and industry be conducted to determine what benefits car buyers will receive for the added costs.

Today's new car buyer pays an average of $400 to meet current safety standards, including about $155 for added bumper protection, GM said.

Bumpers will have to be strengthened in years to come under present laws.

GM also complained about proposals for stronger seats, stricter emission standards, better gasoline mileage and stronger brakes.

190

PROCEDURE

This activity is for all students in the journalism class since even those who are adept at coping with inferences made by others need assistance in symbolizing, satirizing, or caricaturing some action or concept of popular interest. Students select one of the clippings provided by the teacher or find a news story of their own. After digesting the data, they portray it visually. The teacher is looking for conceptualization, not artistic talent, and students should be so informed.

CHAPTER 6

Fine Arts: Art, Music, and Theatre

If you are starting the book here, you are coming in on the middle of the act. Part I is the curtain raiser; it builds up to the use of the fine arts section.

Creative people—those who live their art by the esthetic criteria of beauty and value—recognize the meaning of language in all of its forms: from words to painting and sculpture, to melody and harmony, to comedy and tragedy. The fine arts faculty works with learners to help them become interpreters, expressing what is within themselves and what they perceive, their final products to be read by all who will.

An artist interprets with oils, water colors, chalk, charcoal, clay, metals, and other media. With them he or she symbolizes feelings about what is "out there." However, because of their youth, students in art classes have only limited experiences with what is "out there." What will they interpret? Using familiar resources such as newspapers and magazines as idea generators, art students can express themselves about many life situations. These and other resources are suggested as catalysts in this section.

Sociologists and economists tell us that in the not too distant future Americans will be searching for ways to fill untold leisure hours. It is a rare music teacher these days who does not have that prediction in mind as he or she plans diverse and multifaceted activities for students. While a small percentage of students are candidates for musical careers, all of them are potential music lovers, whether performing or nonperforming. For all of them the language of music, on the one hand signs and symbols and on the other foreign words and phrases, presents difficulty in varying measures. Consequently, almost all the music activities in this section have growth in vocabulary as the target.

For students of the theatre, verbal and nonverbal communications are partners. Sometimes they work together harmoniously, and sometimes the nonverbal makes a liar of the verbal. As drama students study the use of gestures and tie them to the script, drama coaches draw on life situations for practice materials. That seems appropriate since drama reflects society. Some of the resources offered as practice materials in the theatre activities include advice to the lovelorn columns, menus, pictures, billboards, and ads.

ART

SUBJECT AREA

Art

GRADE LEVEL

9–12

NAME OF ACTIVITY

Art in Its Time

OBJECTIVE OF ACTIVITY

To reinforce the placement of artists, movements, art forms, techniques, influences in their appropriate chronological order in the historical development of art.

STUDENT PREPARATION

If used as illustrated, this activity serves as a technique for review toward the end of the semester after students have studied various periods in art history.

TEACHER PREPARATION

Prepare the game boards (illustrated) and question cards for each of the major periods. Have art history references, such as books, slides, and illustrations or reproductions, available for the students. Since this type of activity is motivating for many students, it is suggested that the game board be made of wood or other durable material. By making different sets of cards, the teacher can reinforce learning data in various categories. For instance, divisions of the board might be labeled Sculpture, Paintings, Architecture, Ceramics, and Miscellaneous.

PROCEDURE

Students work in teams of two or three. Each team rolls the dice and moves according to the number that appears on the toss. The label on the square where the team stops determines the stack from which the team draws a question card. Each team has three minutes to answer a question. If the players do not answer correctly (answers are on the backs of cards), they forfeit their turn. If the answer is correct, the team rolls the dice again. If their turn sends a team beyond the finish mark, the entire board is worked through again. The winning team is the first to end on the Start-End square.

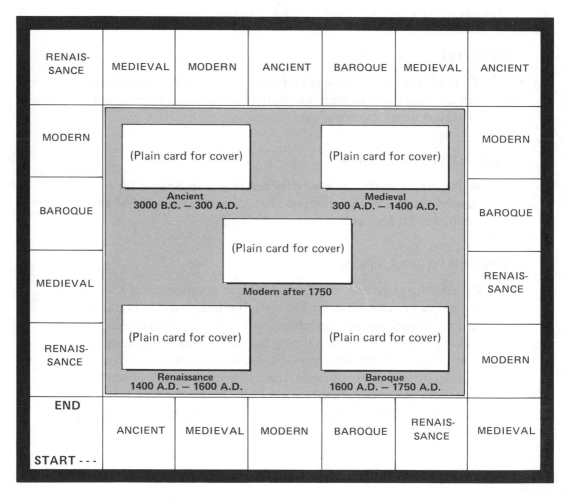

Art in Its Time Game Board.

▶SUBJECT AREA

Art

GRADE LEVEL

7–12

NAME OF ACTIVITY

Humorous Titles

OBJECTIVE OF ACTIVITY

To invoke humor and involvement in the art and power of words.

STUDENT PREPARATION

None.

TEACHER PREPARATION

To set the stage, introduce the whole class to some of the witty and/or obscure titles which artists have named their works. Paul Klee would be an excellent choice, particularly his "Two Men Met, Each Supposing the Other To be of Higher Rank," or "The Twittering Machine," or "Super-check!" Mel Ramos also has some witty titles, such as "Mysta of the Moon" or "The Virna-burger." Display a series of unusual and unfamiliar reproductions, identified by number.

PROCEDURE

After thoroughly examining the reproductions, students invent their own titles for each. Categories for titles might include unique, longest, imaginative, descriptive, outlandish. Students whose titles are judged "the most" in each of the categories are awarded the prints of their choice.

SUBJECT AREA

Art

GRADE LEVEL

7–12

NAME OF ACTIVITY

Sketching Relationships

OBJECTIVE OF ACTIVITY

Urging students to stretch to the nth of their imagination can be accompanied by a warming-up exercise. The objective of this activity is to help students see relationships in words as a precursor to depicting relationships in ideas.

STUDENT PREPARATION

Paper and pencil.

TEACHER PREPARATION

Prepare a list of seemingly unrelated words in sets of three. Examples:

- cup, rain, popcorn
- flower, book, silver
- umbrella, bicycle, leaf

PROCEDURE

Students are given sets of three words and a short time period in which to jot down as many ways as they can to show how three words in one set are related. They select what they consider to be the best of their interrelationship suggestions and make a sketch depicting the relationships. The teacher may want students to show their sketches on an opaque projector and share the inventing or creating process that preceded the sketching. (See illustration.) The student saw rain falling hard enough to bounce up from a sidewalk (as popcorn bounces), leaving a ring like the top of a cup in its wake.

Example of One Student's End Product Using the Words Cup, Rain, and Popcorn.

SUBJECT AREA

Art

GRADE LEVEL

7–12

NAME OF ACTIVITY

Illustrated Word

OBJECTIVE OF ACTIVITY

To promote vocabulary interest and introduce composition; to combine dictionary browsing and art work.

STUDENT PREPARATION

The student has collected the materials for whatever medium he chooses.

TEACHER PREPARATION

Have a dictionary available for each student in the class.

PROCEDURE

Students browse through the dictionary in quest of a word. It must be a word completely new to the individual. A word can be chosen on the basis of its sound when pronounced, its particular meaning, or possibly the significance it holds for the student. Students should be encouraged to give lavish thought and attention to selecting the perfect word, considering possibilities, weighing alternatives. When the student has chosen a word and feels he understands it fully, he illustrates it, incorporating the written word into his design. Ample time should be given for this task. A class critique upon completion gives students a chance to share their words and their experiences.

Art

GRADE LEVEL

9–12

NAME OF ACTIVITY

Color Book

OBJECTIVE OF ACTIVITY

To foster symbolic interpretation given to colors.

STUDENT PREPARATION

None.

TEACHER PREPARATION

Attach postcard-size reproductions of paintings to 4 × 6″ cards. Prepare a cover and directions, as illustrated. Punch two holes on the left side of the cards to house rings to facilitate page-turning.

PROCEDURE

This is an individual activity. The student studies the reproductions and chooses one for which she thinks the artist used certain colors for their symbolic significance. Then she writes two or three paragraphs describing the aspects of the painting that caused her to decide colors were used because of the symbolism attached to them.

Example of directions that are typed on 4 × 6″ cards:

Directions

The symbolic interpretation given to colors has not been the same for every culture nor in every period of history. In any case, we can

Example of a Color Book Card.

find many points of agreement, regardless of time and place, in the symbolic interpretation of colors.

Here are some examples:

- white: innocence, purity, also coldness
- black: night, mourning, death, evil
- blue: faithfulness, depth, chastity
- green: hope, growth, immaturity
- yellow: envy, hate
- gold: sun, riches, joy
- red: blood, passion
- purple: ruler, majesty
- violet: mourning, resignation, dignity
- gray: inferiority, age

Your task is to look at the pictures. Pick *one* in which you think the artist used certain colors for their symbolic significance. Then in two or three paragraphs describe the artist's subject in terms of the symbolic meanings of the colors. Note that not all of the pictures necessarily have colors chosen for symbolism.

SUBJECT AREA

Art

GRADE LEVEL

7–12

NAME OF ACTIVITY

"Whatchamacallit" Has a Name

OBJECT OF ACTIVITY

Learning the names of trade tools needs constant reinforcement
from the art instructor or else "whatchamacallit" becomes the name
for everything in the art room. This activity, designed for crafts
class, induces students to learn and call tools and equipment by
their proper names.

STUDENT PREPARATION

The student has seen the instructor demonstrate the use of tools
and equipment and has heard their names.

TEACHER PREPARATION

On a sheet of durable cardboard sketch tools/equipment used in
crafts, such as

debubblizer	bristle brush wheel
dapping block	torch key
kiln	flexible shaft machine
bracelet mandrel	vacuum casting machine
centrifuge	chasing hammer
mallet	planishing hammer
oxyacetylene torch	ring mandrel
striker	horn anvil

Cover the cardboard with a piece of acetate and provide a marking
pencil.

PROCEDURE

This is an individual activity performed by students who have difficulty remembering the names of tools and other pieces of equipment. The student identifies the piece of equipment by writing its name across it on the acetate. He takes the board to the instructor for checking and verbalizes the use of the objects.

▶SUBJECT AREA

Art

GRADE LEVEL

7–12

NAME OF ACTIVITY

Feeling Color

OBJECTIVE OF ACTIVITY

To enable students to discover that words by themselves can be pleasant or neutral in connotation until a dash of color is added.

STUDENT PREPARATION

None.

TEACHER PREPARATION

Make two sets of 3 X 5″ cards. On one set label in large black letters words used with color words. Examples:

feather	mail
letter	goods
streak	tape
slip	sky
shirt	brick

On the other set label in large blue letters words like these:

spoon	blossoms
branch	lady
rule	heart
thumb	oyster
ribbon	cross

205

PROCEDURE

The two sets of cards are shuffled together and stacked face down. A student draws a card from the top of the deck. If it is written in black ink, she supplies a color word that makes the word negative in connotation, for example, yellow streak. If the word is written in blue ink, she adds a color word that gives the word a positive connotation, for example, green thumb. If the student is correct, she keeps the card. If she is not, her opponent has an opportunity to add a color word. If neither student is correct, the card is put on the bottom of the deck. The winner is the student with the most cards.

SUBJECT AREA

Art

GRADE LEVEL

9–12

NAME OF ACTIVITY

You Be the Teacher

OBJECTIVE OF ACTIVITY

To promote self-study of art terms and concepts. This activity is self-directing and self-correcting.

STUDENT PREPARATION

None.

TEACHER PREPARATION

Cut a spiral notebook in half vertically. Then split each page so the two halves of one sheet can be turned separately. (See the accompanying sketch.) On the half sheets on the left portion, write

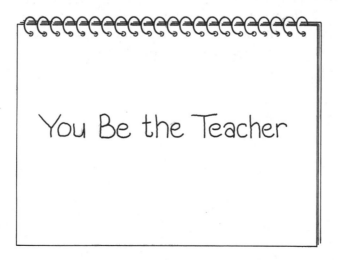

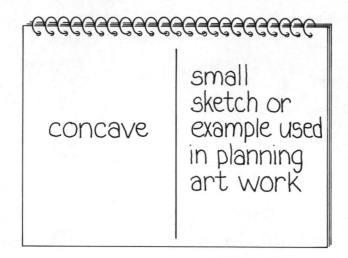

Divided Notebook for Self-Study.

art terms or phrases that are important to the unit's or semester's study. On the half sheets on the right side write definitions. Position definitions so they are not across from matching terms. On the back side of each definition page, write the answer.

PROCEDURE

This activity is designed as a study technique for one student to use at a time. He matches the term on the left with the correct definition on the right. He checks his accuracy by looking at the correct answer on the back of each definition sheet.

SUBJECT AREA

Art

GRADE LEVEL

7–12

NAME OF ACTIVITY

Descriptors

OBJECTIVE OF ACTIVITY

To extend use of descriptive words, adjectives, and observational skills.

STUDENT PREPARATION

None.

TEACHER PREPARATION

Attach a reproduction to a piece of cardboard larger than the picture by three or four inches on all four sides. Display it in the room on an easel or on the wall.

PROCEDURE

At their leisure students observe the reproduction closely, attending to color, composition, proportions, details, content, and other features. Their task is to think of a descriptive term that is applicable. When a student has decided on an adjective, she prints it with her name on the cardboard framing the picture. (See possible result.) The teacher may wish to culminate the activity with a class discussion.

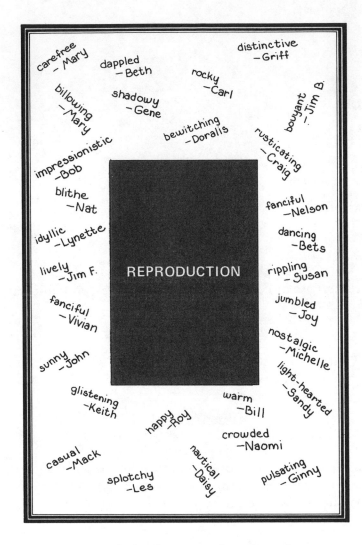

Sample Student Descriptor Board.

▶SUBJECT AREA

Art

GRADE LEVEL

9–12

NAME OF ACTIVITY

Armchair Tourist

OBJECTIVE OF ACTIVITY

Beginning art students, like beginning composition writers, often have difficulty thinking of a scene to depict. This type of activity is a pump-primer. Specifically, it develops the skills of interpreting someone else's words and visualizing an end product.

STUDENT PREPARATION

None.

TEACHER PREPARATION

Clip articles from newspapers and magazines that vividly describe a locale, particularly an area which students have not personally seen. The travel sections of Sunday editions are good sources, as are travel magazines and airline giveaway magazines. Prepare a motivational paragraph designed to stimulate imagining (see example). Mount each clipping and laminate for durability.

PROCEDURE

The instructor may wish all of the art class to be involved in the activity. If so, sufficient articles have been collected. Or the activity may be reserved for those students who verbalize difficulty in thinking of a scene. The students read the article (the example could be the basis of six or eight drawings) and depict visually something the writer has described.

Copan Ruins sign of prehistoric genius

COPAN — Ruins are all that remain of the great Maya city of another era.

Wandering about the temples, pyramids, "stelae" (sculptures of stone columns) and their related altars, one can only marvel at the cultural genius of these prehistoric people.

Their brilliance remains not only in their sculpture and architecture, but in mathematics, astronomy, hieroglyphics (written on thin three bark), even an almanac advising best days for planting, fishing and hunting. The Maya even evolved an accurate calendar.

THE COPAN. Ruins stand silent and peaceful in the National Archeological Park. the jungle held at bay beyond its boundaries. A guide book takes you from one work to another, explaining and detailing structures that have been here since before 500 B.C.

(Archeologists say the first inhabitants were here around 3,000 B.C. The Maya were well on their way toward building a highly complex civilization by 5 0 0 B.C.; reached their cultural peak after 300 A.D.; crumbled in 800 A.D., when the jungle closed in upon their buildings. It is estimated that 100,000 people resided in the larger cities.

Many Honduras descendents of the Maya speak the distinct language developed by this race centuries ago.

There are more Maya ruins in Mexico, Guatemala and part of El Salvador. Copan is where the civilization developed and flourished. and is one of the first to be known.

One of the earliest reports on Copan was recorded by a Spaniard explorer in 1576. A later archeologist refers to Copan as the "Alexandria of the Maya world" and the "one of the most valuable archeological r e l i c s of American culture."

RESTORATION was not undertaken until 1934, an agreement between Carnegie Institute of Washington and the Honduras government. It included not just the statues and buildings, but changing the destructive course of the Copan River in this peaceful and fertile valley.

O n e enters t h e park through an elegant avenue flanked by temple foundations leading to the Ceremonial Court, a l a r g e amphitheater seating some 50,000, with enormous stairways on three sides.

Within are nine stelae each constructed o v e r vaults apparently intended for the deposit of such religious offerings as clay vessels, jade beads, etc., altars and a sacrificial stone.

THERE IS also a Central Court with more monuments; a Ball Court (for religious games); the Court of the Hieroglyphic Stairway, 63 carved steps a n d balustrades, with five statues on decorated thrones, centered by a great stone altar. Some 30 dates have been interpreted from the carvings, the oldest date about 544 A.D.; the most recent, 744 A.D.

The stairway leads to the temple atop the pedestal, small but considered a priceless architectural gem, revealing a glorious role in the great city.

There is also an Acropolis containing pyramidal bases, temples, terraces, platforms and patios, the West Court, w i t h more, temples, a "spectators grandstand" (five stairways connected to a temple), more stelae, an East Court, tombs, cemetery units, tunnels, all masterfully carved.

"Awesome" is an overworked, understated word to describe the sensations of seeing the Copan Ruins, what remains of the goals and ideals of a vanished civilization.

A Sample Newspaper Article for Armchair Tourist.

212

Example:

Armchair Tourist

Faraway places with strange sounding names invite daydreaming and even escape from the humdrum of our everyday surroundings. Even though you can't hop a boat today as Gauguin did, seeing through someone else's eyes is possible. Read about the remains of a flourishing Maya city in Honduras and draw any one of the scenes described.

►SUBJECT AREA

Art

GRADE LEVEL

7–12

NAME OF ACTIVITY

Police Artist

OBJECTIVE OF ACTIVITY

Although most students in art class will not earn their living with masterpieces on canvas or see their creations on the walls of art galleries, they should be aware that other avenues in art will net profit and satisfaction. Advertising, television, and movie industries are known for their use of artists. An overlooked source of employment are the thousands of law enforcement departments throughout the country. The objective of this activity is to enable students to visualize and to interpret relationships between a verbal description of an eye witness and reality.

STUDENT PREPARATION

Charcoal and other media for sketching.

TEACHER PREPARATION

Clip newspaper articles in which people wanted by the police are described by eye witnesses (see examples). Occasionally photographs of suspects are published after they have been apprehended. Clip them also. Invite a police artist to meet with the class to discuss his job and their job opportunities.

PROCEDURE

Students sketch portraits of suspects who have been described in newspaper clippings. They check their sketches against a newspaper photograph if one has been published or watch television newscasts after a suspect has been taken into custody. If feasible, students take turns having a day with the local police artist.

Pair sought in robbery of city motel

A young man and woman who referred to themselves as Bonnie and Clyde were being sought throughout the Southwest Saturday after the robbery of a Phoenix motel and kidnaping of a night clerk, police reported.

Jimmy Hogan, 27, night clerk at the Desert Hills, 2707 E. Van Buren, was in satisfactory condition in Maryvale Samaritan Hospital where he was being treated for head injuries, officials said.

The robbers took $270 in cash from the motel, investigators said, and forced Hogan to give them a diamond ring, a turquoise ring and a gold watch.

Detective Sgt. Joe Lease said the young couple checked into the motel Thursday. Witnesses said the two caused disturbances in the motel bar Friday night. For this reason, and because they had run up a high bar bill, Hogan telephoned them to ask them to pay their bar charges, Lease said.

As the woman talked to him across the desk about the bill, Hogan told officers, the man slipped behind him and rammed what he believed was a pistol against his back.

The two put Hogan between them on the front seat of their white 1970 Oldsmobile and forced him to keep his head between his knees as they drove to Tonopah, where they used a length of pipe to beat him on the head, Lease said Hogan related.

Then they drove another 25 miles west, pulled off on a side road and again beat him until the man said, "Well, he's dead now," Hogan told Lease. They dragged Hogan from the car and drove west on Interstate 10.

Hogan said he managed to flag down a truck and the driver gave him a ride to Tonopah, where they found a highway patrolman.

Lease said the man being sought was about 26, 6 feet, with a medium build and shoulder-length, dishwater blond hair. He has a scar on his nose between his eyes.

His companion was about 22, 5 feet 3, 100 pounds, with shoulder length blonde hair. She wore gold wire-framed glasses.

During the drive, Lease said Hogan told officers, the two called each other Bonnie and Clyde.

The rear seat of their car was loaded with clothing and other items.

Bank robber doffs clothes in getaway

A long-nosed, pimply-faced robber took about $4,300 from the First National Bank office at 5033 N. Seventh St. Tuesday, then did a partial strip-tease as he fled across the rear parking lot, investigators said.

Police and Federal Bureau of Investigation agents said witnesses told them the robber pushed a note and beige cloth drawstring-type bag toward a teller. The note threatened the teller's life and ordered her to put $10,000 into the bag.

Detective Hayden Williams said the man put his hands in his pockets as though he might have a gun, but no weapon was seen. Williams said witnesses told officers the robber ran out the back door of the bank. Investigators who followed his trail said they found buttons which apparently showered from the robber's chest as he began ripping off the shirt, sweater and tie.

Detectives Jack Hackworth and Jim Thompson were checking the neighborhood when Thompson caught a glimpse of a sweater atop a metal canopy in the parking lot of a nearby group of office condominium suites. Detective Jack Hackworth climbed to the top of the canopy, where he recovered the sweater, a tie and a nearly buttonless shirt.

A note, apparently the one used in the holdup, was found in the shirt pocket. Hackworth said the note was dirty and had been folded and refolded many times, as though the robber might have made many false starts before going through with the holdup.

Witnesses said the robber was white, about 22 years old, 5-foot-6, with a small frame, full, conservatively-cut brown hair, small brown eyes and an acne complexion.

Excerpts from Newspaper Articles Describing Suspects.

SUBJECT AREA

Art

GRADE LEVEL

7–12

NAME OF ACTIVITY

Logos

OBJECTIVE OF ACTIVITY

This activity has a two-fold objective:

1. To promote the skill of visualizing through the use of everyday resource materials, in this example, the telephone book.
2. To foster the skills of classifying and alphabetizing.

STUDENT PREPARATION

The student has had a unit on the functions of a commercial artist.

TEACHER PREPARATION

Clip examples of logotypes used by companies as their trademarks on stationery, advertising, and other official printing from the telephone book. (See illustrations.) Furnish a telephone book for each student in the class (available from telephone companies after they pick up outdated books).

PROCEDURE

After studying examples, students use the Yellow Pages to find additional examples of logos. Then they find ads containing no logos from which they select the names of local companies and businessmen in varying occupations, such as department stores, dress shops, men's clothing stores, lumber yards, garages. After narrowing their choices to five, students design logos for local businesses. As a final step of the activity, they call on the business houses and make a gift of the logos they designed.

Sample Logos from the Yellow Pages.

SUBJECT AREA

Art

GRADE LEVEL

7–12

NAME OF ACTIVITY

Cartooning

OBJECTIVE OF ACTIVITY

To promote translating the main idea of written language into pictorial language.

STUDENT PREPARATION

Students read newspapers for the purpose of finding an article or feature story whose main idea can be depicted pictorially.

TEACHER PREPARATION

As you teach the unit on cartooning, place special emphasis on main idea, theme, or message.

PROCEDURE

Each student chooses two or three articles from newspapers in the classroom or from personal copies in the home. In fact, every part of the newspaper can be used as a resource. (See examples.) After deciding the main idea of each of his choices, the student uses that idea as the basis for his or her cartoon. The sophistication of the end result usually depends on the student's personal knowledge and experience. It is possible that two students may use the same written material, and the results will be entirely different. At the completion of the assignment, cartoons are prominently displayed.

Brooklynese is flourishing in New Orleans, y'all

Associated Press

NEW ORLEANS — Dis, dat, mudda, fadda, woik and y'all.

It's pure Brooklynese, reported dying out in New York City but flourishing with a southern drawl in a New Orleans melting pot called the Irish Channel.

Brooklynites have all but abandoned their distinctive accents, says Francis Griffith, a retired speech professor at Long Island's Hofstra University who has studied Brooklynese for four decades.

Words like Joisey, Williamsboig and moider, he says, have practically disappeared from the Brooklyn idiom.

But in the tough Irish Channel district, which stretches near the Mississippi river front, they still ogle da goils, flush da terlet and try to find Foist Street.

No one seems to know when they began mangling vowels and slashing consonants in the finest Brooklyn tradition.

"Some say a boatload of workers came down from New York before the turn of the century and stayed, but that's just a theory," says Dr. George Reinecke, a professor of English at the University of New Orleans.

Most of the residents are descendants of Irish, German, Italian, and more recently, Cuban immigrants, who missed an Ellis Island landing either by accident or choice. There also are a sizable number of blacks.

They live in a tacky but architecturally rich sliver of the city wedged between the French Quarter downtown and the plush Garden District uptown.

Their politicians dole out favors with Tammany Hall panache. Their priests, ministers and rabbis march arm in arm in the St. Patrick's Day parade. And they take delight in coining expressions that would shine with the best of Brooklyn.

"Fru-fru" means fancy, "oofty-goofty" is nonsense. "Where ya at?" means "How are you?" And when someone says "Da job was ta ta," he means it was free.

Reinecke says the beat of the language is as strong as ever. Oysters will always be "ersters," church "choich."

His favorite: "Wrap da toikey in tin ferl and baste it wid oilive erl."

SAN DIEGO (AP) — Naturalist Euell Gibbons exchanged looks with a gibbon named Euell after the ape was named in his honor at the San Diego Zoo.

Gibbons juggled four wild hickory nuts in a vain effort to gain the attention of the ape, an eater of fruits and nuts. But the gibbon, which sports a stand of white whiskers on each side of its face, refused to go closer than six feet during the ceremony.

Sample Articles for Illustration.

Today's chuckle

How come politicians who claim the country is ruined are trying so hard to get control of the wreck?

MUSIC

▶SUBJECT AREA

Music

GRADE LEVEL

7–12

NAME OF ACTIVITY

The Two-timer

OBJECTIVE OF ACTIVITY

To enhance students' understanding of equivalents as set by the meter in which a piece is to be played.

STUDENT PREPARATION

The student has had instruction in meanings and values of notes and rests.

TEACHER PREPARATION

Construct a sturdy activity board about 12 X 18″ so that it can serve several activities in the nature of this one. On a black background construct a puzzle board consisting of sixteen squares. The puzzle board is made by pasting black felt strips over an area of white felt. (See example.) On the lower portion of the activity board attach a pouch of heavy, clear plastic. Cut notes and rests from black felt and store them in the plastic pouch. Write instructions on a 3 X 5″ card and place it on the board.

PROCEDURE

The student arranges the notes and rests so that each row, vertically and horizontally, makes (in this case) a 2/4 measure. Accuracy is verified by the instructor.

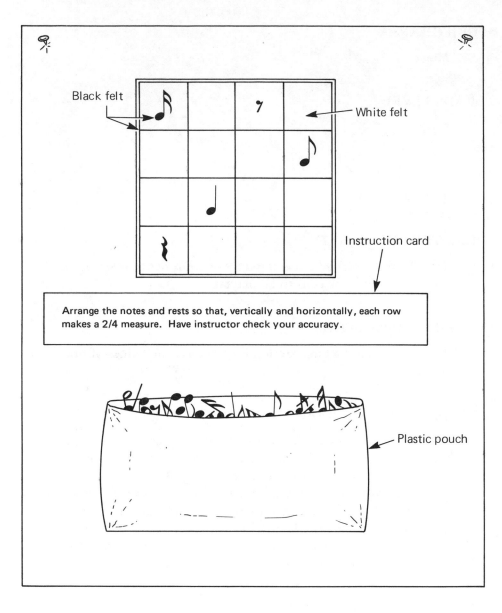

Black felt

White felt

Instruction card

Arrange the notes and rests so that, vertically and horizontally, each row makes a 2/4 measure. Have instructor check your accuracy.

Plastic pouch

Music Activity Board.

▶SUBJECT AREA

Music

GRADE LEVEL

7–12

NAME OF ACTIVITY

Cluster Memory

OBJECTIVE OF ACTIVITY

To develop vocabulary by encouraging students to categorize and classify; to reinforce correct spelling.

STUDENT PREPARATION

The student has heard the terms discussed and performed.

TEACHER PREPARATION

This is a whole-class activity that involves the students in identifying terms that are the properties of a major concept, in this example, instruments. Ditto a list of the forty or more instruments used in band and orchestra performances. Have an overhead projector and transparencies ready.

PROCEDURE

The instructor announces the category by writing on the transparency:

PERCUSSION

Students scan the names of instruments on the ditto and jot down those they believe are percussion instruments. Then one by one they present a term, and the teacher fits it into the word *percussion* on

the transparency. As an example, the first student offers *triangle* as
the initial word. The teacher adds it this way:

```
                    T
                    R
P E R C U S S I O N
                    A
                    N
                    G
                    L
                    E
```

The student who offered the term describes the instrument or shows
it. Another student says *glockenspiel,* and the teacher fits it into the
schemata:

```
                    T
                    R
P E R C U S S I O N
                    A
                    N
                    G L O C K E N S P I E L
                    L
                    E
```

The procedure continues until eventually all of the percussion
instruments appear in the diagram. The brass, woodwind, and string
families can be studied in the same manner since the teacher has
included the names of all orchestra instruments on the ditto.

VARIATION

This type of activity can be used to reinforce terminology at all
sophistication levels. For example, the instructor is introducing a
unit on harmony. He uses the technique to give students an overall
picture of the terms (and their meanings) they will be using. It is
important that students know and recognize the words in print to
help assure their independence in continuing to learn. The teacher
writes on a transparency:

HARMONY

The students use the text or the handouts on harmony the teacher has prepared and find technical words that belong to the harmony family. As the teacher fits each word into the schemata, he explains the new term and discusses its relationship to harmony and to other family words. As the schemata progresses:

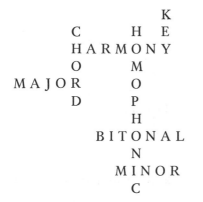

```
                    K
        C       H   E
        H A R M O N Y
        O       M
M A J O R       O
        D       P
                H
            B I T O N A L
                N
            M I N O R
                C
```

SUBJECT AREA

Music

GRADE LEVEL

7–12

NAME OF ACTIVITY

Reverse Crossword Puzzle

OBJECTIVE OF ACTIVITY

To facilitate learning terminology and symbols.

STUDENT PREPARATION

The student has been introduced to both terms and symbols during the course of classroom instruction.

TEACHER PREPARATION

The symbolic language of music, like the language of mathematics and science, is precise and strictly fixed. In addition, the language of music in word form is literally foreign. Consequently alternate learning techniques need to be designed to aid students in mastering terminology. The reverse crossword, one such aid, is made by selecting terms important to or contributing to a concept under study. The concept of tempo has been chosen for demonstration. When you have chosen the terms, fill them into spaces, crossing letters of words where you can find overlaps. Prepare a set of instructions. Make a copy of the puzzle and directions page for each student (see examples) since this activity is used for a reinforcement early in the study of a particular concept.

PROCEDURE

With the completed puzzle in front of him, the student writes the symbols and/or definitions, using a glossary or a music dictionary when necessary. When the clue page is completed, students take turns performing a definition on their instruments.

Reverse Crossword Puzzle.

Reverse Crossword Puzzle

DIRECTIONS

In this puzzle the terms relating to tempo are already filled in, but there are no definitions. Look at each of the across and down words, note its position, and write a meaning by the term's corresponding number. Check your glossary if you get stuck. You will have a turn performing a definition when the class members finish their puzzles. Some terms are not performable, for example, 4A, 17A, and 25D.

Down	Across
1.	2.
3.	4.
5.	6.
8.	7.
14.	9.
15.	10.
16.	11.
18.	12.
20.	13.
22.	15.
24.	17.
25.	19.
	21.
	23.
	25.
	26.
	27.

▶SUBJECT AREA

Music

GRADE LEVEL

7–10

NAME OF ACTIVITY

Inharmonious Terms

OBJECTIVE OF ACTIVITY

Intermediate and junior varsity band members often have difficulty with the specialized language of music, including foreign terms. This activity is designed for those who need additional assistance in comprehending terminology.

STUDENT PREPARATION

The student has met the terms in her course of study.

TEACHER PREPARATION

On a dittoed sheet jumble the letters of key terminology that students are required to know. In an adjacent column, write the meaning, examples, or clues for the term. Leave the third column blank. (See examples. Jumbled word puzzles lend little to comprehension unless words are tied to their meanings.)

PROCEDURE

The class can begin this activity while waiting for a bell to ring for class dismissal. When the class meets again, the instructor shows the key on a transparency so students may check their own puzzle-solving.

Example of activity sheet:

Inharmonious Terms

1. namhory   science of combining chords   _____

2. etanand   moderately slow and even movement   _____

3. calidentac   indicating sharps, flats, or naturals   _____

4. rnosiporges   way in which chords follow one another   _____

5. thacmrico   example: C to C sharp   _____

6. icodtina   five whole steps and two half steps   _____

7. natcec   stress given certain notes   _____

8. osrcddi   not in harmony   _____

VARIATION

Directional terms are often used on scores in their abbreviated forms. ABBREVIATED INHARMONIOUS TERMS can be the subject of another activity.

Examples:

1. z.piz   "Look, ma, no bow."   _____

2. src.ec   "Turn up the volume."   _____

3. .imd   getting softer   _____

4. tr.i   getting slower   _____

5. cal.ec   getting faster   _____

SUBJECT AREA

Music

GRADE LEVEL

7–12

NAME OF ACTIVITY

Music Categories

OBJECTIVE OF ACTIVITY

To further skill in categorizing or classifying and to motivate use of reference material.

STUDENT PREPARATION

None.

TEACHER PREPARATION

Prepare a format on a ditto which will allow students to list the specifics of general categories such as composers, instruments, works, musical directions, and musical symbols (see example). Have music reference materials available.

PROCEDURE

This is a whole class, small group, or individual activity. The student writes a word in each category that begins with the letters of the key word; in this example, the key word is MUSICAL. He may use dictionaries, glossaries and other reference material, but the words must be spelled correctly.

One student's grid may look like this when completed:

Music Categories

	Composers	Instruments	Works	Musical Directions	Symbols
M	Mozart	mandolin	Marriage of Figaro	moderato	mordent
U	Unger	ukulele	Unanswered Question	un poco calando	up-bow
S	Strauss	saxophone	Swan Lake	sforzando	sharp
I	Ibert	. . . .	Il Trovatore	inversion	inverted turn
C	Chopin	cello	Così fan tutte	crescendo	clef
A	Antes	accordion	Aida	arpeggio	alla breve
L	Liszt	lyre	L'Elisir d'Amore	lento	long appoggiatura

►SUBJECT AREA

Music

GRADE LEVEL

10–12

NAME OF ACTIVITY

Evaluating the Reviewer

OBJECTIVE OF ACTIVITY

Music students often are required to evaluate a performance. Evaluating the Reviewer develops that skill by evaluating the music critic who writes for the local newspaper.

STUDENT PREPARATION

Guided by the music instructor, the class has drawn up and has used a set of criteria on which to judge a musical performance.

TEACHER PREPARATION

A natural follow-up to having students evaluate and make judgments on a musical performance is to have them evaluate and make judgments on professional reviews of concerts. Together with the students, draw up a set of standards by which to judge a critic's writings. Evidence-gathering should be based on objective criteria.

Examples:

1. Is the critic an authority in the field of music?
   Evidence:
2. Does his or her writing reveal knowledge of merits and faults of musicians' performances?
   Evidence:
3. Does he or she use emotion-laden, biased, or prejudicial words in the review?

Evidence:

Explain the class project to the business manager of the performance and enlist his aid in getting a ticket price that will enable all students to attend. He may issue free passes.

PROCEDURE

On the night of the concert, students do their own evaluation of the performance, using the set of criteria they helped draw up. They make notes on which they will write their own reviews and have the reviews ready for class use.

When the review of the critic is published in the newspaper, copies are obtained for every member of the class. Students then evaluate the critic's review, using the criteria set up.

In the final step of this activity, the reviews written by the students are given out randomly, identified by only a number. One way to insure anonymity is to have students identify their reviews by numbers instead of by their names. Another way is for the teacher to assign numbers after obliterating names. Using the same criteria on which they judged the professional critic, students evaluate the reviews of their peers. The results are analyzed in class.

Music

GRADE LEVEL

7–12

NAME OF ACTIVITY

Light the Board

OBJECTIVE OF ACTIVITY

To motivate self-study of the vocabulary of music and to provide instant feedback on accuracy.

STUDENT PREPARATION

None.

TEACHER PREPARATION

Make the electrical board using the directions and schematic provided. Use plywood and suitable framing to make the board sturdy. Size is optional. The completed electrical board can serve as a medium for self-study of a variety of materials: musicians and their compositions, symbol identification, or periods in music history, to name a few possibilities.

Prepare questions and put them on the board with two-sided tape (to make it easy to change the questions). For example, in the box at top left the choices of answers and key word are

getting gradually slower   diminuendo
getting gradually louder
getting gradually softer

235

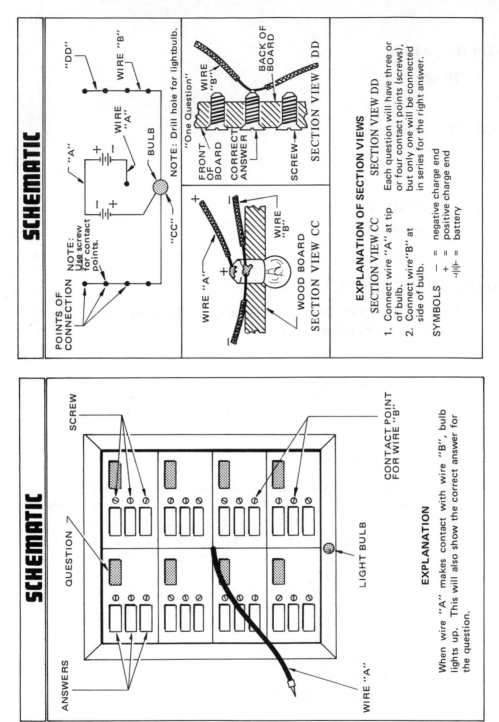

Schematic for an Electrical Board.

PROCEDURE

This is an individual activity. The student reads the key word and touches the screw next to his choice of answer with the terminal at the end of wire "A." If the answer is correct, the bulb at the bottom of the board lights up. If the answer is wrong, the student tries one of the other two choices in order to find the correct meaning.

▶SUBJECT AREA

Music

GRADE LEVEL

7–9

NAME OF ACTIVITY

Music Jigsaw Puzzle

OBJECTIVE OF ACTIVITY

To facilitate learning non-English terms on musical scores.

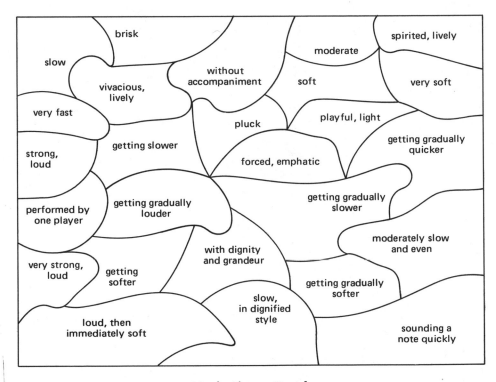

Music Jigsaw Puzzle.

STUDENT PREPARATION

The student has had instruction in the meanings of the non-English terms.

TEACHER PREPARATION

Draw a jigsaw puzzle (see example) on a piece of lightweight cardboard. In each section write the definition of a different musical term, for example, brisk, without accompaniment, moderately slow and even. Before cutting the cardboard into pieces, cover it with a piece of paper transparent enough for the outline of the pieces to be visible. On the transparent sheet print each term that corresponds to the definition so that the term is within the boundary lines of the definition's puzzle piece. (See example.) Mount the transparent sheet on heavy backing. This is the board to which the student

adagio allegro moderato spiritoso

a cappella pianissimo

vivace piano

presto

pizzicato scherzo

ritardando sforzando accelerato

forte

crescendo rallentando

solo

andante

decrescendo grandioso

fortissimo

diminuendo

largo

forte—piano staccato

Music Jigsaw Puzzle Key.

matches the puzzle pieces. Cut the jigsaw puzzle containing the definitions into pieces.

PROCEDURE

The student who has had difficulty associating meanings with non-English terms on musical scores can use this board to master terminology. She reads the definition on each puzzle piece and places it on top of the appropriate term on the board. If she has correctly placed the pieces, the puzzle will fit together when she finishes.

THEATRE

SUBJECT AREA

Theatre

GRADE LEVEL

10–12

NAME OF ACTIVITY

Lend Me Your Ear

OBJECTIVE OF ACTIVITY

To use something in students' everyday world—in this case, personal advice columns—to stimulate interpretation and character projection.

STUDENT PREPARATION

Each student selects a letter from a personal advice column that appears in the newspaper.

TEACHER PREPARATION

None.

PROCEDURE

The student works with a team member in this activity. He studies the letter he has clipped until he can talk it through without the clipping. However, he should not memorize. With the stage set with counselor-counselee props, student no. 1 of the team role-plays the writer of the letter and presents his case to his partner. The partner ad-libs his response. The role shifts to student no. 2 who role-plays the writer of the letter which he has selected and receives ad-lib advice from his partner.

VARIATIONS

A pair of students reads and enacts an interview between a winning or losing football coach and sports writer, printed testimony given by a person to a congressional investigating committee, or an interview of a movie star by a Hollywood columnist.

SUBJECT AREA

Theatre

GRADE LEVEL

10–12

NAME OF ACTIVITY

Dramatic Route

OBJECTIVE OF ACTIVITY

To facilitate students' learning of basic concepts and skills necessary for reading and acting plays.

STUDENT PREPARATION

The student has had an introductory lesson on basic drama concepts.

TEACHER PREPARATION

Prepare a diagram such as the one illustrated. Mount it on a piece of wood for durability. Drill a hole at the intersection and ends of lines (there will be thirteen) and make two wooden pegs that fit the holes. Prepare cards with questions on one side and answers on the reverse. (Examples of the types of questions are given.)

PROCEDURE

Two students participate in the activity. The cards are stacked in a pile, question side up, and are covered with a blank card. A player draws a card, reads and answers the question. If she gives the correct response, she moves her peg from bottom center in the direction of top center one hole per correct answer. If she answers incorrectly, her peg remains where it is. When a player is stalled in the center, the other player may pass to the right or left in order to gain a center position. The player whose peg reaches the top hole and returns to starting position first is the winner. Disputes on correct

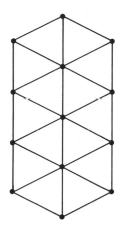

Diagram for Dramatic Route.

answers are settled by referring to the answer on the reverse side of the card.

Examples of types of questions:

Typed on question side	*Typed on answer side*
What is the chief tool of the dramatist?	Dialogue.
What is the meaning of "stage right?"	The actor's right.
A "cross" (sometimes abbreviated X) represents what movement?	A movement of a character from one part of the stage to another.
What is the second major concept of the drama?	The power to induce emotion.
What is the concept of empathy?	The imaginative projection of one's own consciousness into another being.
What is the first major concept of the drama?	Conflict.
When does a new episode begin?	Whenever an important character enters or leaves the scene.
When is a climax reached in a drama?	It is that instant of greatest conflict, greatest doubt, greatest suspense that precedes the falling action and the play's conclusion.

SUBJECT AREA

Theatre

GRADE LEVEL

10–12

NAME OF ACTIVITY

Shakespeare Eating House

OBJECTIVE OF ACTIVITY

Theatrical neophytes sometimes have difficulty assuming the distinctive qualities of characters, particularly those in Shakespearean plays. Although characters in modern theatre may be counterparts of characters in the early theatre, a four-hundred year span of time presents hurdles for adolescents. The objective of this activity is to enable students to relate distinguishing traits of characters in a Shakespearean play to something in their everyday life. This example uses food as the medium.

STUDENT PREPARATION

The play has been studied. This activity is used at the time qualities of characters are discussed prior to role enactment.

TEACHER PREPARATION

Prepare a ditto giving directions to students to create a menu for the Shakespeare Eating House which depicts the physical and/or personal qualities of characters in the Shakespearean play being studied. (See example.)

PROCEDURE

Each student selects three characters from the play. In order to climb inside the characters the student likens each of the three to food or dishes usually found on menus, such as meats, vegetables,

246

appetizers, salads, sandwiches, beverages. The student names the menu item for a character and describes the item with the character's particular qualities, personal or physical. The drama coach can anticipate much variety in the descriptions because they will reflect the students' opinions of food. When the task is finished, members of the class share their creations with their peers.

Example of drama coach's ditto:

Shakespeare Eating House

This restaurant includes on its menu foods named for characters in the Shakespearean dramas. For this assignment you must see the characters from *Hamlet* as food. Describe them as meats, vegetables, appetizers, beverages, sandwiches, salads, or any other food that would appear on a menu. Describe three characters from *Hamlet* and give your reasons for relating the person to the food you chose.

My version of Ophelia is given as an example. However, you might see Ophelia as a different type of food, which is as it should be because you and I are different people with different culinary tastes.

Vegetable Dishes

Ophelia

Tender, delicate mushrooms, sauteed gently in butter, over a bed of delectable tomato cubes.

tender delicate gentle	adjectives which describe Ophelia
mushrooms	tender and delicate also fit mushrooms; mistaken mushrooms, toadstools, can cause coma and death, related to Ophelia's madness
tomato	slang term for well-developed, good looking girl

SUBJECT AREA

Theatre

GRADE LEVEL

10–12

NAME OF ACTIVITY

Theatre Talk

OBJECTIVE OF ACTIVITY

To acquaint students with the language of the stage proper and other parts of the theatre.

STUDENT PREPARATION

The student has studied the key words after introduction and demonstration by the drama coach.

TEACHER PREPARATION

On a piece of graph paper enter the letters of the key words backwards (to increase concentration), forwards, diagonally, vertically, and horizontally in scattered positions. At the bottom of the sheet, give descriptions of the terms. (See example.) For variation, sketch the devices instead of describing them. Ditto copies for the entire class. Make an answer key.

PROCEDURE

Activities like Theatre Talk are teaching/learning devices that students can use profitably while the coach is working on stage with individual actors or small groups. The student circles or draws a box around each term after reading the description. The key is used for self-check.

VARIATION

Many students will enjoy making their own puzzles for classmates to use. Both decoding and encoding are learning experiences.

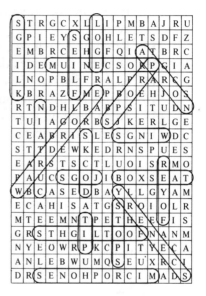

Theatre Talk Puzzle and Key.

Theatre Talk

Draw a circle around the terms for the following descriptions:

1. Space behind and above the stage with devices for handling scenery and lights.
2. The arch or wall that separates the stage from the auditorium.
3. The lobby of the theatre.
4. Spaces on the right and left of the stage.

5. Storage places for scenery.
6. Usually the front of the main floor reserved for musicians.
7. Narrow flats used in set building.
8. Floodlights.
9. Part of the stage in front of curtain.
10. A box with seats, sometimes the front sections of the lowest balcony.
11. A seat in a box at the theatre.
12. Furniture, ornaments, decorations used in a stage setting by an actor.
13. Room in which costumes are kept.
14. Drapery that hides the stage from the view of the audience.
15. Lights that line the lower front of the stage.
16. Lights focused on small areas of the stage.
17. Items used on stage to represent a particular scene or setting.
18. Sound amplifiers.

Key:

1. Flies
2. Proscenium
3. Foyer
4. Wings
5. Docks
6. Pit
7. Jogs
8. Kliegs
9. Apron
10. Loge
11. Box seat
12. Props
13. Wardrobe
14. Curtain
15. Footlights
16. Spots
17. Scenery
18. Microphones

▶SUBJECT AREA

Theatre

GRADE LEVEL

10–12

NAME OF ACTIVITY

The Body Talks

OBJECTIVE OF ACTIVITY

To use pictures in students' everyday lives for the study of body gestures.

STUDENT PREPARATION

Students find pictures in which subjects are using body movements to express an idea or emotion. The picture should be from anywhere in the students' everyday world, from magazines, newspapers, posters, billboards (students' snapshots), comic books, handbills.

TEACHER PREPARATION

Provide an overhead projector.

PROCEDURE

Each student shares with the class what he or she learned from reading the gesture shown in the picture. Some time is allowed for class members to comment on their interpretations of the photograph as they view it projected on the screen or wall.

VARIATION

A more sophisticated class in theatre can write a short script to accompany each photograph. With the picture projected on the screen, each student (in a spotlight) imitates the gestures and speaks the lines he or she has written. Time should be allowed for input from the other members of the class.

SUBJECT AREA

Theatre

GRADE LEVEL

10–12

NAME OF ACTIVITY

Mime

OBJECTIVE OF ACTIVITY

To reinforce the ability to follow directions as a student brings his personal experiences to a pantomiming role.

STUDENT PREPARATION

The student has observed films of Marcel Marceau, the French pantomimist, Tony Montanaro, Red Skelton and/or Sid Caesar.

TEACHER PREPARATION

Prepare pantomime cards (see examples). Obtain a timer.

PROCEDURE

The class is divided into two teams by assigning each student a number. Students with odd numbers form team 1, students with even numbers, team 2. A toss of the coin decides which team performs first. The teacher keeps score and takes care of the timer, which is set for one or more minutes depending on the intricacy of the role. Team 1's first player draws a pantomime card. If the player's teammates correctly identify his portrayal, the team receives a point. But if the timer catches the player before his team identifies the role and before he has had time to put the card back on the table, the team forfeits the point. Teams alternate portraying a mime, and the one with the highest number of points wins.

Examples of miming categories:

I Work-A-Day

- A gardener pulling weeds.
- A police officer giving a ticket to a speeder.
- A judge bringing a court to order.
- An Avon lady making a house call.
- A dentist filling a tooth.
- A landscape artist planting a tree.
- A nurse giving a patient a shot.
- Boy in supermarket sacking groceries.
- A beauty operator blow drying a customer's hair.
- A first grade teacher in a primary chair in reading circle.
- Attendant at filling station servicing a car.
- An optometrist adjusting glasses.

II Fun Day

- Swimmer on the high dive.
- Romantic young man paddling a canoe with girl aboard.
- Grandma on her three-wheeled cycle.
- Man on motorcycle driving an obstacle course.
- A man with a coin detector finding money.
- Future Farmer receiving a ribbon for his prize hog.

III An Unday

- A freeway traveler discovering a flat tire.
- A smoker burning a hole in his coat.
- A woman feeling a snag turn into a runner.
- A person walking across grass as automatic sprinkler turns on.

SUBJECT AREA

Theatre

GRADE LEVEL

10–12

NAME OF ACTIVITY

Following the Director

OBJECTIVE OF ACTIVITY

To develop an actor's ability to follow the direction of a director and to sharpen observational abilities of students in the class.

STUDENT PREPARATION

None.

TEACHER PREPARATION

Prepare direction cards to be used by students as they participate in the activity. Each card contains six different directions and also contains a script line. (See additional sample script lines.) Example:

```
1. FEARFULLY
2. WITH CONCERN
3. CURIOUSLY
4. SARCASTICALLY
5. ANGRILY
6. HUMOROUSLY


There goes Ray.
```

Ditto score sheets similar to the one illustrated.

PROCEDURE

Each student performs as the rest of the class fills in the score sheet. The actor selects five cards from the director who is sitting out of eye contact with the rest of the class. The director writes the script lines on his score sheet, and the actor goes front and center, keeping his cards in the order recorded on the director's score sheet. When he is ready to begin, the actor looks to the director who holds up one, two, three, four, five, or six fingers. The actor says the script line in accordance with the direction. For instance, if the director holds up four fingers, the actor says the line sarcastically. The members of the class score the direction they think the actor was following; the director also scores the interpretation. The actor moves to the next card and repeats the procedure until all five lines have been spoken. At the end of his performance, score sheets are passed to the director who will use them later in conferring with the actor. Each member of the class takes a turn.

Examples of script lines:

What is your name?
What did I do?
Why don't you take a bath?
She's disgusting.
You're only sixteen.
Do you really want me to leave?
Why are you doing this?
My mother and father are getting a divorce.
Where are you going?
We lost the game last week.
That's your boyfriend/girlfriend.
I got fired today.
It's a boy.
When?
Now.
Do you overeat?
Who are you?
How long are you going to keep up this nonsense?
Are you going to shoot him?
This is the last time I'm going to tell you.

Don't come back.
Do you really want to leave me?
What are you doing?
Is that a promise?
I can't figure out what to do.
Am I insane?
Are you marrying him?
Where is everybody?
Why?
Yes.
No.

Example:

Score Sheet

DIRECTIONS

As the actor expresses his line, check (✓) the direction you think he was given by the instructor. The score sheet has one column for each of the five lines an actor performs. Write the name of the actor and the lines spoken in the order in which they were spoken.

Actor:

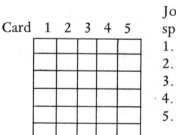

	Card	1	2	3	4	5
FEARFULLY						
WITH CONCERN						
CURIOUSLY						
SARCASTICALLY						
ANGRILY						
HUMOROUSLY						

Jot down lines in order spoken.
1.
2.
3.
4.
5.

SUBJECT AREA

Theatre

GRADE LEVEL

10–12

NAME OF ACTIVITY

Target: S.R.O.

OBJECTIVE OF ACTIVITY

Not every member in the theatre class gets a part in the play at hand. One task non-performing actors draw is publicity. This activity suggests that the drama coach make publicity a focus for teaching/learning and that she expect performance as excellent as that expected from the actors. The objective of Target: S.R.O. is to foster first-rate publicity techniques.

STUDENT PREPARATION

Members of the publicity committee have received instruction on techniques of advertising from the drama coach or her surrogate, the journalism instructor. Weeks prior to the opening of the play, students collect newspaper advertisements for theatrical performances to study techniques of design, paying special attention to the language used by professional ad copywriters. (See examples.)

TEACHER PREPARATION

None.

PROCEDURE

After instruction and self-study, each member of the publicity committee roughs out five ads for the school newspaper and five posters, using the techniques evident in the professional advertisements. The roughs are exhibited before the theatre class, designers' names remaining a secret. After top roughs for the newspaper ads and the posters have been selected, the designer who had the largest number of roughs accepted receives the Addy Award. All members of the publicity committee complete the preparation of the final copy.

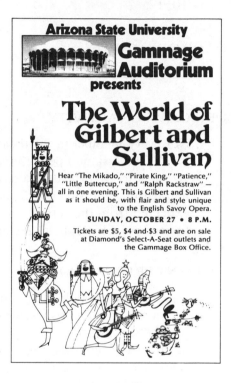

Some Examples of Professionally Designed Ads.

SUBJECT AREA

Theatre

GRADE LEVEL

10–12

NAME OF ACTIVITY

The Person I Am

OBJECTIVE OF ACTIVITY

To assist actors and actresses to get into the skins of characters they are playing by interpreting descriptions and actions of corresponding characters.

STUDENT PREPARATION

The student has been assigned a role, has read the script, and has internalized how the director has said the role should be played.

TEACHER PREPARATION

If the cast were presenting the "Life of Helen Keller," you would have not only the lead but other members of the cast read one or more biographies, as well as Keller's autobiography, to get insights into the nature of Miss Keller. When plays are chosen that are nonbiographical, you probably regret not being able to use this excellent teaching-learning technique. You can, however, assign players to read fiction (nonfiction) portraying persons whose characteristics correspond to your direction of how a character should be played. Write a series of inference questions which enable the players to get insights into the nature of the roles into which they have been cast.

PROCEDURE

After the director has determined how characters are to be played, he gives the players directed reading assignments. The players read the materials guided by the inference questions the director has written.

If you are starting the book here, you are coming in on the middle of the act. Part I is the curtain raiser; it builds up to the use of the foreign languages section.

CHAPTER 7

Foreign Languages

This section focuses on teaching/learning activities designed for students of French, Spanish, and German. Certainly other languages are being taught in schools throughout the country, but the suggestions here are immediately applicable to the study of all foreign languages. The influence of varied ancestors of United States citizens is present in almost every facet of American life, a strength to be capitalized on in the classroom.

While textbooks are contributors to the success of foreign language students, the attractiveness of everyday materials is not to be overlooked. So, a number of unceremonious resources are employed for activities that facilitate merging the teaching of reading skills with the teaching of content: packagings of exported products, menus, telephone books, baseball, newspapers, proverbs, recipes, and other realia.

The skills promoted in this section bear a remarkable likeness to those in the English section: vocabulary, of course; the skills of problem solving, interpreting, collecting, and organizing data; following printed directions; and the use of glossaries and dictionaries. You will want to check out the fifty or so activities in the English section for further practice materials for your students.

FRENCH

SUBJECT AREA

French

GRADE LEVEL

Levels I and II

NAME OF ACTIVITY

May I Take Your Order? (Que Voulez-vous Commander?)

OBJECTIVE OF ACTIVITY

To simulate a real situation that allows students to use their knowledge of French as they weigh price tags and extenuating circumstances and to reinforce use of a French/English dictionary or glossary.

STUDENT PREPARATION

The student has attained a working vocabulary in the French language.

TEACHER PREPARATION

Examples of all phases of this activity are illustrated. Print a menu that might be encountered in a French restaurant on a large piece of tagboard. Prepare a glossary of terms used on the menu and create situation or problem cards.

PROCEDURE

This activity is housed in the learning center if it is to be used by individual students. All situation or problem cards demand that the student choose an appropriate meal from the menu in accordance with certain restrictions, such as cost, food allergies, food likes and dislikes. She also totals the amount of her tab in American dollars.

The student selects a situation card and proceeds to order from the menu, making notations of her selections later to be checked by the teacher. If the activity is used with a whole class, the menu and the glossary are dittoed and a different situation or problem card is given to each member of the class. When students have completed their menu selections and bill computations, they share their rationale with the entire class and receive corrections and/or reinforcements.

Example of menu:

Que Voulez-vous Commander?

Hors d'Oeuvre

Anchois	3 Frs.
Crêpes Fourrées Gratinées	4 Frs.
Quiche au Fromage	3 Frs.
Saucisson en Croûte	3 Frs.

Consommé

Bouillabaisse-Mediterranée	4 Frs.
Potage Crème d'Asperges	2 Frs.
Potage Crème de Champignons	3 Frs.
Soupe à l'Oignon	3 Frs.

Poisson

Filets de Sole Bonne Femme	8 Frs.
Homard à l'Americaine	12 Frs.
Truites à la Meunière	10 Frs.

Volaille

Caneton aux Navets	10 Frs.
Coq au Vin à la Bourguignonne	12 Frs.
Poulet Rôti	8 Frs.

Viande

Bifteck Marchand de Vins	10 Frs.
Boeuf à la Mode	10 Frs.
Cassoulet	8 Frs.
Foie de Veau Sauté	8 Frs.
Gigot d'Agneau Rôti	12 Frs.
Rôti de Porc Boulangère	12 Frs.

Légumes

Asperges au Naturel	5 Frs.
Champignons Grillés	4 Frs.
Petits Pois Frais à la Française	3 Frs.
Pommes de Terre Dauphinoises	3 Frs.
Tomates à la Provençale	3 Frs.

Gâteaux

Clafoutis aux Cerises	4 Frs.
Crème Caramel	2 Frs.
Paris-Brest	3 Frs.
Tartes aux Fraises	4 Frs.

Glossary: French—English

Hors D'Oeuvres	*Appetizers*
Anchois	Hot Anchovy Canape
Crêpes Fourrées Gratinées	Filled French Pancakes

Quiche au Fromage	Open Faced Cheese Tart
Saucisson en Croûte	Sausage Baked in Pastry Crust

Consommés	*Soups*
Bouillabaisse-Mediterranée	Fisherman's Soup with Hot Pepper Sauce
Potage Crème d'Asperges	Cream of Asparagus Soup
Potage Crème de Champignons	Cream of Mushroom Soup
Soupe à l'Oignon	French Onion Soup

Poisson	*Fish*
Filets de Sole Bonne Femme	Fillets of Sole with Mushroom and Wine Sauce
Homard à l'Americaine	Lobsters Simmered with Wine, Tomatoes and Herbs
Truites à la Meunière	Trout Sauteed in Butter

Volaille	*Poultry*
Caneton aux Navets	Duck with Turnips
Coq au Vin à la Bourguignonne	Chicken Simmered in Red Wine with Onions and Mushrooms
Poulet Rôti	Roast Chicken

Viande	*Meat*
Bifteck Marchand de Vins	Sauteed Steak with Red Wine Sauce
Boeuf à la Mode	Pot Roast of Beef Braised in Red Wine
Cassoulet	Casserole of White Beans Baked with Meats
Foie de Veau Sauté	Sauteed Calf's Liver
Gigot d'Agneau Rôti	Roast Leg of Lamb
Rôti de Porc Boulangère	Glazed Roast Loin of Pork

Legumes	*Vegetables*
Asperges au Naturel	Boiled Asparagus
Champignons Grillés	Broiled Mushrooms

Petits Pois Frais a la Française	Fresh Peas Braised with Onions and Lettuce
Pommes de Terre Dauphinoises	Scalloped Potatoes with Cheese
Tomates à la Provençale	Tomatoes Baked with Bread Crumbs and Garlic

Gâteaux	*Cakes*
Clafoutis aux Cerises	Cherry Cake
Crème Caramel	Caramel Custard
Paris-Brest	Cream Puff Pastry Ring with Whipped Cream Filling
Tartes aux Fraises	Fresh Strawberry Tarts

Currency Exchange
5 francs = $1.00
****

Examples of situation or problem cards:

Order dinner for yourself but remember that you are allergic to milk and milk products.

This is your niece's fifth birthday. Order a "birthday lunch" for her and three little friends of the same age.

Order a mid-afternoon snack that costs less than $1.00.

An American teenager is visiting you; hamburgers and French fries are not on the menu. What will you order for him?

Order two dinners. One dinner is for a diabetic friend, the other is for you, but you are on a low cholesteral diet.

You are taking two children to lunch. One child is allergic to chocolates and hates fish and mushrooms. The other child has a small appetite. What will you order for each child and for yourself?

SUBJECT AREA

French

GRADE LEVEL

Level I

NAME OF ACTIVITY

Laissez les Doigts

OBJECTIVE OF ACTIVITY

To provide opportunity for students to increase their knowledge of French terms, using materials in their everyday lives.

STUDENT PREPARATION

None.

TEACHER PREPARATION

Obtain enough telephone books for each student in the class. They often are available from telephone companies after new directories are delivered each year. Prepare a ditto for the activity which includes directions and a list of French words for various business men and women. (See example.)

PROCEDURE

The students look up telephone numbers for the job classifications listed on the ditto. In addition to writing the telephone numbers in numerals, they write them in words, for example, 949-1242, and neuf-quatre-neuf-un-deux-quatre-deux. In some instances, there will be no classification in the telephone book for the terms listed. Students are expected to think of other categories which might contain a telephone number for the person listed on the ditto. For example, for *le prêtre* students would need to look under churches to find the telephone number for a rectory of a Catholic church; for *la bonne,* the telephone number would be that of an employment agency.

Example of ditto:

Laissez les Doigts

Laissez les doigts faire une promenade a travers les pages jaunes.*

DIRECTIONS

Using your telephone book, find numbers for the professional and service persons listed. In addition to writing the numbers in numerals, write them in words. The first entry is an example.

Person	Telephone Number	Listed Under
le plombier	949-1242 neuf-quatre-neuf-un-deux-quatre-deux	Plumbers
le coiffeur		
les pompiers		
le chirurgien		
l'avocat		
la coiffeuse		
la masseuse		
le docteur		
le boucher		
le professeur		
la bonne		

*Telephone Advertisements and Excerpts Reprinted with Permission of Mountain Bell.

▶SUBJECT AREA

French

GRADE LEVEL

Level I

NAME OF ACTIVITY

You're a Frenchman Already

OBJECTIVE OF ACTIVITY

This type of activity is a strong reinforcement to dispel the uneasiness that often fills the first few days in a foreign language class. Its objective is to impress on students that they already know and use many French terms, cognates, in other words. It also fosters use of context clues.

STUDENT PREPARATION

None.

TEACHER PREPARATION

On 3 X 5" cards print a French cognate and a very simple French sentence in which the cognate is used.

Example:

chaise-longue
La chaise-longue est bleue.

On the reverse side type the translation of the sentence.
Hundreds of English and French words are spelled exactly alike (or

have a slight variation) and have the same meaning. Just a few examples are:

cabinet	cantaloup	catastrophe
câble	capable	cavité
cadavre	cape	célébration
cadence	capital	censure
café	capsule	centre
cage	capture	cérémonial
calamité	carafe	certain
calibre	caramel	chaîne
calme	carcasse	champion
calorie	cardinal	chance
camp	caresse	chaos
Canadien	caricature	chaperon
canal	carnaval	charme
cancer	carton	chic
cannibale	caste	chocolat
canoë	catalogue	cigarette

(And that's just part of the c's.) Have French/English dictionaries at hand.

PROCEDURE

The class is divided into groups of five. Each group is given a stack of fifteen cards which are dealt in threes to each. Individual players look at their words, and if they don't know the meaning for the French-English look-alikes, they can check the dictionary. Then they try to translate the simple sentences. After a time limit, each student shows his cards one at a time to others in his group, gives his meaning of the word and his translation of the sentence. Another student verifies the sentence with the translation on the back. At the completion of a round the fifteen cards are traded with a nearby small group.

SUBJECT AREA

French

GRADE LEVEL

Level I

NAME OF ACTIVITY

Quelle Heure Est-il?

OBJECTIVE OF ACTIVITY

To promote the ability to assign English equivalents to French words and French equivalents to English words as well as to develop a working sight and speaking vocabulary.

STUDENT PREPARATION

The student has been introduced to French numbers.

TEACHER PREPARATION

The activity requires two decks of cards. Draw the face of a clock with hands pointing to a specific time on pieces of green tagboard. Examples:

Make approximately twenty-five cards and at the bottom of each, print *Quelle heure est-il?* Using the same size card in another color, print the answers in French, for example, *Il est midi; Il est huit heures.*

PROCEDURE

Quelle Heure Est-il? is played by five students. Five green cards are dealt to each player. The orange cards are placed in the center of the table. The first player draws a card from the stack. If she can match it to one in her hand, she lays them face up in front of her. She may

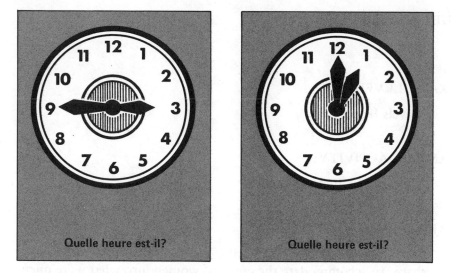

"Quelle Heure Est-il?" Cards.

then select another orange card. If she can match this card, she may place it in front of her and draw another. If not, the turn goes to the next player. If a player, at her turn, cannot match her drawn card, she places it at the bottom of the stack. The student who is the first to match all cards is the winner. Ten points are given for each matched set. The winner has the highest number of points.

▶SUBJECT AREA

French

GRADE LEVEL

Levels II and III

NAME OF ACTIVITY

Nommez La Femme

OBJECTIVE OF ACTIVITY

The French language may need to be revamped, or added to perhaps, to accommodate the entry of women into what were once
exclusively male domains. This activity serves to reinforce the skills
of problem-solving and inventing, as it provides an opportunity to
exercise suffixes.

STUDENT PREPARATION

None.

TEACHER PREPARATION

Set up problems which call for students to create names for women
entering professions and services which heretofore have been dominated by men. Type on 3 × 5″ cards such problems as this:

Nommez La Femme

French does not include a word for a woman butcher. Le
boucher is declined as a masculine noun. Create a word to
describe a female who enters the butcher trade. Cautions: La
boucherie is the word for butcher shop. La bouchere usually
describes a butcher's wife. What other alternatives?

274

PROCEDURE

Students work in small groups to solve the problem situations created by the teacher. Each group has its own problem and shares the solution it finds with the rest of the class. As a follow-up, students write their own situation cards. They scan French dictionaries for male nouns that have no female counterparts. A result might be:

Nommez la Femme

Diplomate is a masculine. As more and more women enter the diplomatic service, a feminine noun needs to be created for them. What are some alternatives?

NOTE

Should the male students in the class find this activity less than motivating, the teacher can assign them to create new words for men engaged in a profession or trade formerly dominated by women. Examples are feminine nouns such as la infirmière, or hospital nurse; la couturière, or dressmasker; la gouvernante, or housekeeper.

SUBJECT AREA

French

GRADE LEVEL

Levels I and II

NAME OF ACTIVITY

Baseball French

OBJECTIVE OF ACTIVITY

To help students become skillful and articulate in transposing the verbs of the French language when used in sentences.

STUDENT PREPARATION

The student has some knowledge of the structure of French verbs.

TEACHER PREPARATION

Prepare a chart with a baseball diamond or draw the figure on the chalkboard or transparency to be used on an overhead projector. Prepare sentences that contain French words at the level at which the students can perform successfully. Provide buttons, cardboard squares, or pipe cleaner figures to be used on the bases.

PROCEDURE

The teams are chosen. The teacher or monitor reads a sentence in English. If the first batter of team one can translate the sentence correctly in the present tense, he makes a first base hit. The second batter of team one is allowed to translate the sentence in past tense. If she answers correctly, she goes to first base and advances her teammate to second base. The third player attempts to translate in future tense. If successful, he goes to first base and advances each teammate one base. The fourth batter has a turn to translate in imperfect tense. If she answers correctly, she has brought the first player home and scored a run. This process continues until there are three misses or outs. The runs made are recorded on a score sheet, and the second team comes to bat. Team two now has a chance, and the players follow the same procedure with a new sentence. The number of innings which represents a game are determined before the competition begins.

VARIATION

To allow physical as well as mental exercise, the teacher may wish to draw a large baseball diamond on butcher paper and place it on the classroom floor. The players then stand on the bases when they have scored a hit and move to succeeding bases as their teammates get hits.

SPANISH

▶SUBJECT AREA

Spanish

GRADE LEVEL

Level I

NAME OF ACTIVITY

Aquí Se Habla Español

OBJECTIVE OF ACTIVITY

To strengthen interpreting skills by way of writing skills.

STUDENT PREPARATION

None.

TEACHER PREPARATION

Clip line drawings of produce, meats, and packaged goods from grocery ads. Ten drawings for each group of five in the class would be sufficient. Put the clippings in an envelope with the directions (see example) written on the front.

PROCEDURE

In groups of five, students design a grocery store ad in Spanish, complete with line drawings, prices, descriptions, store hours, address, phone number, length of sale, and other details requested by the instructor. When the ad is completed, a speaker for each group shares its creation with the rest of the class.

NOTE

This activity can be varied by focusing on other retail establishments, such as pharmacies, car dealers, department stores, jewelry stores, clothing stores, farm implements, variety stores.

Line Drawings for Use in a Spanish-Language Ad.

Example of directions on front of envelope:

> ### AQUÍ SE HABLA ESPAÑOL
>
> Directions: In this envelope are line drawings of ten items which Mr. Garcia wishes to feature at El Mercado Garcia this weekend. Design the ad for him, using the clippings, prices, descriptions, amounts, store hours, dates of sale, address, and phone number.

SUBJECT AREA

Spanish

GRADE LEVEL

Level I

NAME OF ACTIVITY

Realia

OBJECTIVE OF ACTIVITY

To foster vocabulary building.

STUDENT PREPARATION

None.

TEACHER PREPARATION

Obtain labels and packagings of products that are exported to or manufactured in Spanish-speaking countries. If you live in a state bordering Mexico, your treasure hunt can take you personally south of the border. If you teach in a state where a trip is not feasible, contact Spanish teachers in towns that do border Mexico. An obliging faculty member will spearhead a drive to get the labels for you.

Company	Example Label
1. Kellogg Company	Hojuelas de Maiz (illustrated)
2. Del Monte Foods	Ejotes Verdes Cortados (illustrated)
	Vegetales Mixtos (illustrated)
	Guisantes con Zanahorias (illustrated)
3. Colgate-Palmolive	Palmolive de Lujo con crema de oliva
	Ultra Brite para la blanca, blanca sonrisa

4. General Foods Corp.   Gelatina Jell-o con vitamina C
5. Proctor & Gamble   Crest la pasta dental con chispas
         azules con fluoristán
6. Nabisco   Galletas Ritz con queso

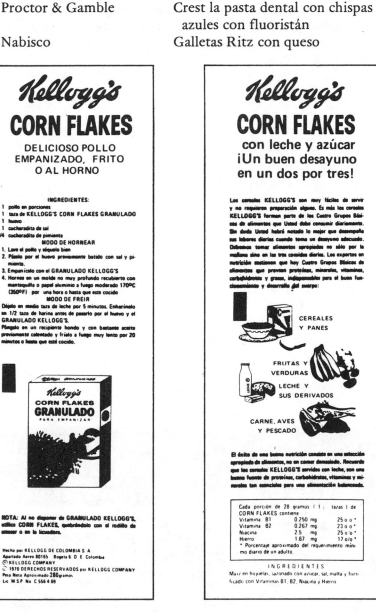

Container for Corn Flakes Printed in Spanish (Courtesy of the Kellogg Company)

When you receive the labels, assemble them in such a way that they resemble the actual product. For example, paste a can label around a simulated can of cardboard; reassemble boxes into their original shapes. Remodel one corner of the classroom into a mercado and stock your shelves.

PROCEDURE

How to get best use of the classroom grocery store is bounded only by your imagination as you design activities using the realia. Vocabulary development would be just a starter. A few other considerations might be developing ability to

1. follow directions (for example, the side panel of the Kellogg's box has a recipe for Delicioso Pollo Empanizado)
2. interpret (for example, Kellogg's box discusses vitamins, minerals, proteins, and carbohydrates)
3. distinguish fact from opinion (any straight advertising used on the packagings)

Students themselves will be motivated to design activities when an enterprising teacher has arranged such an ambiente.

Label for Can of Cut String Beans (Courtesy of Del Monte Corporation)

Label for Can of Mixed Vegetables (Courtesy of Del Monte Corporation)

Label for Can of Peas and Carrots (Courtesy of Del Monte Corporation)

SUBJECT AREA

Spanish

GRADE LEVEL

Levels II and III

NAME OF ACTIVITY

Multiple Dictionary Entries

OBJECTIVE OF ACTIVITY

To assist students in assigning appropriate Spanish meanings to English words and appropriate English meanings to Spanish words based on use in sentences.

STUDENT PREPARATION

The student has had experience in using a Spanish/English and English/Spanish dictionary.

TEACHER PREPARATION

Write both English and Spanish sentences containing words that have several meanings. Write a context clue in English for each sentence. (See examples.) Have dictionaries available.

PROCEDURE

Using an English sentence to be translated into Spanish, the student uses the dictionary to find various vocabulary words that may be unknown to him. He or she checks all of the definitions against the context clue provided by the teacher and decides on the appropriate translation. The same procedure is used for translating a Spanish sentence into English.

Examples of sentences and context clues given to students:

English to Spanish

1. The apple was falling from the tree where it had grown red and juicy.
   Context clue: We are talking about a ripe apple falling from the tree where it has grown.
2. The lecture was held in a classroom that was not fit for scholars.
   Context clue: We are talking within scholastic circles.

Spanish to English

3. El puerco, grande y gordo, atravesó la carretera.
   Context clue: We are talking about an animal dashing across an interstate highway.
4. En el desierto, el hombre moribundo pedía un trago de agua.
   Context clue: This sentence describes a desert scene with a weather-beaten man dragging himself across the hot sand in the last stages of life.

Examples of teacher's notes which may be used for further clarification at completion of assignment:

English to Spanish

1. The apple was falling from the tree where it had grown red and juicy.
   Context clue: We are talking about a ripe apple falling from the tree where it has grown.
   Student choices:
   1. La manzana   caía
                     bajaba
                     descendía
                     derribaba
   2. del árbol donde había   crecido
                                nacido
                                desarrolládose
                                formádose
                                aumentádose

3. roja y   jugosa
            zumosa
            sucosa

Answer: (sentence most commonly used in Spanish) La manzana caía del árbol donde había crecido roja y jugosa.

2. The lecture was held in a classroom that was not fit for scholars.
   Context clue: We are talking within scholastic circles.
   Student choices:
   1. La   conferencia
            lectura
            disertación
   2. tuvo lugar
      se tuvo
      se detuvo
      se mantuvo
   3. que no   era adecuado para
                era equipado para
                era vestido para
                era ajustado para

   Answer: La conferencia tuvo lugar en un salón de clases que no era adecuado para hombres eruditos.

Spanish to English

3. El puerco, grande y gordo, atravesó la carretera.
   Context clue: We are talking about an animal dashing across an interstate highway.
   Student choices:
   1. The   pig
             dirty
             brute
   2. big
      great
      extensive
   3. and   fat
             thick

    4. ran across
       placed across
       bet
       interferred
    5. the   highway
             road
             street

Answer: The big, fat pig ran across the highway.

4. En el desierto, el hombre moribundo pedía un trago de agua.
Context clue: This sentence describes a desert scene with a weather-beaten man dragging himself across the hot sand in the last stages of life.
Student choices:
    1. In the   desert
               deserted
    2. the man   dying
                near death
    3. asked for
       demanded
       ordered
    4. a   drink
           shot
           gulp
           misfortune

Answer: In the desert, the dying man asked for a drink of water.

▶SUBJECT AREA

Spanish

GRADE LEVEL

Levels II and III

NAME OF ACTIVITY

Rewrite Man

OBJECTIVE OF ACTIVITY

To assist students in organizing their own words, phrases and sentences according to patterns appropriate for Spanish and different from English.

STUDENT PREPARATION

The student has some knowledge of putting sentences together in Spanish so that he can rewrite, in his own words, a newspaper article written in Spanish.

TEACHER PREPARATION

Make a copy of an article(s) from a Spanish newspaper for students in the class.

PROCEDURE

The student reads the article in Spanish and rewrites the article in his own Spanish words. In individual conferences the teacher and student doublecheck grammar, composition, and spelling. As a culminating activity, the teacher lifts examples of the most commonly made errors from the rewrites and discusses them, using an opaque or overhead projector and concealing student identity.

▶SUBJECT AREA

Spanish

GRADE LEVEL

Levels I, II and III

NAME OF ACTIVITY

Cultural Proverbs

OBJECTIVE OF ACTIVITY

To assist students with the vocabulary of Spanish proverbs as they learn some culture of Spanish people by way of proverbs.

STUDENT PREPARATION

None.

TEACHER PREPARATION

Proverbs may be found throughout Spanish texts used in all three levels of Spanish courses. Use 3 X 5" cards for this activity. On one side print or type a Spanish proverb.

Example:
Antes que te cases, mira lo que haces.
On the reverse side of the card, print the literal translation of the Spanish.

Example:
Before you get married, look at what you are doing.
On the same side of the card, print the English version of the proverb.

Example:
Look before you leap.
Cover the English version with a cardboard flap.

PROCEDURE

Students work in pairs. The player reads the front side of the card while the other student is reading the literal translation on the back side to check for accuracy. If the player has translated correctly, both students try to think of the English version of the proverb. When they agree on what it might be, they lift the flap to check their guess. Then the players reverse roles.

Additional examples of Spanish sayings:

1. Cada chango por su mecate.
   Each monkey through his own rope. (To each his own.)
2. A quien madruga, Dios le ayuda.
   God helps him who gets up early. (God helps him who helps himself.)
3. Si no te gusta, trágatelo.
   If you don't like it, swallow it. (If you don't like it, lump it.)
4. Uno pone y Dios dispone.
   Man proposes and God disposes.
5. Pediche pero no robiche.
   A beggar but not a thief.
6. El perro que ladra no muerde.
   The dog that barks does not bite. (A barking dog doesn't bite.)
7. Más vale pájaro en mano que cien volando.
   A bird in hand is worth more than a hundred flying. (A bird in the hand is worth two in the bush.)
8. Poquito porque es bendito.
   A small amount because it is blessed. (Good things come in small packages.)
9. Dios te lo pague porque yo no puedo.
   May God pay you for it because I can't. (God repays.)
10. Al pobre dale de tu pan, pero al triste dale de tu corazón.
    To the poor give of your bread, but to the sad give of your heart.
11. Si le viene el saco, póngaselo.
    If the coat fits, put it on. (If the shoe fits, wear it.)

GERMAN

SUBJECT AREA

German

GRADE LEVEL

Level I

NAME OF ACTIVITY

Quick Vocabulary

OBJECTIVE OF ACTIVITY

In *Teacher* Sylvia Ashton Warner offered the theory that students learn words when they have some affective attachment to the words. Language teachers who want their students to build vocabulary quickly might test Mrs. Warner's hypothesis. The objective of this multi-phased activity is to promote vocabulary growth in first-year German students.

STUDENT PREPARATION

None.

Phase I

TEACHER PREPARATION

Provide 3 X 5″ cards or slips of paper.

PROCEDURE

This activity should take place at the beginning of the term. The teacher asks each student to think about an English word in his everyday life that is important to him for one reason or another. While students are engaged in seat work, the teacher visits each student, asks him the English word he has chosen and inquires about its importance. The instructor writes the English word on the 3 X 5″ card and then the German word. Some of the words that might emerge as important might be Kampf, lieben, Familie, Sahneneis, Nahrung. What has happened? Because each student has chosen a word important to him, his likelihood of remembering it is strong. The teacher has given each student personal attention and has learned something of a personal nature. The student has the beginning of a vocabulary file. The activity should be repeated frequently.

Phase II

TEACHER PREPARATION

Provide 3 × 5" cards and dictionaries.

PROCEDURE

The students look up the names of objects in the classroom in German/English dictionaries, write the German word on a 3 × 5" card and tape it to the object, for example, Fenster, Kreide, Wandtafel. Then each student finds the German equivalents of words that represent objects in his home. Each student prepares his own 3 × 5" cards to take home and tape to the objects, for example, Kühlschrank, Stuhl. The labels stay on the objects at home until the student learns them. (The teacher may wish to apprise parents of this activity. Most will enjoy the opportunity to learn some German themselves.)

Phase III

TEACHER PREPARATION

Provide 3 × 5" cards and dictionaries.

PROCEDURE

On the chalkboard the teacher has written a sentence that gives the direction for the activity. It might be "If you had three wishes in German, what would they be for?" The students use their dictionaries and put the English words and their German companions on vocabulary cards. Other stimulators might be "Write all the German words you can think of that tell what you like today," or "Describe your boyfriend or girlfriend in German."

NOTE

The students' vocabulary cards become their resource when they begin to put words into sentences and sentences into paragraphs.

▶SUBJECT AREA

German

GRADE LEVEL

Levels I and II

NAME OF ACTIVITY

Affe See; Affe Read; Affe Do

OBJECTIVE OF ACTIVITY

This activity promotes the skills of

1. Collecting and organizing realia and data,
2. Making a how-to demonstration,
3. Following printed directions, and
4. Writing directions.

STUDENT PREPARATION

Each student is assigned to make a how-to demonstration in German. He collects objects that are plentiful and inexpensive, enough for each student in the class to have his own. (The teacher should emphasize that the student's choice of demonstration must be guided by availability of realia. For example, *How To Change a Tire* is inappropriate for this activity; whereas *How To String Puka Shells* would be appropriate for a student who had collected them on a trip to Hawaii.) The student prepares what he is to say in German and also writes the directions in German on a transparency.

TEACHER PREPARATION

None.

PROCEDURE

After a student makes his how-to presentation, he passes realia to members of the class and puts the transparency on the overhead projector. The rest of the class proceeds to follow the printed directions.

▶SUBJECT AREA

German

GRADE LEVEL

Levels II and III

NAME OF ACTIVITY

Feinschmecker

OBJECTIVE OF ACTIVITY

The foremost objective of this activity is to reinforce student ability to follow directions. In addition, Feinschmecker provides an opportunity to translate from English to German, while learning more about the culture of the German people.

STUDENT PREPARATION

None.

TEACHER PREPARATION

Provide German cookbook(s) or recipes written in English. Make arrangements with the chairman of the home economics department to use the kitchen on a specified date.

PROCEDURE

The class is divided into groups. Each group is assigned one course of a German meal to plan. The students use the cookbooks and recipes to decide on their selections and make a grocery list of supplies needed. They translate the English recipes into German (see example of a main course dish) and shop for the groceries. If possible, the purchases should be made in a store specializing in German foods so the students can speak in German. On the appointed day, students use the kitchen facilities to prepare the meal from the German-language recipes and serve themselves and the home economics students whose facilities they are preempting.

299

THE REPUBLIC'S *Recipe File*

LUKSHEN KUGEL

(Cheese and Noodle Pudding)

1 pound broad egg noodles

1 pound cottage cheese

5 eggs, lightly beaten

11 cups golden raisins

1 cup dairy sour cream

½ cup melted butter ▾ or margarine, divided

¼ cup sugar

4½ teaspoons g r o u n d cinnamon

2 teaspoons grated lemon peel

1¾ teaspoons salt

¼ teaspoon ground nutmeg

¾ cup corn flake crumbs

Cook noodles according to package directions. Drain, rinse, and place in a large mixing bowl. Combine remaining ingredients except ¼ cup of the melted butter and corn flake crumbs. Pour seasoned cheese mixture over noodles; mix gently but thoroughly. Spoon noodle mixture into a buttered 13-½ x 9 x 2-inch baking dish. Combine remaining ¼ cup melted butter with corn flake crumbs. Sprinkle over noodle mixture. Place in a preheated moderate oven (375 degrees F.) for 30 minutes. Remove from oven and let stand 10 minutes before cutting. Serve as a main dish or main dish accompaniment. YIELD: 8 to 12 portions

Recipe for Translation.

If you are starting the book here, you are coming in on the middle of the act. Part I is the curtain raiser; it builds up to the use of the health section.

CHAPTER 8

Health

Much of the family budget is earmarked for keeping the body sound or returning it to peak condition. While students use their share of the budget on trips to physicians, ophthalmologists, and orthodontists, their real concern about family health and health budget will not come until long after textbooks have been forgotten.

Therefore it makes sense for teachers to supplement the textbook regularly and often with materials from the everyday world. More than ever before popular news sources like the daily newspaper include factual information, advice columns, and advertisements that touch on the problems of keeping Americans healthy. So do magazines. New discoveries may take three, four, even five or more years to get into health textbooks, but information on new methods, ideas, and products is regularly provided in

301

the daily media. Product packages and labels themselves make excellent teaching materials.

All types of resources are fair game for improving the vocabulary and comprehension skills of students, such as the ability to interpret, compare, evaluate and make judgments, classify, collect and make sense of data, follow printed directions. Some of these resources are demonstrated here. You will find that many of the activities in the home economics and science sections will provide useful learning experiences for health students.

▶SUBJECT AREA

Health

GRADE LEVEL

7–12

NAME OF ACTIVITY

Linking Terms

OBJECTIVE OF ACTIVITY

To reinforce vocabulary closely associated with a particular unit. The area of study demonstrated is cardiovascular diseases.

STUDENT PREPARATION

None.

TEACHER PREPARATION

None.

PROCEDURE

This is a whole-class activity which involves the students in identifying vocabulary words that are associated with the topic in beginning stages of the unit on, for example, cardiovascular diseases. Using a transparency, the teacher writes

H
E
A
R
T

The students turn to the appropriate section in their textbook and scan it to select technical words that are unfamiliar to them. As they find a word, they jot it down. Then one by one they present a word they have found, and the teacher fits it into the word *heart* on the transparency. As an example, the first student offers *artery* as the initial word. The teacher adds it this way

```
H
E
A R T E R Y
R
T
```

and explains the term, using a visual of the cardiovascular system. Another student says the word *rheumatic,* and the teacher fits it into the schemata,

```
H
E
A R T E R Y
R        H
T        E
         U
         M
         A
         T
         I
         C
```

and explains the term. The next student offers *hypertension* as a new term. As he or she fits it into the appropriate position, the teacher discusses its meaning.

```
H Y P E R T E N S I O N
E
A R T E R Y
R        H
T        E
         U
         M
         A
         T
         I
         C
```

This activity is an introduction to the terms that are associated with cardiovascular diseases. The teacher reinforces meanings of the terms as he or she teaches the unit.

SUBJECT AREA

Health

GRADE LEVEL

9–12

NAME OF ACTIVITY

The Great Escapes

OBJECTIVE OF ACTIVITY

To enable students to interpret and portray defense mechanisms in light of experiences familiar to them.

STUDENT PREPARATION

The student has completed a unit on mental health.

TEACHER PREPARATION

Prepare assignment cards, each describing one of the defense mechanisms sometimes used by people to cope with their problems. (See examples.) Assign students to groups.

PROCEDURE

The class is divided into seven groups, and each group is given one assignment card prepared by the teacher. Members of each group write a short skit that portrays a mechanism in action. The preparation time limit is five minutes. After each skit is presented, the rest of the class identifies the mechanism and, led by the teacher, discusses ramifications of the use of the mechanism and alternate routes the characters in the skit could have taken.

Examples of assignment cards:

1. The escape mechanism your group is to portray is COMPENSA-TION/SUBSTITUTION.

   When a person uses this technique, he tries to make up for some lack in his personality by overstressing another trait. Sometimes a person uses compensation to gloss over something he has done or has not done.

   Each member of your group should contribute ideas for portraying compensation in action. Write a script or prepare to ad lib a situation after you have decided on its factors. Make sure each member of the group has an acting role.

2. The escape mechanism your group is to portray is DAYDREAM-ING.

   Some people choose to avoid unpleasant life situations by slipping into an imaginative world of their own creation. We all daydream to some extent, but fantasy becomes a defense mechanism when it is carried to extremes.

   Enact for the class a situation portraying fantasy. Write a part for each member of your group.

3. RATIONALIZATION is the defense mechanism your group is to portray.

   Saving face is important enough to some people that they cover up disappointing results of an act with some kind of a lame explanation. The cover-up might have some truth in it, but it isn't the real reason, the one that the rationalizer wants to keep hidden.

   Your classmates will try to determine the identity of this defense mechanism from the little skit that you create. Write a role for each member of your committee.

4. The defense mechanism your group is to portray is PROJEC-TION.

When a person uses this technique to cope with tensions, she assigns to someone else the feelings, thoughts, or attitudes she has but wishes to hide.

Make up a skit to show how a person goes about setting up a scapegoat. All members of your group should have some role in the portrayal.

5. IDENTIFICATION is the defense mechanism your group will show.

One way to cover up your deficiencies or to even hide them from yourself is to take on the qualities or characteristics of another person: hero worship to the extreme. Sometimes you can associate with a group whose qualities are admired in order to "be somebody."

Portray this mechanism in a skit, having all members of your group playing a role.

6. REPRESSION is the defense mechanism your group is responsible for depicting.

This escape is used by a person who cannot cope with the reality of a situation, so he rejects from his consciousness painful or disagreeable ideas, memories, feelings or impulses.

Your task is to create a situation which portrays a person in the act of repressing. Find parts in your skit for all members of your group.

7. The escape mechanism your group is to portray is REGRESSION.

When a person cannot cope with a real situation in the present, he or she escapes to the past by adopting earlier real-life behaviors, even those as far back as childhood.

Your classmates will try to identify the mechanism you are attempting to enact. Your skit should have a part for all of the members of your group.

SUBJECT AREA

Health

GRADE LEVEL

7–12

NAME OF ACTIVITY

Board of Health

OBJECTIVE OF ACTIVITY

To familiarize students with the specialized vocabulary of nutrition and to reinforce their knowledge of nutritional data.

STUDENT PREPARATION

The student has had class instruction on proper eating habits for healthful living.

TEACHER PREPARATION

Prepare the game board (illustrated) and markers to represent players. On 3 X 5" cards write thirty to forty questions on nutrition, dividing the questions equally among two-space, three-space, and four-space values. (See examples.) Type the answers on the back of each card.

PROCEDURE

Players can number from two to five. When it is his turn, a player selects the top card from one of four stacks, depending on the number of spaces he would like his marker to move. If he answers correctly, he advances his marker the number of spaces the card directs. His answer is verified by another player who reads to the group from the back of the question card. The player must comply with the directions in the spaces on the board when his marker lands on them. The winner reaches the finish line first.

309

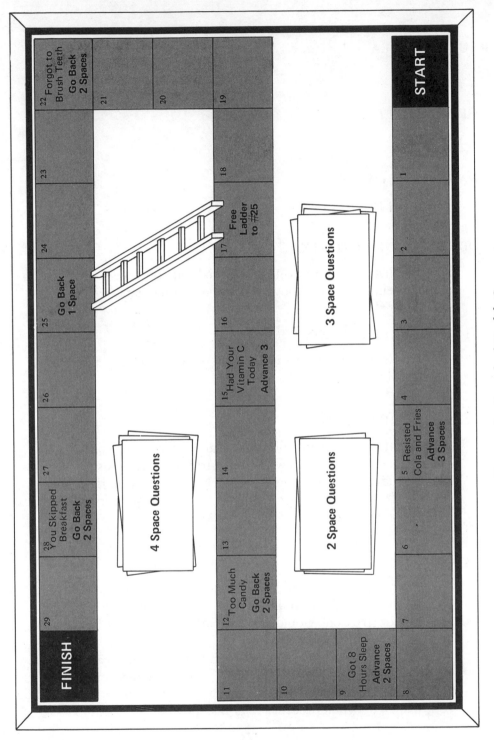

Format for Board of Health Game.

Examples of two-space questions:

· How often should you eat a serving of vitamin C? (every day)
· Dark green and yellow vegetables are good sources of _____. (vitamin A)
· Two empty-calorie foods are _____ and _____. (pop, gum, candy)
· How often should you eat a serving of vitamin A? (every other day)

Examples of three-space questions:

· How many servings from the meat group should you eat every day? (two or more)
· How many servings from the bread-cereal group should you eat every day? (four or more)
· How many servings a day do teenagers need from the milk group? (four or more cups)
· How many servings from the vegetable-fruit group should you eat every day? (four or more)
· How many eggs make one serving? (two)

Examples of four-space questions:

· Quick energy for GO power is provided by _____ or sugar. (carbohydrates)
· How many cups of ice cream equal one serving of milk? (two cups)
· Name the five nutrients needed to be healthy. (proteins, carbohydrates, vitamins, minerals, and fats)
· Name two foods that are highest in percentage of protein. (meat, fish, poultry)
· What food has the highest percentage of carbohydrates? (sugar)

▶SUBJECT AREA

Health

GRADE LEVEL

7–12

NAME OF ACTIVITY

Mismatch

OBJECTIVE OF ACTIVITY

To reinforce students' skill in classifying and in making word associations.

STUDENT PREPARATION

The class has studied units from which categories are drawn.

TEACHER PREPARATION

Select categorical terms that have been used in health class. Make a list of the terms and possible responses, which are to be given to scorekeepers, for example:

CATEGORY	POSSIBLE RESPONSES
muscles	biceps, triceps, trapezius, deltoid, gluteus maximus, and such
digestive system	small intestine, large intestine, stomach, gall bladder, liver, to name a few

PROCEDURE

One student serves as scorekeeper and pronounces the categorical terms for two teams of three or four each. As he or she pronounces the term, each team member secretly writes one property of the term. Points are awarded each time all members on the same team have written different, but correct, properties on their papers. Students will search their memories for the lesser known properties. Instead of writing pupil when the category is eye, for example, students will be motivated to choose sclera or choroid coat. Since the entire class has been divided into teams and scorekeepers, the teacher may wish to set a time limit rather than point-number ceiling for the activity.

SUBJECT AREA

Health

GRADE LEVEL

10–12

NAME OF ACTIVITY

Medical Tic-Tac-Toe

OBJECTIVE OF ACTIVITY

This old children's game serves as a motivation for learning the value of prefixes and roots in identifying medical specialties.

STUDENT PREPARATION

The student has had instruction in the unit relating to specialties in medical practice.

TEACHER PREPARATION

Since only a few of the specialities usually are discussed in health texts, extend the students' knowledge by adding specialities you have found in the telephone directory of a large city (available at libraries and at offices of telephone companies). Prepare questions and answers that have to do with the various prefixes and root words contained in the labels that identify medical specialists, for example, neuro (nerve) logist. Type question and its answer on a 3 X 5" card. (See examples.)

PROCEDURE

The players consist of two contestants, a moderator, and nine panel members. The rest of the class is divided into two rooting groups for the contestants and shares in the prize. The moderator reads the questions, rules on the correctness of the answers, and places the Xs and the Os on the tic-tac-toe graph on the chalk board. The contestants take turns picking a panel member to answer the moderator's question. The contestant must then agree or disagree with the panel member's answer. If he agrees and the answer is correct, he receives an X in the spot in the graph that corresponds to the position in which the panel member is seated. If the contestant agrees and the answer is incorrect, he receives an O. Panel members sit in three rows of three:

1	2	3
4	5	6
7	8	9

The first contestant to complete a row either horizontally, vertically, or diagonally wins the game and shares the prize with his rooters.

Examples of Tic-Tac-Toe questions and answers:

1. Q: This specialist treats diseases of the nose. Add logist to the root word for nose. An animal is identified by the same root.

    A: Rhinologist.

2. Q: Ophthalmo was borrowed from the Greeks. What part of your body would an ophthalmologist treat?

    A: Eye.

3. Q: This doctor is an expert in diseases peculiar to women, especially diseases of the reproductive organs. Add a root meaning female to logist and the doctor's title is _____.

    A: Gynecologist.

4. Q: To bleed profusely is to hemorrhage. A physician who treats this and other conditions of the blood is called a _____.

    A: Hematologist.

5. Q: A highly specialized doctor treats the disorders of babies at their birth. A prefix meaning new joins a root word meaning birth to form the name of this specialist.

    A: Neonatologist.

6. Q: This specialist once was known as a hand worker; he was called a chirurgeon. Change part of the word to get his modern name.

    A: Surgeon.

7. Q: The Greeks used the term ortho for straight, upright, correct. This specialist tries to straighten children's deformities.

   A: Orthopedist.

8. Q: This doctor specializes in administering certain drugs, either locally or generally, for the purpose of inducing insensibility.

   A: Anesthesiologist.

9. Q: An oncologist deals with a mass or bulk, according to the Greek definition of the root onco. What does he specialize in?

   A: Tumors.

10. Q: To paraphrase an old song: "I've Got You Under My Derma." What is the area of expertise of a dermatologist?

    A: Skin.

►SUBJECT AREA

Health

GRADE LEVEL

9–12

NAME OF ACTIVITY

Drug Terms

OBJECTIVE OF ACTIVITY

To help students cope with the special vocabulary and slang of drug terms.

STUDENT PREPARATION

The student has read about drugs and participated in class discussion.

TEACHER PREPARATION

Make a crossword puzzle using the drug terms and slang that have been introduced in the unit. (See example.)

Crossword Puzzle Form for Drug Terms.

317

PROCEDURE

Students work the crossword puzzle using the dictionary of drugs or glossary of text.

Across

1. Pills that slow down the body functions.
6. Abbreviation for overdose.
9. Term for diluting a drug.
10. A drug used in medicine to relieve pain.
11. Slang term for Dexedrine.
12. Natural compound much stronger than marijuana.
16. 2.2 pounds of marijuana.
19. Turn _____.
21. Abbreviation for lysergic acid diethylamide.
22. Slang term for narcotic agent.
23. To shoot a drug.
24. Slang for lysergic acid diethylamide.
25. Slang for a person who shoots drugs into a vein.

Down

1. Slang for anything unsatisfactory.
2. Slang for a marijuana cigarette.
3. Tune _____.
4. Pills that speed up the body functions.
5. Slang for Methedrine.
6. Medical term for taking too much of a drug at one time.
7. One of the main reasons someone tries drugs.
8. Active ingredient in cough medicine often abused.
12. Most expensive addictive drug.
13. Slang for a marijuana cigarette.
14. Slang for seconal pills.
15. Slang for marijuana.
17. Slang for equipment needed to shoot up.
18. One who sells drugs.
20. Slang for marijuana.
21. Approximately 1 ounce of marijuana.

Key:

Across	Down
1. Barbiturates	1. Bummer
6. OD	2. Reefer
9. Cut	3. In
10. Morphine	4. Amphetamines
11. Dexie	5. Speed
12. Hashish	6. Overdose
16. Kilo	7. Curiosity
19. On	8. Codeine
21. LSD	12. Heroin
22. Nark	13. Joint
23. Fix	14. Reds
24. Acid	15. Pot
25. Mainliner	17. Fit
	18. Pusher
	20. Tea
	21. Lid

SUBJECT AREA

Health

GRADE LEVEL

7–12

NAME OF ACTIVITY

Under the Kitchen Sink

Part I

OBJECTIVE OF ACTIVITY

The principal objective of this activity is to develop the skills of interpreting, comparing, problem-solving, evaluating, and judging.

STUDENT PREPARATION

None.

TEACHER PREPARATION

Create a situation such as the one in the example on which students can make a judgment. Prepare the activity on a transparency for overhead projection or ditto it.

PROCEDURE

In small groups students respond to the questions on the activity. Reports from small groups probably will indicate weaknesses in one or more of the responses and will direct attention to the need for the experiences in parts II and III of this activity.

Example of a vignette:

Under the Kitchen Sink

Your mother has gone to the shopping center, and you find your little brother and sister playing with the cans and bottles under the kitchen sink. After you take them to the family room to play, you go back to the kitchen to put things away and realize how dangerous and how numerous these products are. You make this list:

1 bottle liquid dish soap	1 bottle ammonia
1 bottle liquid all-purpose detergent	1 can crystal toilet bowl cleaner
1 box crystal bleach substitute	1 can crystal drain opener
1 spray can fabric finish	1 box crystal lye
1 spray can starch	1 bottle liquid drain opener
1 box crystal soil and stain remover	1 spray can ant and roach killer
1 bottle liquid bleach	1 bottle shoe cleaner
1 box water softener	1 bottle floor polish
1 box washing powder	1 bottle window cleaner
1 spray can furniture polish	1 spray can air freshener
1 can powdered bleach and cleaner	1 spray can oven cleaner

You know that some of these products could be harmful or fatal to humans and that boxes, cans, and bottles are attractive to curious and exploring children. As you look at the length of the list and read the labels, you face some decisions.

1. What makes these products child-harmers?
2. Are there some that are more dangerous than others? Try to categorize them.
3. What would you have done if you found Darin and Lisa putting some of the contents of cans or bottles in their mouths?
4. What will you do about the products in your home? List as many alternatives as possible.

Part II

OBJECTIVE OF ACTIVITY

The need for more information and additional skills is likely to be an outcome of part I. This activity is designed to assist students in the skill of collecting and organizing data.

STUDENT PREPARATION

Notebook, pencil, and permission of grocery store manager.

TEACHER PREPARATION

None.

PROCEDURE

Pairs of students have the task of collecting data on items usually kept under the sink that may be harmful or fatal to humans, especially children. Each pair has been assigned one classification, for example, drain openers, clothes washing detergents, dish washing detergents, starch products, bleaches, insect killers. The paired students collect data by examining the printing on the boxes, cans and bottles on the grocery shelves. (The teacher may wish to help them organize by giving them a format to follow: type of product, brand name, presence of a caution, specific wording of caution, antidotes (internal, external, eyes), presence of the word *poison* or of the skull and crossbones symbol.) Students are to keep each report on a separate card or piece of paper.

Reports are discussed in class.

Part III

OBJECTIVE OF ACTIVITY

To develop the skill of organizing data.

STUDENT PREPARATION

Students have reports on products.

TEACHER PREPARATION

Lead the class in a discussion on what to do with all their separate cards or pieces of paper. The goal is to lead students to a decision on amassing their data for personal use. Because there are hundreds of harmful products that could be kept under sinks, have secretarial help standing by (teacher aide, typing class, members of future teachers' organization).

PROCEDURE

Students prepare their information neatly so that it can be reproduced on 4 × 6″ cards from a stencil. When the cards are completed, each student punches holes in the upper left hand corner and inserts a ring in the set of cards and takes them home to be used if needed.

Example of one report:

TYPE OF PRODUCT: crystal toilet bowl cleaner
BRAND NAME:
CAUTION:

- Danger: Harmful if swallowed.
- Damaging to eyes.
- Irritating to skin.
- Keep out of reach of children.

ANTIDOTES:

- External: Flood surface with water, using soap freely, then cover with moist Magnesia or Baking Soda.
- Internal: Give Milk of Magnesia, chalk, or whitening suspended in much water, milk, or raw egg white. Call physician.
- Eyes: Wash thoroughly with water. Call physician.

POISON: Not printed on can.
SKULL AND CROSSBONES: Not printed on can.
LABEL DIFFICULT OR EASY TO READ: Difficult, small type, printed in light blue.

▶SUBJECT AREA

Health

GRADE LEVEL

7–12

NAME OF ACTIVITY

Nutrition Mobile

OBJECTIVE OF ACTIVITY

To have examples of important terms of nutrition hanging in sight of the class.

STUDENT PREPARATION

None.

TEACHER PREPARATION

Using string or piano wire and cardboard, make the mobile. The category used on the example is NUTRIENTS. Clip pictures of examples of foods containing vitamins, carbohydrates, fats, proteins, and minerals. Label the pictures with the nutrient for which the food is a source.

PROCEDURE

The mobile, hanging in the room, is a prominent resource for students who need to doublecheck examples of terms as they study privately or participate in class instruction.

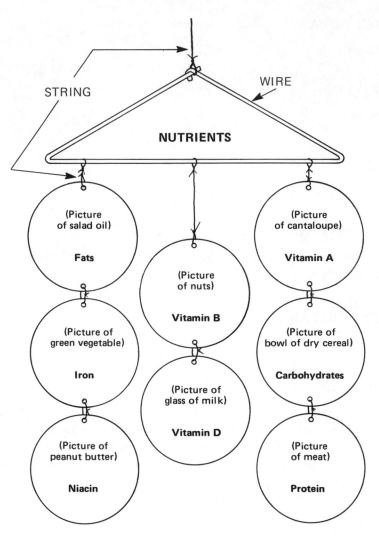

Nutrients Mobile.

SUBJECT AREA

Health

GRADE LEVEL

7–12

NAME OF ACTIVITY

Reading Medicine Bottles

OBJECTIVE OF ACTIVITY

In a poll of 10,000 users of nonprescription drugs, the New York State Pharmaceutical Society found that 85 percent of the respondents did not read the labels on products they purchased. This activity has two objectives, both important to health care:

1. To facilitate interpretation of information on labels of medicine bottles or packages, and
2. To increase skill in following directions.

Part I—Nonprescription Medications

STUDENT PREPARATION

The student has observed (on transparencies) the location of information on labels of nonprescription medicine bottles or packages and has heard the teacher explain the meaning of that data.

TEACHER PREPARATION

In addition to preparing the transparencies, collect a variety of labels from across-the-counter medicine bottles and packages. The example illustrated is a flattened cardboard carton for Pepto-Bismal tablets. Paste each label on an 8½ X 11″ piece of cardboard. On small slips of paper type or print these terms:

dosage	ingredients
expiration date	strength
accepted standards	warning
manufacturer	volume
name of medication	explanation of medication
purpose	

Put the slips of paper in an envelope with a number of thumb tacks and attach envelope to the cardboard on which a label has been mounted. Prepare a key as illustrated and secure it in an envelope attached to the back of the cardboard.

PROCEDURE

This is an individual activity. The student reads the label thoroughly and thumbtacks each slip of paper adjacent to the appropriate information on the label. In some instances there may be slips left over if manufacturer does not provide the data. The student checks his accuracy with the key provided.

Example key is on page 329.

Part II—Prescription Medications

STUDENT PREPARATION

The student has observed (on transparencies) information given by physicians concerning medication they have prescribed. The student has heard the teacher's explanation of the information.

TEACHER PREPARATION

In addition to preparing the transparencies, ditto a variety of simulated labels, using fictitious names for physicians, pharmacies, and patients. Use one ditto for each simulated label and write questions on the data provided. (See example.)

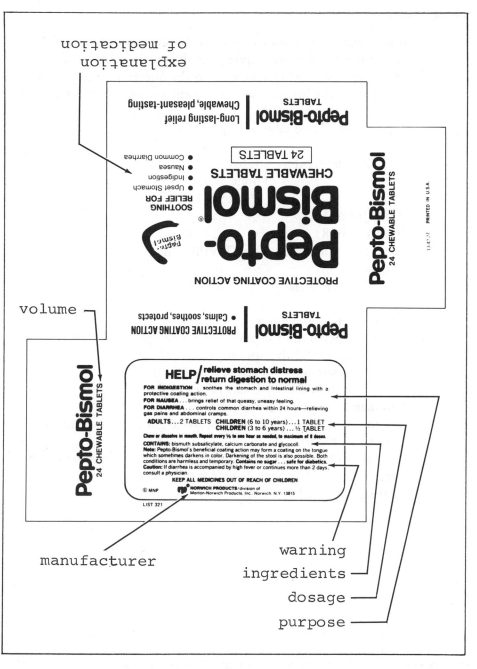

Sample Medical Label.

PROCEDURE

Each member of the class works with the same simulated label, answering the teacher-made questions. When the class has completed the task, the teacher elicits answers to the questions and points to the location of the information on a transparency made of the ditto.

Example of simulated label and questions:

> XYZ Drug Center, Anytown, U.S.A.
> Phone 123-1234
> Date 4/19/77
>
> FOR   John Doe
> NO.   312 608
> One tablet four times a day (Erythrocin
> 250 mg.)
> DR.   John Physician

1. Who is the person who is ill?
2. Which physician did the person describe his symptoms to?
3. What medicine did the doctor prescribe?
4. What is the strength of each tablet?
5. How often should the patient take a tablet?
6. Who manufactured the medicine?*
7. May the patient go to the drug store to get more tablets when he runs out of them?
8. Why does XYZ Drug Center print its telephone number on the label?
9. What's wrong with the patient?

*The rationale for questions for which data is not given is to impress upon students what the label does not say, as well as what it does.

SUBJECT AREA

Health

GRADE LEVEL

9–12

NAME OF ACTIVITY

Who Says?

OBJECTIVE OF ACTIVITY

To reinforce the skill of evaluating evidence of the authority of a writer and the validity of the source of information and/or opinion.

STUDENT PREPARATION

The student has had instruction on criteria by which to measure the authority of a writer.

TEACHER PREPARATION

Collect ten newspaper and magazine articles containing data and/or opinions on any aspect of health. Assign a number to each. Rank order the clippings from most authoritative to least and state the reasons. For example, an article on acne by a dermatologist would merit a higher ranking than an article by a columnist quoting an anonymous researcher. Put your ranking and reasons in an envelope to be used later by students. Provide a means by which the student can record his or her own rank ordering. (See example.)

PROCEDURE

This is an individual activity in which the student reads the articles looking for criteria which make the declarer of statements on health an authority. He puts the ten articles in rank order from the highest credentials to the lowest and states reasons for his choices. He checks his opinion against that of the instructor.

VARIATION

Several students make their choices and compare them with each other, defending their opinions, before checking the opinion of the teacher.

Example of dittoed sheet on which student does his work:

Who Says?

DIRECTIONS

Who do you believe?

Look at the credentials of the writers. Rank the articles in order from most believable to least believable. Write down the numbers of the articles in the order of your choice and next to each number state your reason(s) for the ranking.

When you have completed the task, look in the envelope accompanying the clippings and compare your ranking with mine. If we differ, let's discuss it.

1. Article #_____. Reason:
2. Article #_____. Reason:
3. Article #_____. Reason:
4. Article #_____. Reason:
5. Article #_____. Reason:
6. Article #_____. Reason:
7. Article #_____. Reason:
8. Article #_____. Reason:
9. Article #_____. Reason:
10. Article #_____. Reason:

If you are starting the book here, you are coming in on the middle of the act. Part I is the curtain raiser; it builds up to the use of the home economics section.

CHAPTER 9

Home Economics

The language of home economics is probably more complex than that of any other discipline in the higher grades, simply because it is the most extensive. Consider the expertise needed by the home economics teacher and students: under the general rubric of home economics are the languages of mathematics, nutrition, psychology, art, business, even foreign languages.

For this reason, you must take extra precautions against allowing students to be overwhelmed by language problems. Some students enroll in your class to find the success they have missed in print-oriented courses only to find that the need for reading is of primary importance in your class too. They will need a great deal of guidance and practice in reading/thinking skills for success this semester and later as home managers.

In actuality, students are serving their apprenticeships as future home-makers while they are in school. As you help students become discerning, discriminating, and critical readers, bring reality into the classroom as much as possible, use newspapers and magazines to supplement the textbook. Some techniques for simultaneously bringing the outside in and strengthening language-coping skills are demonstrated in this section. Since your subject area incorporates so many factors of other disciplines, you will want to check all the activities in this text for possible use in your classroom.

Foods

SUBJECT AREA

Foods

GRADE LEVEL

7–12

NAME OF ACTIVITY

Pigsaw Puzzle

OBJECTIVE OF ACTIVITY

To foster the identification of the wholesale and retail cuts of pork and the improvement of chart reading.

STUDENT PREPARATION

The student has studied the cuts of pork and the location of the cuts either in the text or on a pork chart.

TEACHER PREPARATION

Draw the carcass of a pig on a piece of cardboard and identify each section, for example, ham, belly, spareribs, fat back, clear plate. Cut the sections apart, jigsaw fashion. Clip each retail cut from the chart, such as fresh picnic, smoked hock, bacon, center loin, and paste each clipping on lightweight cardboard. Arrange to have several copies of weekend grocery ads in the classroom.

PROCEDURE

The student has three tasks:

1. The jigsaw parts, representing the wholesale cuts of pork, are assembled.
2. Then the student scans the grocery ads, making notations of the prices on the clippings of the retail cuts.

3. Next the student places the clippings on the appropriate sections of the carcass.
4. As a final activity, the student draws conclusions about the most expensive and least expensive wholesale cuts.

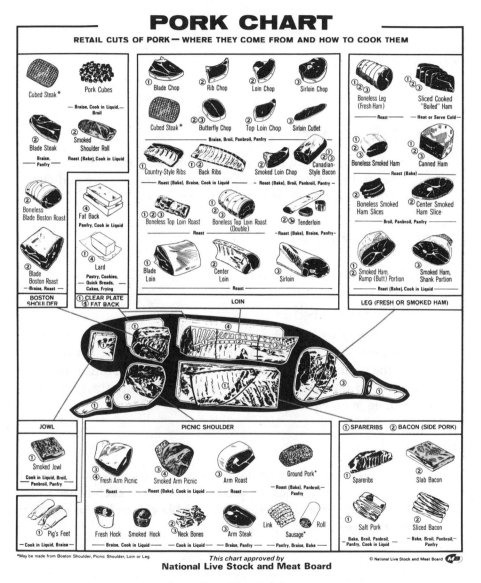

Chart Detailing Pork Cuts.

SUBJECT AREA

Foods

GRADE LEVEL

7–12

NAME OF ACTIVITY

What Is It?

OBJECTIVE OF ACTIVITY

To extract information from recipes; to understand and visualize the steps and results of printed instructions; to compare and contrast different methods of food preparation.

STUDENT PREPARATION

None.

TEACHER PREPARATION

Cut out five or six recipes with pictures. (See examples. Colored pictures are more life-like.) Mount the examples on stiff paper and assign the same number to each picture and its accompanying recipe. After printing the number on each, separate the two. Put everything in an envelope.

PROCEDURE

On receiving an envelope containing five or six separated recipes and pictures, the student lines the pictures up next to each other and reads the recipes for clues which will enable him or her to match the appropriate recipe with its picture.

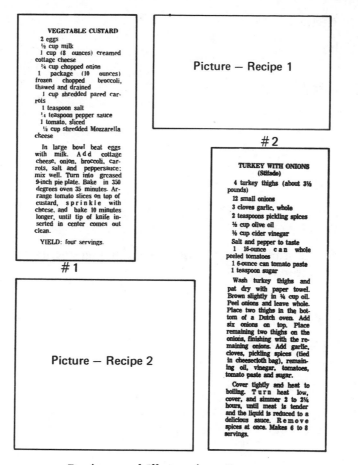

VEGETABLE CUSTARD

2 eggs
½ cup milk
1 cup (8 ounces) creamed cottage cheese
¼ cup chopped onion
1 package (10 ounces) frozen chopped broccoli, thawed and drained
1 cup shredded pared carrots
1 teaspoon salt
¼ teaspoon pepper sauce
1 tomato, sliced
½ cup shredded Mozzarella cheese

In large bowl beat eggs with milk. Add cottage cheese, onion, broccoli, carrots, salt and peppersauce; mix well. Turn into greased 9-inch pie plate. Bake in 350 degrees oven 35 minutes. Arrange tomato slices on top of custard, sprinkle with cheese, and bake 10 minutes longer, until tip of knife inserted in center comes out clean.

YIELD: four servings.

#1

Picture — Recipe 1

#2

TURKEY WITH ONIONS
(Stifado)

4 turkey thighs (about 3½ pounds)
12 small onions
3 cloves garlic, whole
2 teaspoons pickling spices
½ cup olive oil
½ cup cider vinegar
Salt and pepper to taste
1 16-ounce can whole peeled tomatoes
1 6-ounce can tomato paste
1 teaspoon sugar

Wash turkey thighs and pat dry with paper towel. Brown slightly in ¼ cup oil. Peel onions and leave whole. Place two thighs in the bottom of a Dutch oven. Add six onions on top. Place remaining two thighs on the onions, finishing with the remaining onions. Add garlic, cloves, pickling spices (tied in cheesecloth bag), remaining oil, vinegar, tomatoes, tomato paste and sugar.

Cover tightly and heat to boiling. Turn heat low, cover, and simmer 2 to 2½ hours, until meat is tender and the liquid is reduced to a delicious sauce. Remove spices at once. Makes 6 to 8 servings.

Picture — Recipe 2

Recipes and Illustrations Format.

SUBJECT AREA

Foods

GRADE LEVEL

7–12

NAME OF ACTIVITY

Send in a Sub

OBJECTIVE OF ACTIVITY

To provide student practice in associating ingredients with their appropriate substitutes.

STUDENT PREPARATION

Prior instruction.

TEACHER PREPARATION

Make two sets of cards. On one set print in red ink ingredients and quantities. On the other set, print in green ink appropriate substitutions.

Examples:

Red	*Green*
1 teaspoon double acting baking powder	1 1/2 teaspoon phosphate or tartrate; or 1/4 teaspoon baking soda plus 1/2 cup buttermilk or sour cream
1 square unsweetened chocolate	3 tablespoons cocoa plus 1 tablespoon shortening
1 cup cream	3 tablespoons butter plus 7/8 cup milk

PROCEDURE

After the cards are mixed, the student matches the ingredients and substitutions.

Foods

GRADE LEVEL

7–12

NAME OF ACTIVITY

Breakfast Bowl

OBJECTIVE OF ACTIVITY

To facilitate extracting information from graphs, tables, and charts.

STUDENT PREPARATION

None.

TEACHER PREPARATION

Cut the sides from five or six cereal boxes and mount them on a heavy piece of cardboard. Prepare a number of questions that can be answered by reading the information on the boxes. The questions should be written so that one-third are relatively easy, one-third are average, and one-third are difficult or complicated. The easy questions are worth ten points; type them on white cards. Type the average questions worth twenty points on yellow cards, the difficult questions worth thirty points on green cards. (See examples.) Make a pocket for the questions and attach it to the piece of cardboard for storage.

PROCEDURE

The cards are placed in three stacks according to point values. The first player takes the top card from the stack of her choice. She wins the points if she answers correctly within a given time limit. If she answers incorrectly or her time runs out, she receives no points for that round. The second player proceeds, then others in turn. The

Lucky Charms
...is a part of this good breakfast

NUTRITION INFORMATION PER SERVING

Serving Size......1 ounce (1 cup)
Servings per Container.........9

	1 ounce Lucky Charms	Lucky Charms plus ½ cup Vitamin D milk
Calories......	110	190
Protein, grams	2	6
Carbohydrate, grams......	24	30
Fat, grams...	1	5

PERCENTAGE OF U.S. RECOMMENDED DAILY ALLOWANCES (U.S. RDA)

Protein.......	4	10
Vitamin A.....	25	30
Vitamin C.....	25	25
Thiamin......	25	30
Riboflavin....	25	35
Niacin........	25	25
Calcium......	2	15
Iron..........	25	25
Vitamin D.....	10	25
Vitamin B₆....	25	30
Vitamin B₁₂...	25	35

INGREDIENTS

Oat flour, sugar, corn syrup, corn starch, dextrose, wheat starch, salt, gelatin, calcium carbonate, sodium phosphate, sodium ascorbate, natural and artificial flavors, niacin, artificial colors, iron, gum acacia, vitamin A palmitate, pyridoxine (vitamin B₆), riboflavin, thiamin, vitamin B₁₂ and vitamin D.

General Mills, Inc.
General Offices
Minneapolis, Minnesota 55440
Made in U.S.A.
NET WT 255 grams

Trix
is part of this good breakfast

And so is **toast**. Bread is a source of food energy needed for walking, running, playing, sitting and even resting. Bread also provides several B vitamins, iron and protein. The amount of food energy you need depends on your size, age and how active you are.

Start each day right with a good breakfast. Remember the better you treat your body, the better it'll treat you.

NUTRITION INFORMATION PER SERVING

Serving Size......1 ounce (1 cup)
Servings per Container.........8

	1 ounce Trix	Trix plus ½ cup Vitamin D milk
Calories........	110	190
Protein, grams..	1	5
Carbohydrate, grams........	25	31
Fat, grams.....	1	5

PERCENTAGE OF U.S. RECOMMENDED DAILY ALLOWANCES (U.S. RDA)

Protein.........	2%	8%
Vitamin A......	25%	30%
Vitamin C......	25%	25%
Thiamin.......	25%	30%
Riboflavin.....	25%	35%
Niacin.........	25%	25%
Calcium.......	*	15%
Iron..........	25%	25%
Vitamin D......	10%	25%
Vitamin B₆.....	25%	30%
Vitamin B₁₂.....25%		35%

*Contains less than 2 percent of the U.S. RDA of this nutrient.

INGREDIENTS

Degermed yellow corn meal and oat flour, sugar, corn syrup, wheat starch, salt, monoglycerides, sodium ascorbate, artificial colors, natural and artificial flavors, niacin, iron, gum acacia, calcium carbonate, vitamin A palmitate, pyridoxine (vitamin B₆), riboflavin, thiamin, vitamin B₁₂ and vitamin D.

General Mills, Inc.
General Offices
Minneapolis, Minnesota 55440
Made in U.S.A.
NET WT 226 grams

Cereal Box Panels Containing Nutrition Information

King Vitaman
+ Milk
Nutrition

If your kids love cereal and milk for breakfast, good for them! Good for you, too, because cereal and milk complement one another nutritionally.

To understand exactly what we mean we suggest you study the information below. It shows you exactly how much of the U.S. Recommended Daily Allowance (U.S. RDA) of each nutrient your children get from just one bowl of King Vitaman and ½ cup of Vitamin D Milk.

PERCENTAGE OF U.S. RECOMMENDED DAILY ALLOWANCES (U.S. RDA)

FOR ADULTS AND CHILDREN 4 OR MORE YEARS OF AGE	PER 1 OZ. CEREAL	PER 1 OZ. CEREAL PLUS ½ CUP VITAMIN D FORTIFIED WHOLE MILK
PROTEIN	2%	8%
VITAMIN A	50%	50%
VITAMIN C	60%	60%
THIAMINE	60%	60%
RIBOFLAVIN	60%	70%
NIACIN	60%	60%
CALCIUM	*	10%
IRON	60%	60%
VITAMIN D	60%	70%
VITAMIN E	50%	50%
VITAMIN B_6	50%	50%
FOLIC ACID	60%	60%
VITAMIN B_{12}	60%	60%

FOR CHILDREN UNDER 4 YEARS OF AGE	PER 1 OZ. CEREAL	1 OZ. CEREAL PLUS ½ CUP VITAMIN D FORTIFIED WHOLE MILK
PROTEIN	2%	15%
VITAMIN A	100%	100%
VITAMIN C	90%	90%
THIAMINE	120%	130%
RIBOFLAVIN	120%	150%
NIACIN	130%	130%
CALCIUM	*	15%
IRON	100%	100%
VITAMIN D	60%	70%
VITAMIN E	150%	150%
VITAMIN B_6	140%	170%
FOLIC ACID	120%	120%
VITAMIN B_{12}	120%	130%

* CONTAINS LESS THAN 2% OF THE U.S. RDA FOR THIS NUTRIENT.

INGREDIENTS: Sugar, corn flour, vegetable oil, oat flour, rice flour, brown sugar, salt, corn starch, sodium ascorbate (a vitamin C source), corn oil margarine with lecithin (an emulsifier) and artificial flavor, iron, vitamin E, niacinamide (one of the B vitamins), artificial coloring, pyridoxine hydrochloride, riboflavin, thiamine, vitamin A, folic acid, vitamin D, vitamin B_{12}.

For additional nutrition information, write to: Consumer Services Department, The Quaker Oats Company, Chicago, Illinois 60654.

Our guarantee: Your money back if not satisfied.

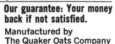

Manufactured by
The Quaker Oats Company
Chicago, Ill. 60654, U.S.A.

Kellogg's ®
RICE
KRISPIES ®

Kellogg's Rice Krispies is labeled in accordance with federal standards for nutrition labeling as established by the U.S. Food and Drug Administration.

These toasted puffs of rice are fortified with eight important vitamins and iron.

NUTRITION INFORMATION PER SERVING

SERVING SIZE: ONE OUNCE (1 CUP) RICE KRISPIES ALONE AND IN COMBINATION WITH ½ CUP VITAMIN D FORTIFIED WHOLE MILK.

SERVINGS PER CONTAINER: 10

	RICE KRISPIES 1 OZ.	WITH ½ CUP WHOLE MILK
CALORIES	110	190
PROTEIN	2 g	6 g
CARBOHYDRATES	25 g	31 g
FAT	0 g	4 g

PERCENTAGE OF U.S. RECOMMENDED DAILY ALLOWANCE (U.S. RDA)

	RICE KRISPIES 1 OZ.	WITH ½ CUP WHOLE MILK
PROTEIN	2	10
VITAMIN A	25	25
VITAMIN C	25	25
THIAMIN	25	25
RIBOFLAVIN	25	35
NIACIN	25	25
CALCIUM	*	15
IRON	10	10
VITAMIN D	10	25
VITAMIN B_6	25	25
FOLIC ACID	25	25
PHOSPHORUS	2	10
MAGNESIUM	2	6
ZINC	2	2

*CONTAINS LESS THAN 2 PERCENT OF THE U.S. RDA OF THIS NUTRIENT.

INGREDIENTS: MILLED RICE, SUGAR, SALT AND MALT FLAVORING WITH VITAMIN A, SODIUM ASCORBATE, ASCORBIC ACID, THIAMIN (B_1), RIBOFLAVIN (B_2), NIACINAMIDE, VITAMIN D, PYRIDOXINE (B_6), FOLIC ACID AND IRON ADDED. BHA AND BHT ADDED TO PRESERVE PRODUCT FRESHNESS.

Rice Krispies is a trade mark (Reg. U.S. Pat. Off.) of Kellogg Company, for its delicious brand of oven-toasted rice cereal.

**MADE BY KELLOGG COMPANY
BATTLE CREEK, MICHIGAN 49016, U.S.A.
© 1973 BY KELLOGG COMPANY
® KELLOGG COMPANY**

SNAP, CRACKLE, POP™

THIS PACKAGE IS SOLD BY WEIGHT, NOT VOLUME. SOME SETTLING OF CONTENTS MAY HAVE OCCURRED DURING SHIPMENT AND HANDLING.

Cereal Box Panels Containing Nutrition Information.

used cards are set aside until the game is over. Each player may choose only two cards from the ten-point stack during a game. The first player to accumulate 100 points wins.

Examples of ten-point questions:

· What company manufactures Lucky Charms?
· What is the first, or main, ingredient in Rice Krispies?
· How would you address a letter to Quaker Oats Company?
· One cup of Trix equals how many ounces?

Examples of twenty-point questions:

· Of these three cereals, Rice Krispies, Lucky Charms, and Trix, which one is lowest in fat?
· What is another name for riboflavin? How did you find out?
· How much protein does one-half cup whole milk add to King Vitamin?
· What does USRDA stand for?

Examples of thirty-point questions:

· Why is BHA added to cereal?
· Determine why all three breakfast food companies give information on the amount of essential nutrients needed by a person per day and the amount a particular cereal provides.
· Compare the percentages of USRDAs for persons under four years of age and over four. What conclusions can you draw?
· Check the ingredients on any one of the packages. Why do you think there are ingredients whose names are totally unfamiliar to you?

Clothing

▶SUBJECT AREA

Clothing

GRADE LEVEL

7–12

NAME OF ACTIVITY

Person, Place, and Thing Words

OBJECTIVE OF ACTIVITY

To remember meanings of terms by associating them with the stories behind the words.

STUDENT PREPARATION

Prior introduction of terms.

TEACHER PREPARATION

Have various word history books available in the Clothing Room or in the school library.

PROCEDURE

The student may be provided with the words for this exercise or may opt to use the word history books to find various clothing terms. The student finds a history for a word and then categorizes it on a sheet similar to one shown here. Examples of clothing terms that have word histories:

Juliet cap (person word)	Chantilly (place)
cardigan (person)	denim (place)
Gibson girl fashions (person)	argyle (thing)
mercerized thread (person)	basket weave (thing)
silhouette (person)	lumberjack (thing)
damask (place word)	

347

PERSON, PLACE, AND THING WORDS

Person Words	Place Words	Thing Words

►SUBJECT AREA

Clothing

GRADE LEVEL

7–12

NAME OF ACTIVITY

Do-It-Yourself Crossword

OBJECTIVE OF ACTIVITY

To give students an opportunity to use fabric terms and to explain what they mean in their own words.

STUDENT PREPARATION

The student should have some previous knowledge of textiles.

TEACHER PREPARATION

Give students a list of twenty-five to thirty textile terms. Provide handouts, booklets, and/or books students may refer to as needed. Distribute a sheet of graph paper with fairly large squares to each person in the class.

PROCEDURE

Students are given these directions:

Make your own crossword puzzle, using these terms

acetate	wool
cashmere	acrylic
polyester	cotton

(Note to teacher: Add to the list terms you or the text have introduced.)

On a separate sheet of paper give your own definition or explanation of what each term means. Dictionaries, textbooks, pamphlets, and booklets on the table may be used as resources. Here is an example for cotton:

Across

2. Natural fiber widely grown in the United States. Comfortable

because of its coolness.

Connect all terms with each other by at least one letter.

Example:

```
      A C R Y L I C
      C           A
      E     W     S
      C O T T O N H
      A     O     M
      T     L     E
P O L Y E S T E R R
                  E
```

▶SUBJECT AREA

Clothing

GRADE LEVEL

7–12

NAME OF ACTIVITY

Sewing by Metrics

OBJECTIVE OF ACTIVITY

Eventually pattern makers will adopt the metric system of measurement, as some food packing firms have. This activity gives students practice in translating standard measurements on patterns to metric measurements.

STUDENT PREPARATION

The student has had training in metrics and some practice in the conversion of standard measurement.

TEACHER PREPARATION

None.

PROCEDURE

Using their own patterns or those that are in the clothing laboratory, students convert all measurements on the back side of the pattern envelope to meters. After taking their own body measurements in inches and converting the inches to meters, they compute the amount of material, facing, and decorations needed in terms of metrics.

SUBJECT AREA

Clothing

GRADE LEVEL

7–12

NAME OF ACTIVITY

Private Practice

OBJECTIVE OF ACTIVITY

To give students alternative methods for learning the vocabulary of patterns and symbol meanings.

STUDENT PREPARATION

The student has heard the teacher explain the terms used on patterns and has seen demonstrations of symbol meanings.

Part I

TEACHER PREPARATION

Prepare a sheet containing pattern symbols and write four choices for the meaning of each symbol. (See example.) Attach the sheet to a piece of cardboard for sturdiness and cover the face with a piece of transparent plastic. Attach a string holding a grease pencil to the activity. To make the self-check key, lay a piece of transparent tissue over the sheet and draw a circle around each correct answer. Prepare a pocket on the back of the cardboard in which to store the key.

PROCEDURE

Using the grease pencil, the student circles one of the four choices for each symbol, then takes the key from the envelope, lays it over the activity sheet and checks accuracy. When the self-check is completed, the plastic is cleaned with a tissue.

Example of activity sheet:

Pattern Symbols Self-Check

DIRECTIONS

With the grease pencil, circle the correct term for the symbol.

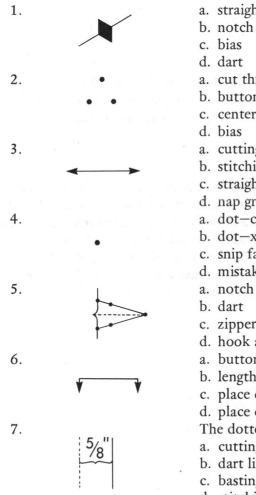

1. a. straight grain
    b. notch
    c. bias
    d. dart

2. a. cut three
    b. buttonhole placement
    c. center front
    d. bias

3. a. cutting line
    b. stitching line
    c. straight grain
    d. nap grain

4. a. dot—circle it
    b. dot—x through it
    c. snip fabric here
    d. mistake in the pattern

5. a. notch
    b. dart
    c. zipper
    d. hook and eye

6. a. buttonhole placement
    b. length of zipper
    c. place on fold
    d. place on bias

7. The dotted line is the
    a. cutting line
    b. dart line
    c. basting line
    d. stitching line

8.

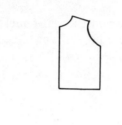

    a. bodice back
    b. sleeve front
    c. bodice front
    d. skirt back

9.

XXXXX

Looks like which hand stitch?
    a. catch stitch
    b. diagonal basting
    c. blind stitch
    d. blind hem

Part II

TEACHER PREPARATION

On 3 X 5″ cards, draw symbols 1, 3, 4, 5, 6, and 7 shown in part I, as well as any other symbols that call for performance. In a box place swatches of material, needle, thread, and scissors.

PROCEDURE

The student takes each card in turn and performs the task the symbol indicates. For example, he chooses symbol 1 which calls for a notch, selects a swatch and proceeds to cut a notch. The card is placed with the piece of fabric for the teacher to check later. Then the student proceeds to the next symbol card. (Very little is lost if a student misreads a symbol when using a small swatch, but an error on $4.98 per yard material could be costly.)

SUBJECT AREA

Clothing

GRADE LEVEL

7–12

NAME OF ACTIVITY

Sketch It

OBJECTIVE OF ACTIVITY

To give students an opportunity to visualize from printed descriptions. Success in completing an attractive dress, shirt, or pant suit is related to a student's success in visualizing what the finished product will look like.

STUDENT PREPARATION

None.

TEACHER PREPARATION

Clip ads that have detailed descriptions of the clothing illustrated from newspapers and magazines. (Note the descriptions of the pantsuit shown by Switzer's and the bucsuede suit in the Hanny ad.) Clip the descriptions from the ads. Mount each description to the left side of a piece of cardboard and cover the cardboard with plastic. Provide a crayon or marking pencil. Assemble swatches of fabrics in a box.

PROCEDURE

The student reads the word description of the clothing and sketches her conception of the article. (Artistry should be minimized so all students will feel comfortable with the activity, not just those who have artistic talent.) When the sketch is completed, the student selects swatches of fabric she considers appropriate for the apparel

Switzer's

4 Pc. Wardrober

You get the Dacron¹ polyester/wool herringbone pant and pleated skirt plus the color matched cardigan jacket and shell with Nordic intarsia design.

The washable polyester removable dickey is a fashion bonus.

Blue, beige. 8-18.

$96 complete

and discusses the results with the teacher, who may or may not wish to show the student the original sketch. The plastic covering is wiped clean for the activity to be used again.

Child Development

Child Development

GRADE LEVEL

10–12

NAME OF ACTIVITY

Test Posters

OBJECTIVE OF ACTIVITY

To set up an evaluation that gives students an instrument through which they can demonstrate ability to interpret, to draw inferences, and to apply concepts.

STUDENT PREPARATION

The student has studied the unit in the child development text that discusses the physical, emotional, social, and intellectual development of the child from ages three to six.

TEACHER PREPARATION

Make two posters, one containing pictures taken from various magazines showing the settings and furnishings of bedrooms for girls of preschool age, the other poster showing bedrooms for boys of the same age. Be sure to include pictures of children in various activities to aid recall of concepts discussed in the unit. Pictures in color enhance the attractiveness of the posters, which should be large enough to be clearly visible to a group of students. Prepare test questions. The questions are of this nature:

1. Describe the advantages and disadvantages of the rooms of these four little girls on the basis of what we learned in this unit.
2. Evaluate the rooms of these five little boys on the basis of the principles learned in the unit.

This type of testing gives creative students an opportunity to express insights.

PROCEDURE

The students study the posters and answer the essay questions prepared by the teacher.

SUBJECT AREA

Child Development

GRADE LEVEL

10–12

NAME OF ACTIVITY

Evaluating Day Care Centers

OBJECTIVE OF ACTIVITY

To assist students in developing the skills of judging and evaluating against a standard.

STUDENT PREPARATION

The student has read appropriate areas in the child development text and has listened to the teacher's class presentations.

TEACHER PREPARATION

Prepare a ditto describing situations observed by a mother as she visited a fictitious child care center preparatory to choosing a center for her daughter. (See example.) Prepare another ditto which serves as student's answer sheet. (See example.)

PROCEDURE

Evaluating Day Care Centers can be an individual activity or one for an entire class. The student reads the vignette prepared by the teacher, judges the individual parts of the vignette in light of what has been presented in class and in the text, and evaluates each of the situations found at a fictitious day care center.

Example of Vignette

In Search of a Child Care Center

DIRECTIONS

Read through this paragraph. Note that each sentence is numbered. On the second page state what is good practice or poor practice about the situation described in each sentence and state your reason.

SETTING

Jane is looking over several day care centers for her three-year-old daughter, Tammy, to stay in while Jane works. This is what she saw at one center.

1. The main playroom was painted in lively colors while the rest área was painted in more subdued colors. 2. Jane noticed that all the children's tables and chairs were miniature in size, keyed to the children's bodies. 3. The toys were safely placed on high shelves away from a child's reach. 4. The 23 three year olds and the teacher seemed to be having fun playing outside. 5. Upon noticing a child climbing up a ladder leaning against the building, the teacher yelled, "Don't climb on that ladder!" 6. The children who were riding tricycles were in a special area for trike riders only. 7. The gravel-covered play yard was enclosed by a fence. 8. In the sandbox the instructor was showing several children how to make a house. 9. Satisfied that she had seen enough, Jane went home.

Example of Student Sheet

Determine good practice or poor practice described in each sentence and write your reason.

1. _____

   _____

2. _____

_____

3. _____

_____

4. _____

_____

5. _____

_____

6. _____

_____

7. _____

_____

8. _____

_____

9. _____

_____

Examples of Responses

1. Good practice. Playrooms should be painted in cheerful and gay colors. Rest areas should not have "busy" colors.
2. Good practice. Equipment should be child-sized. This gives the child the feeling that he can cope with his world.
3. Poor practice. Toys should be easily accessible to children.

Interpersonal Living

SUBJECT AREA

Interpersonal Living

GRADE LEVEL

9–12

NAME OF ACTIVITY

Lucy's 5-cent Psychiatry Booth

OBJECTIVE OF ACTIVITY

To evaluate and make tentative judgments on given data and ideas.

STUDENT PREPARATION

None.

TEACHER PREPARATION

Clip various question-and-answer columns from newspapers and various magazines. Paste the question on one sheet and the answer on another and assign to them a matching code.

PROCEDURE

A team of students chooses one "question" clipping. One member reads the clipping aloud (the clipping may be passed around later as members need to check a detail). Based on just the data in the clipping, students make suggestions for a solution to the problem, giving reasons for the advice offered. One member of the team records suggestion. After each team member offers a solution, the recorder leads a discussion for the purpose of getting a possible consensus. If a consensus cannot be reached, a majority and minority report may be made. Then the group gets the "expert's" response clipping and compares. Further discussion may ensue.

▶SUBJECT AREA

Interpersonal Living

GRADE LEVEL

11–12

NAME OF ACTIVITY

Insights

OBJECTIVE OF ACTIVITY

To give students opportunities to evaluate and make judgments.

STUDENT PREPARATION

None.

TEACHER PREPARATION

Clip an assortment of reader's letters from newspapers and various magazines. Select the types of letters that are submitted to advice columnists, suggestion boxes, and letters to the editor. Paste the reader's letter (not the response) on a sheet of paper. Across the top of the paper, type something like this:

> We will be better equipped to handle interpersonal problems if we try to gain some insight into why relationships are good or poor.

PROCEDURE

The student selects those letters in which he feels people involved have developed good relationships and explains in writing or in teacher conference why he has made that judgment. The student also selects those letters which imply poor relationships and suggests possible improvements. The teacher responds.

NOTE

The student should understand that he is not being asked to solve problems, only to identify good and poor interpersonal relationships.

Home Management

Home Management

GRADE LEVEL

9–12

NAME OF ACTIVITY

Household Products

OBJECTIVE OF ACTIVITY

To encourage students to read and interpret descriptions often carried in fine print on containers of cleansing and beautifying products used in the home.

STUDENT PREPARATION

The student has participated in a unit on products used in the home for jobs such as cleaning, polishing, tinting.

TEACHER PREPARATION

Arrange on a table or counter a display of ten to fifteen nonfood household products. Provide students with a dittoed sheet containing terms such as biodegradable, chlorine, sodium hydroxide, or phosphorus. Provide space after each term for student's entry.

PROCEDURE

Students examine the containers, reading the fine print, to find the terms on the dittoed list. They (1) note the name of the product, (2) write the purpose, benefit or caution listed for the term on the container, and (3) draw a conclusion from what they learned. An unabridged dictionary may be used as a resource.

SUBJECT AREA

Home Management

GRADE LEVEL

10–12

NAME OF ACTIVITY

Consumer's Directions

OBJECTIVE OF ACTIVITY

Large and small electrical appliances are accompanied by booklets
or brochures giving the consumer specific directions for use and care
of the products. Within a short time the booklets often wind up lost
or in the bottom of an overcrowded drawer, and expensive appliances are mistreated. Phase I of this activity gives students an
opportunity to follow directions on a simply made product. Phase II
involves interpreting and following directions given in booklets
accompanying electrical appliances.

STUDENT PREPARATION

None.

Phase I

TEACHER PREPARATION

Prepare a set of directions for making a wall holder for brochures
that accompany electrical appliances. (See example.) Duplicate
copies.

PROCEDURE

On receiving a copy of the directions, students gather their materials
and proceed to make the do-it-yourselfer. The teacher examines the

TLC
For Appliances

Wallholder for Brochures.

holders carefully in order to identify students who need additional training and practice in following directions.

Example of handout for phase I:

Holder for Appliance Booklets

Appliances which will be expensive items in outfitting your home often suffer because consumers disregard the directions for care and use of the appliance. This attractive holder you will create is designed to hang on the wall of the kitchen as both an ornamental and useful decoration. (See drawing.)

Cut a piece of burlap or canvas measuring 16 × 21½ inches. Cut a piece of scrap material the same dimension to use as a lining. Sew the two pieces together, using a half-inch seam.

Trace these letters from material matching the lining:

TLC.

(stands for tender loving care)

FOR APPLIANCES

Attach to the top half of the canvas or burlap.

Obtain a piece of masonite 15 inches by 1/2 inch. Complete the holder by sewing the burlap or canvas to gussets on each side and attaching the masonite at the bottom of the holder.

Wrap two wire coat hangers with ribbon to match the letters and lining and sew one to each top of the holder with matching yarn. The tops of the wire hangers hook over a cup hanger attached to the wall. Your brochures will be easily accessible when needed.

Phase II

TEACHER PREPARATION

Gather enough booklets usually packed with appliances so that each student has a different one. Distribute the booklets and assign each student to design questions to test a person's ability to follow directions given for care and use of that particular appliance.

PROCEDURE

After the questions are completed, they are placed in the booklet. Then the booklets are passed to peers who answer the student-designed questions. The question designer is the authority on accuracy of the answers.

CHAPTER 10

Industrial and Vocational Arts

If you are starting the book here, you are coming in on the middle of the act. Part I is the curtain raiser; it builds up to the use of the industrial and vocational arts section.

Industrial and vocational students in secondary schools actually are serving a two-way apprenticeship.

For some of them, ideas are germinating about possibilities of spending their adult "work" hours in electronics, or automotives, metals, graphic arts, mechanical drawing, woods. All of them, however, are serving an apprenticeship for filling "leisure" hours that are predicted to be abundant in this country. It was recently estimated that by the 1980s Americans would be spending in excess of 250 billion dollars on leisure time or fun activities.

So it is a rare industrial arts teacher these days who sees himself (or herself) solely as a vocational teacher. He also sets goals and plans student activities as an avocational leader. In effect he arranges the environment so students not only can learn to do for today, but also can understand how to continue learning to do for the rest of their lives. This ongoing learning can take place only when students are skillful at assigning meaning to the language of the various vocational-avocational arts. As adults, they will encounter the language most often in written form—in newspapers, in magazines, in expository articles, in how-to-do-it manuals, and in advertising.

The use of these and other media is demonstrated in this section in activities that foster vocabulary and such skills as evaluating, problem solving, following directions, and classifying. Industrial and vocational arts seem to have many languages. Math language, for instance, is a part of the industrial arts language; so is the language of science, social studies, art, safety, business, and of course, native English. You will want to find many avenues for helping students cope with the language(s) of industrial and vocational arts.

Woodworking

SUBJECT AREA

Woodworking

GRADE LEVEL

7–12

NAME OF ACTIVITY

New Shop Products

OBJECTIVE OF ACTIVITY

To give students experience in proceeding logically through decision-making steps, namely

1. to verbalize problems,
2. to critique pros and cons of new products associated with woods,
3. to predict degree of success of the new products.

STUDENT PREPARATION

None.

TEACHER PREPARATION

Popular science magazines regularly inform their readers of new products. Clip pictures and descriptions of new inventions that are related to working with woods. Write the magazine for permission to reproduce the pictures and descriptions. Prepare questions appropriate to the objectives of this activity. (See example of description.)

PROCEDURE

Working in small groups, class members role-play the meeting at which the board of directors of the company made the decision to manufacture the product. Small groups try to reach consensus on the questions. When small groups submit their reports, the entire class, under the guidance of the teacher, tries to reach consensus, much as a decision-making body for a corporation does.

New Product

Sawhorses Are Adjustable, Foldable

(Picture of sawhorses showing elevator rails)

Handy Horses fold up to less than five-inch thickness for storage. Unfolded, they have elevator rails that adjust from 22½ to 39 inches high. The rails have built-in calibrations to insure a level working surface. Wood sawhorses come unfinished with a wall hanger and a diagonal brace for stability when horses are raised and spread far apart. $28.50 a pair from Croton Craft, 2 Memory Lane, Croton-on-Hudson, N.Y. 10520.*

Example question for Objective 1:

1. What are some of the problems with regular sawhorses that the inventor tried to overcome?
   (Possible answers: sawhorses are awkward to store; when not in use, get in the way of other work; height sometimes uncomfortable for some jobs; if working area is not level, regular sawhorses aren't either)

Example of question for Objective 2:

2. List good features of the adjustable, foldable sawhorses and poor features.
   (Possible favorable answers: sawhorses can be raised to height comfortable to worker; fold to store)
   (Possible unfavorable answers: the price per each approximately twice the cost of building your own; metal more serviceable than wood)

*From *Popular Mechanics* © 1974 by The Hearst Corporation

Example of question for Objective 3:

3. What is your prediction for success of this product?
   (Possible answers: fair—good features, but price seems higher
   than many woodworkers might want to pay; however, compared
   to metal sawhorses, you can get two of these for the price of one
   metal one)

SUBJECT AREA

Woodworking

GRADE LEVEL

7–12

NAME OF ACTIVITY

In a Word

OBJECTIVE OF ACTIVITY

To reinforce learning of shop vocabulary.

STUDENT PREPARATION

None.

TEACHER PREPARATION

Construct puzzle from key words under study. Ditto enough copies
for every member of the class.

PROCEDURE

The puzzles are distributed during the last few minutes of class
while students are waiting for the bell to ring. Even better results
come when students develop their own puzzles to share with class
members.

"In a Word" Puzzle.

In a Word

Across
1. Used to cover joints and decorate
4. Glue
6. Used in cutting wood
8. Final step in fine polishing
11. Durable, hard, transparent finish
12. Type of joint used in construction
15. Grade of sandpaper

Down
2. Rod used to reinforce joints
3. Glue together
5. Cutting with the grain
7. Twisting of wood by moisture
9. Reducing moisture naturally
10. Type of pine that yields a hard, durable wood
13. Product of trees used in points, finishes and in the textile and plastics industries
14. Abrasive tool

Key:

Across	Down
1. molding	2. dowel
4. adhesive	3. laminate
6. quarter	5. rip
8. pumice	7. warp
11. varnish	9. air-dried
12. dovetail	10. slash
15. grit	13. resin
	14. file

SUBJECT AREA

Woodworking

GRADE LEVEL

7–12

NAME OF ACTIVITY

It's There Somewhere

OBJECTIVE OF ACTIVITY

To acquaint students with important shop terms.

STUDENT PREPARATION

The student has studied key vocabulary words after introduction and demonstration by the teacher.

TEACHER PREPARATION

On a piece of graph paper enter the letters of the key words backwards (to increase concentration) in scattered positions. Fill in the remaining squares with assorted letters. At the bottom of the sheet, give descriptions of the terms. (See example.) For variation, sketch the devices instead of describing them. Ditto copies for the entire class. Make a key.

PROCEDURE

Students use the last five or seven minutes of the class period to match the definitions to terms on the puzzle. They circle or draw a box around each term. If the period ends before students are finished, they may take activity home and turn it in the following day.

IT'S THERE SOMEWHERE

```
r r s e e r e t n i o j o h m g i
e e s o m i n u t i s v a g s i o
i n m t e t g r o f e c r i t g n
n d i m t a v f u d a r e n a l p
t w i t a o e o s e a i b a o a e
h l l n s h r h j o r d a n b r i
p c o a g b a e l k l a c e m d w
m m e i i p y r y v a y u r l h t
a w j i e o o y e o u e o q e a d
l h e r t g f n s y s e c y s a b
c h e r u l e l e v e b o u i k o
g o n l p e t q t o e b t h h u t
e r a w r u e i e u r l i n c t d
e t o u t o n e h t a l a t o h n
```

Draw a box around the terms for the following descriptions:

1. tool for smoothing and straightening the edges of boards
2. cutting hand tool for carving or shaping wood
3. power tool used for rounding edges on molding
4. power tool used to shape table legs
5. power machine that removes rough or excess surface from a board
6. a miter joint in which two pieces of wood meet at other than a right angle
7. thin layers of wood glued together to form plywood
8. a groove into which the end of a board fits
9. a guide for locating proper places to drill holes
10. a device with two movable parts brought together to hold pieces of wood tight
11. a measuring device for truing angles
12. a hand tool, usually used for driving nails

IT'S THERE SOMEWHERE

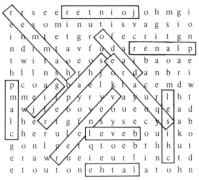

Key:
1. jointer
2. chisel
3. shaper
4. lathe
5. planer
6. bevel

7. veneer
8. dado
9. jig
10. clamp
11. square
12. hammer

▶SUBJECT AREA

Woodworking

GRADE LEVEL

7–12

NAME OF ACTIVITY

In a Flash

OBJECTIVE OF ACTIVITY

Quick recognition of abbreviations and symbols facilitates operations in the woodworking shop. This activity affords practice for students in internalizing this shortened form of vocabulary words.

STUDENT PREPARATION

None.

TEACHER PREPARATION

Prepare flash cards, printing the term on one side and its abbreviation or symbol on the other, such as

- A D (air-dried)
- K D (kiln-dried)
- bd. ft. (board foot)
- S 2 S (surfaced on two sides)
- A-B grades (lumber free from defects)
- _____ ___ _____ ___ (center line)

If some students need help with general math abbreviations (i.e., degree, inch, yard, percent), cards should be made for them also.

PROCEDURE

Working in pairs, students try for a rapid response as they see the abbreviation or symbol on the card. Feedback is given by student flashing cards and viewing correct responses. Time between clean-up and class bell can profitably be used for activities such as In a Flash.

Woodworking

GRADE LEVEL

7–12

NAME OF ACTIVITY

Command Performance

OBJECTIVE OF ACTIVITY

Inability to follow directions sometimes stems from inefficiency in performing according to the action words used in the printed directions, more specifically, the verbs. This activity enables students to follow directions by first performing on paper the task called for by action words. It is less costly to ruin paper than to ruin lumber.

STUDENT PREPARATION

The student has been introduced to the operational words in classroom presentations and demonstrations.

TEACHER PREPARATION

Prepare a large sign for the shop wall which gives students directions for participating in this activity (see example). The types of action words for which students should make sketches are verbs such as:

toenail	countersink	chisel
miter	shim	overlap
trim	bore	route
notch	file	mask
drill	tack	rabbet
coat	sink	round
screw	dado	center
join	groove	mortise
plane	bevel	taper

PROCEDURE

Before a student is allowed to begin a job, he sketches the operation called for by each action word in the printed directions. Artistic merit is not at issue in this activity. (See examples of rough sketching.) The student has only to make his sketch clear enough so the instructor can decide whether or not the student understands the operation before he performs it with a hand or power tool on lumber.

Example of large poster for shop wall:

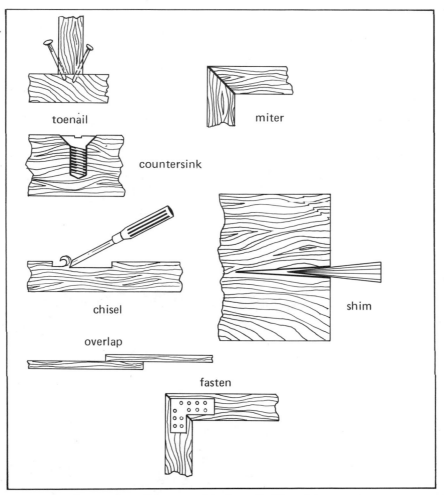

toenail

miter

countersink

chisel

shim

overlap

fasten

Examples of Acceptable Rough Sketching.

Command Performance

Before you use a hand or power tool and lumber, make sure you understand how to perform on the basis of the directions. To show that you do understand what to do, sketch the operation called for by the term and show it to me. You don't need to be artistic.

Woodworking

GRADE LEVEL

7–12

NAME OF ACTIVITY

Slippery Words

Part I

OBJECTIVE OF ACTIVITY

To call students' attention to terms in woodworking for which they already have a different referent. Such "slippery" words are an impediment to comprehension.

STUDENT PREPARATION

None.

TEACHER PREPARATION

Identify terms used in woodworking for which there are different meanings in a student's everyday life, for example, bore. Prepare a ditto (see example) for the first part of this activity.

PROCEDURE

Students, singly or in small groups, assign meanings to terms used in woodworking; the first is an everyday meaning, the second, the shop meaning.

Slippery Words

INSTRUCTIONS

These words you will use in the shop may cause confusion because you have different meanings for them. If you are to be successful in this class, it is important that you learn the shop meanings for these terms. First, write the meaning of the word as it is used in the everyday world. Then, using the dictionary or the textbook, write the shop meaning for the word. A couple of examples are given.

Term	Everyday Meaning	Shop Meaning
1. bore	dull person	to make a hole with a cutting tool
2. jig	a dance	frame for guiding a tool

Other words the instructor might include on the list:

frog	carriage	throat
gain	ash	gauge
plane	arbor	grain
pilot	chisel	spike
grit	bead	bit

Part II

OBJECTIVE OF ACTIVITY

To add visual and kinetic modes of learning "slippery" words.

STUDENT PREPARATION

One half of the class—team 1—prints each term on the board or on a piece of paper. The other half of the class—team 2—assembles the objects that the "slippery" terms name. Items that are not portable, such as a carriage, are to be pointed to.

TEACHER PREPARATION

None.

PROCEDURE

As the instructor calls a word, a member of team 1 raises a sign on which the word is printed or points to it on the board, and another member gives an everyday meaning orally. Then a member of team 2 shows the object, and another member gives the shop definition. Activities such as this one are excellent use of time between clean-up and the bell for next class.

Automotive Mechanics

SUBJECT AREA

Automotive Mechanics

GRADE LEVEL

9–12

NAME OF ACTIVITY

Get in Gear

OBJECTIVE OF ACTIVITY

To facilitate learning new meanings, those applicable to automotive mechanics, for words and concepts for which students have everyday meanings.

STUDENT PREPARATION

The student has been introduced to the terms.

TEACHER PREPARATION

Make a board on which three cardboard gears are displayed. (See the illustration.) On small pieces of lightweight cardboard print or type two sets of words that have a specialized meaning in automotive mechanics and a different meaning in other areas. Staple them to the large gear. Print meanings as the words are used in auto class, and staple them to one of the small gears. Print meanings of the words as they are used in areas other than automotive mechanics, and staple them to the other small gear. (See examples of terms and definitions.)

PROCEDURE

Singly or as buddies, students match the terms on the large gear with the meanings on the "Other Areas" gear. Then they match the terms on the large gear with the meanings on the "Automotive Mechanics" gear. They use textbooks and dictionaries as aids, as well as self-checks.

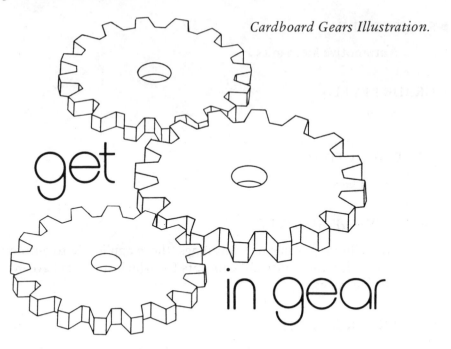

Cardboard Gears Illustration.

Here are some examples of automotive terms for which students might have meanings in everyday life:

1. differential   a set of gears which permit rear wheels to revolve at different speeds
   differential   peculiarity; distinction; feature; earmark
2. governor   a device for automatically controlling the speed of an engine by regulating the intake of fuel
   governor   the elected head of any state in the United States
3. distributor   a mechanical device for distributing electric current to the spark plugs of a gas engine
   distributor   a business firm that distributes goods to customers
4. drum   a metal cylinder
   drum   a percussion instrument
5. shoe   the curved part of a brake that presses against the wheel rim
   shoe   an outer covering for the foot
6. muffler   a device for deadening the sound of escaping gases of an internal-combustion engine
   muffler   a heavy neck scarf

SUBJECT AREA

Automotive Mechanics

GRADE LEVEL

9–12

NAME OF ACTIVITY

Better Mousetraps

OBJECTIVE OF ACTIVITY

Students need guidance in discovering that new techniques, new products, and new inventions are the results of a series of steps, foremost of which is the recognition of a problem. This activity is designed to help students

1. verbalize problems,
2. critique pros and cons of new products,
3. predict degree of success of new products.

STUDENT PREPARATION

None.

TEACHER PREPARATION

Monthly science and automotive magazines feature pictures and descriptions of new products. Clip those features which have a connection with classroom instruction. After obtaining permission from the magazine, ditto copies of pictures, descriptions, and a series of questions written to match the objectives of the activity. (See the accompanying example of a description.)

PROCEDURE

Working in small groups, students role-play the meeting of the board of directors of the company which made the decision to manufacture the product. When the groups are finished, each submits a consensus report. Led by the instructor, the entire class comes to a consensus, combining the best features of group reports.

New Product

Car Jack—Inflatable Rubber Bag

(Picture of girl attaching bag's hose to exhaust pipe)	*(Picture of car on inflated bag and girl removing wheel of flat tire)*

This novel car jack is simply a small rubber bag placed under the car and connected to the exhaust by a hose. The engine is turned on and the bag is blown up within thirty seconds by exhaust gases so that the tire can be changed. The Japanese-made Bull Bag is said to lift three tons approximately 2½ feet. One European distributor: Bull-Bag Vertrief, Birkerstrasse 33, 8 Munich 19, Germany.*

Example question for Objective 1:

1. State problems that may have led the inventor to devise a solution in the form of the Bull Bag.
   (Possible answers: ratchet jack difficult to operate; heavy for old people, infirm persons)

Example question for Objective 2:

2. List the strengths and weaknesses of the Bull Bag.
   (Possible pro answers: easily operated; light-weight)

*From *Popular Mechanics* © 1974 by The Hearst Corporation

(Possible con answers: rubber deteriorates; sharp object could puncture the bag; stiff in cold weather; more storage space needed)

Example question for Objective 3:

3. What is your prediction for success of this product?
   (Possible answers: should be good if price is reasonable, if product is widely advertised)

►SUBJECT AREA

Automotive Mechanics

GRADE LEVEL

9–12

NAME OF ACTIVITY

Dear Abby of the Auto Clinic

OBJECTIVE OF ACTIVITY

To reinforce students' problem-solving abilities.

STUDENT PREPARATION

By the time a student is well into the introductory automotives course he or she should be ready to do the diagnosing and hypothesizing required for this activity.

TEACHER PREPARATION

Request the staff of the school newspaper to print a Dear-Abby-of-the-Auto-Clinic column that invites letters from the student body concerning problems with cars. Have manuals and trouble diagnosis charts available.

PROCEDURE

As questions are turned over to the automotives class from the newspaper staff, the instructor assigns one question to two or three students to prepare the answer for the next publication of the newspaper. Answers will need to be scrutinized carefully by the instructor before publication. The class should have the honor of giving the column an attention-getting name.

SUBJECT AREA

Automotive Mechanics

GRADE LEVEL

9–12

NAME OF ACTIVITY

Slippery Words

OBJECTIVE OF ACTIVITY

To help students recognize that some vocabulary words in automotive mechanics have more than one meaning and to encourage students to use context clues to get meaning.

STUDENT PREPARATION

None.

TEACHER PREPARATION

Prepare the activity using the example or other sentences and vocabulary words. The activity requires ten yellow cards, each containing five incomplete sentences; fifty green cards, each containing a word with its definition and the number of points it is worth when correctly matched with a sentence.

PROCEDURE

Players can number from two to ten. Each player is given one yellow sentence card. In turn, he may draw five green cards. If he is able to match a word to the sentence in which it belongs, he receives the number of points noted on the green card. He may match as many of the five word cards as possible in turn. If he is unable to use any or all of the cards he has drawn, he must place the unused cards at the bottom of the pile face down. The turn passes to the next player. The winner has the highest number of points when all the green cards have been used.

Words for Green Cards (50 cards)

- barrel: the chamber of a pump in which the piston works (10 points)
- barrel: a wooden vessel with bulging sides and flat ends (5 points)
- battery: a combination of two or more galvanic cells electronically connected to work together to produce electrical energy (10 points)
- battery: a large group or series of related things (a battery of questions) (5 points)
- bearing: the support and guide for a sliding shaft, pivot, or wheel (10 points)
- bearing: course, aid, direction (5 points)
- charged: supplied with a quantity of electricity, electrical energy (10 points)
- charged: accused formally (5 points)
- choke: a mechanism which, by blocking a passage, regulates the flow of gas and air (10 points)
- choke: to strangle, stifle, or suffocate; to suppress (5 points)
- clutch: a control, as a pedal, for operating the mechanism which engages or disengages a shaft with or from another shaft or rotating part (10 points)
- clutch: to grasp, seize, claw at, hold tightly (5 points)
- crank: type of arm or lever for imparting rotary motion to a rotating shaft, to rotate by means of a crank (10 points)
- crank: an ill-tempered, grouchy person (5 points)
- distributor: a device which directs electrical current to spark plugs (10 points)
- distributor: one who delivers to market in a particular area usually as a wholesaler (5 points)
- driver: a part transmitting force or motion (10 points)
- driver: a person who drives a vehicle (5 points)
- exhaust: the cylinder of an engine from which steam or gases escape; part of an engine through which the exhaust is ejected (10 points)
- exhaust: to draw out all that is essential in a subject or topic; to treat or study thoroughly (5 points)
- float: a device which regulates the level, supply, or outlet of liquid (10 points)

- float: a vehicle bearing a display in a parade or procession (5 points)
- governor: an attachment to a machine for automatic control of speed (10 points)
- governor: the chief executive or head of a political unit (as a state) (5 points)
- hood: the movable cover used to protect the engine (10 points)
- hood: hoodlum, burglar, gangster (5 points)
- housing: a fully enclosed case and support for a mechanism (10 points)
- housing: shelter, lodging, or dwelling (5 points)
- jack: a mechanical device, one used to raise a heavy body a short distance (10 points)
- jack: a playing card bearing the figure of a man (5 points)
- pilot: a guide for centering or positioning to adjacent parts (10 points)
- pilot: a person qualified to operate an airplane, balloon, or other aircraft (5 points)
- rim: the outer circle of a wheel attached to the hub by spokes; a circular strip of metal forming the connection between an auto wheel and tire (10 points)
- rim: the outer edge, border, margin, or brink of a curved area (5 points)
- seal: to bring (a plug, jack, or socket) into locked or fully aligned position; a closing or fastening that tightly secures parts (10 points)
- seal: a decorative stamp, especially as given to contributors to a charity (5 points)
- seat: a base on which an engine or motor valve rests (10 points)
- seat: something designed to support a person in a sitting position, as a chair or bench (5 points)
- shell: a metal, pressure-resistant outer casing (10 points)
- shell: an attitude or manner of reserve that usually conceals one's emotions, thoughts (5 points)
- shield: a covering usually of metal, placed around electrical devices or circuits (10 points)
- shield: to protect someone or something with or as with a shield (5 points)
- shift: to change gears from one ratio or arrangement to another; a gearshift (10 points)

- shift: a person's scheduled period of work (5 points)
- terminals: mechanical devices by means of which an electric connection to an apparatus is established (10 points)
- terminals: ends of a carrier line (as a railroad, truck, bus) with handling and storage facilities and stations (5 points)
- throttle: a lever, pedal, handle for controlling the flow of fluid to control the speed of an engine (10 points)
- throttle: to choke or to strangle (5 points)
- tire: a ring or band of rubber, either solid or hollow and inflated, placed over the rim of a wheel to provide traction, resistance to wear (10 points)
- tire: to weary, to reduce in strength (5 points)

Sentences for Yellow Cards (10 cards)

1. The _____ granted a pardon to the prisoner.
2. The spark plugs were not receiving the electrical current from the _____.
3. He pushed the _____ in order to control the speed of the engine.
4. Many cars have an automatic _____ for controlling the flow of gas.
5. The empty _____ was used by the movers for packing dishes.

1. Jerome, after shoveling snow for an hour, was beginning to _____.
2. To remove the valve _____ insert, use the proper puller nut and valve seat puller.
3. Insert the _____ into the valve guide, then drive the insert into place.
4. He put up his arm as a _____ against the blows of the attacker.
5. The _____ of the car was not cited at the scene of the accident.

1. A gangster is sometimes known as a _____.
2. A pedal is a control used to operate a _____.
3. The investigator fired a _____ of questions at the suspect.
4. A Christmas _____ was placed on the envelope.
5. He placed the _____ under the car in order to raise it into the air.

1. Harold lived within his own _____ to conceal his emotions.
2. When checking _____ level, be sure it is parallel to the body mounting surface.
3. He preferred to work a night _____ so that he could go to school during the day.
4. The _____ holds the tire in place.
5. The battery _____ were corroded.

1. The group was unable to find its _____ in the vast wilderness.
2. It was necessary for him to _____ the old model car in order to start it.
3. The driver was _____ with criminal negligence.
4. An excessive amount of gases was being ejected from the _____.
5. When disassembling a windup starter, do not attempt to remove the starter spring from its _____.

1. Before repairing the _____ on your engine, check the top speed with a tachometer.
2. Jack served as wholesale _____ for the XYZ Candy Company.
3. The assailant _____ the victim after robbing him.
4. Mary _____ back her tears and tried to smile.
5. The mechanic replaced the _____ of the pump.

1. Before setting out on his trip, he purchased four new _____ for his car.
2. He sat nervously on the edge of the _____.
3. The _____ brought the plane in for a safe landing.
4. He replaced the metal _____, or covering, surrounding the electrical circuit.
5. Drive the valve insert into place with the _____.

1. The mechanic lifted the _____ of the car so that he could check the battery.
2. The woman saw the burglar _____ his throat as she fired the shot.
3. The electrical connections of the cells in the _____ were corroded.
4. The problem seems to be a leak in the transmission _____.
5. In his hand he held the _____ of spades.

1. In disassembling the starter motor, remove the motor support cover from the motor _____.
2. The homecoming queen rode atop a flower bedecked _____.
3. One must _____ gears in order to move the car into reverse.
4. From the _____ of the canyon one views a glorious sight.
5. The railroad _____ were teeming with holiday travelers.

1. To check a ball _____, rotate the part slowly by hand; replace if roughness is noted.
2. Miss Jones, the history teacher, was known as an old _____.
3. When he was unable to start his car, the mechanic _____ the battery.
4. It requires a great deal of talking to_____this subject.
5. In most urban areas, low cost_____is being provided.

►SUBJECT AREA

Automotive Mechanics

GRADE LEVEL

9–12

NAME OF ACTIVITY

All in the Family

OBJECTIVE OF ACTIVITY

To give students an overview of specialized terms that belong in a family, for example, all the terms that have to do with transmission.

STUDENT PREPARATION

None.

TEACHER PREPARATION

None.

PROCEDURE

This is a whole-class activity which involves the students in identifying terms that are the properties of certain parts of the automobile. The activity is used at the beginning of a unit so students get an overall picture of the terms (and their meanings) that they will be verbalizing as they perform. It is important that students know and recognize the words in print to help assure their independence in continuing to learn. The example would be used at the beginning of the unit on transmissions. Using a transparency, the teacher writes

TRANSMISSION

The students turn to the section in the manual or textbook and scan to select technical words that belong to the *transmission* family. As they find a word they jot it down. One by one then they present a word they have found, and the teacher fits it into the word *transmission* on the transparency. As an example, the first student offers *fluid* as the initial word. The teacher adds it this way

```
                          F
                          L
                          U
          T R A N S M I S S I O N
                          D
```

and explains the term, using a visual of the transmission. Another student says the word *automatic,* and the teacher fits it into the schemata

```
                          F
                          L
                          U
          T R A N S M I S S I O N
              U               D
              T
              O
              M
              A
              T
              I
              C
```

and explains the term. The next student offers *dipstick* as a family word. As he fits it into the appropriate position, the teacher discusses its meaning. The procedure continues until more and more and eventually all family words appear in the diagram. The teacher discusses each word's meaning as it is offered and points out the part on a visual.

```
G           F
E           L
A     D     U
TRANSMISSION
   U     P  D
   T     S
   O     T
   M  FILTER
BAND  C
   T     K
   I
   C
```

CHAPTER 11

Mathematics

If you are starting the book here, you are coming in on the middle of the act. Part I is the curtain raiser; it builds up to the use of the mathematics section.

Today more than at any other time in history the study of pure mathematics and applied mathematics are inextricably linked. The fields will become even more interdependent in the decades to come when today's *students* of math become *appliers* of math.

For students to miss learning the significance of mathematics in the modern world as an alive, active, and dynamic field is to dishonor education. How many students know that without mathematics we would not be studying the ocean floor, building swimming pools, designing cars, determining football champions, making telephone calls, or even playing slot machines?

If the answer to the question is not 100 percent then a new look needs to be taken at both the teaching and learning of math. Teachers should examine the kind of "seat work" that spawns robots who compute because 25 problems have been assigned, who find x and didn't even know it was lost, who deal with triangles, rectangles, and cones in calculated isolation. Why? What is the application of this knowledge to the world outside the rungs of the student chair?

Without mathematics the activities in this book could not have been printed. They are activities for the most part that tie math to its raison d'etre as they promote such skills as reading and interpreting equations and graphic materials, evaluating and making judgments, problem solving, guesstimating, recognizing relevant data, and discovering relationships.

Math in General

SUBJECT AREA

Math in General

GRADE LEVEL

7–12

NAME OF ACTIVITY

People Talk Math Every Day

OBJECTIVE OF ACTIVITY

To encourage self-discovery that the language of mathematics, far from being school-centered, is part of our everyday life.

STUDENT PREPARATION

After studying examples given by the teacher, students collect clippings in which the language of mathematics figures. Once alerted, they will find more than they can use in the project. For example, on facing pages in just one edition of a daily newspaper were stories involving math under these headlines:

U.S. crime rate will continue to climb in wake of joblessness, attorney general says

Ford's spending cuts are rejected in House

Confidence in economy rises to 39%, poll shows

Texan sues oil firms for $90 million

Dollar finishes higher on most Europe markets

Auto-firm tax pushed to spur fuel efficiency

New York banks cut lending rates to 8 pct.

Oil firms build up gasoline surplus

low denomination

high yield

anti-inflation

interest rate

passbook

interest

deposit

mortgage

thrift

Big-yield WIN bond is suggested to Ford

Associated Press

NEW YORK — An idea voiced by President Ford — a possible issue of low denomination high-yield "WIN bonds" — has sent another shudder through the nation's cash-strapped savings banks.

Ford said in his Tuesday night speech before the Future Farmers of America in Kansas City that the suggestion came in a letter from James Kincaid of Belleville, Ill. Kincaid proposed an anti-inflation bond purchasable through payroll deductions and paying a competitive interest rate.

The Treasury Department, given the responsibility of studying the suggestion, said Wednesday that the feasibility and mechanics of such a bond hadn't been considered yet.

A spokesman suggested a WIN bond might turn out to be nothing more than the present series "E" savings bond with a higher yield attached, or some other variation. Some banking economists concede small savers probably deserve better than the 6 per cent yields of series "E" bonds and might get it if WIN bonds become a reality.

Whatever form it takes, though, spokesmen for the nation's savings banks, savings and loan associations and mortgage bankers feel the WIN bond could add up to further strong government competition for precious savings dollars.

"It would be just another way of taking more money out of the housing market," a U.S. Savings & Loan League spokesman said.

Currently, he said a savings and loan passbook savings account gets 5.25 per cent interest, while 4-year certificates of deposit are entitled to 7.5 per cent.

He feels that almost any increase in the current 6 per cent interest rate on small-principal government bonds "would be dangerous for us."

"It will cause us to lose more money and this again would make us less able to supply the mortgage market," says a spokesman for the Savings Bank Association of New York.

Some mortgage bankers note that Ford's recent proposals to pump $3 billion into the housing market while at the same time luring savings dollars out of thrift institutions with WIN bonds were at odds with each other.

"You haven't added any new funds here, just more government competition for money," John M. Wetmore, director of research for the Mortgage Banks Association, comments.

---

per cent

statistics

comparable

percentages

average

Under-25 accident rate continues climb in U.S.

The number of accidents involving drivers younger than 25 continues to increase, according to State Highway Division officials quoting from a national study.

They said:

—Such drivers last year made up 22 per cent of the total U.S. driving population, but were involved in 39.4 per cent of all vehicle accidents and 36.3 per cent of all fatal accidents.

—The comparable 1972 percentages for younger drivers were 36.5 and 35.5, respectively.

—In Arizona, 25.5 per cent of all driver's licenses in force last year were in the hands of younger-than-25 drivers, putting the state ahead of the national average.

However, Arizona officials furnished no Arizona accident involvement statistics broken down by age to compare with the national figures.

In Arizona, 55 per cent of the drivers' licenses are held by males, the same as the national average. Ohio leads in male drivers with 60 per cent.

Of 1,474,000 Arizonans old enough to drive, 1,221,771 are licensed.

Hence, of every 1,000 Arizonans of driving age, 829 hold licenses. This puts Arizona in 28th place. Colorado leads with 999 of every 1,000 licensed.

The national average is 790 licensed drivers per 1,000.

TEACHER PREPARATION

Clip two or three articles from today's print media in which some type of mathematics is discussed, for example, statistics, comparison of numbers, or metric equivalents. Paste the clippings on colored art paper. Draw a line under each mathematical term and print the word near its position in the article. (See examples.) Prepare the bulletin board for the new display. Using newspapers, cut out letters for the title, People Talk Math Everyday. Mount the examples on the board.

PROCEDURE

Following the teacher's modeling, students add their clippings from newspapers and magazines that contain mathematical terms to the bulletin board. Each of the teacher's classes is identified by the color of art paper used for mounting. Intraclass competition develops as the bulletin board display nears completion.

SUBJECT AREA

Math in General

GRADE LEVEL

7–10

NAME OF ACTIVITY

Numerals Vacation = Roman Holiday

OBJECTIVE OF ACTIVITY

To read and interpret equations and to apply Roman numerals.

STUDENT PREPARATION

None.

TEACHER PREPARATION

Prepare a chart which reviews Roman numerals and gives an example of the types of equations students will solve. Develop additional equations; print each on one side of an index card and the answer on the other. (See examples.)

PROCEDURE

Students read the equation, substituting the correct Roman numeral for its Arabic equivalent. They may use the chart when necessary. Then they think of a word for the definition given in the equation. Individual students or teams might compete to see who can translate the most equations.

Example of review chart:

Numerals Vacation = Roman Holiday

Roman Numerals:
I = 1   V = 5   X = 10   L = 50   C = 100   D = 500   M = 1,000

Example of Solving an Equation:

$$6 + vex = manly$$

$$VI + RILE = VIRILE$$

Examples of equations:

Side 1 of index card

100 + competent = a heavy wire rope
5 + a malarial fever = not clear
5 + beer = space between mountains
1,000 + type of poem = method
100 + 1/12 of a foot = sure thing
6 + die = like a snake
50 + type of snake = means of climbing
50 + making money = knowledge
100 + floating platform = skill
100 + preposition = lid
100 + type of grain = outer garment

Side 2 of index card

C + ABLE = CABLE
V + AGUE = VAGUE
V + ALE = VALLEY
M + ODE = MODE
C + INCH = CINCH
VI + PERISH = VIPERISH
L + ADDER = LADDER
L + EARNING = LEARNING
C + RAFT = CRAFT
C + OVER = COVER
C + OAT = COAT

SUBJECT AREA

Math in General

GRADE LEVEL

7–12

NAME OF ACTIVITY

Metric Measures

OBJECTIVE OF ACTIVITY

This activity enables students to discover that manufacturers already are using metric designations on their packages.

STUDENT PREPARATION

The student has been introduced to the metric system of measurement.

TEACHER PREPARATION

Display a few cans and packages of products and have students examine them, looking for the words *gram* and *liter.* The position of metric term varies with different manufacturers. Prepare a ditto (see example).

PROCEDURE

After practicing on cans and packages provided in the classroom, students identify brands, products, English weights, and metric weights of products they find in their homes. Class discussion follows when students have completed their investigations.

Metric Measures

Instructions: Look in your kitchen cabinets, refrigerator, bathroom cabinets, and any other place where products are stored in your home. Enter on this sheet all the products which give weights in English measurement and metric measurement. I've listed a few I found in my own home.

Brand	Product	English	Metric
Argo	corn starch	16 oz. (1 lb.)	454 grams
Green Giant	peas	8½ oz.	241 grams
Hills Bros.	coffee	16 oz. (1 lb.)	454 grams
Del Monte	sauerkraut	8 oz.	227 grams
Stokely Van Camp	hominy	14½ oz.	411 grams
Bisquick	baking mix	40 oz. (2 lb. 8 oz.)	1134 grams

Math in General

GRADE LEVEL

7–12

NAME OF ACTIVITY

Grade the Teacher's Paper

OBJECTIVE OF ACTIVITY

Very often charts and graphs in textbooks do not motivate students. To disinterested students the negativism sometimes associated with the textbook is transferred to everything in the textbook. The objectives of this activity are

1. To use everyday resource materials as mediums for reinforcing the skill of chart and graph reading, and
2. To impress on students that the need to interpret graphic materials is a practical ability.

STUDENT PREPARATION

The student has studied the unit on graphic representations.

TEACHER PREPARATION

Clip charts and graphs from newspapers and magazines which appeal to adolescents. Paste each on cardboard. Then write a series of incorrect statements concerning the representation and paste them under the chart or graph. (See examples.)

PROCEDURE

Singly or in pairs, students who need additional experience in extracting data from drawings determine whether the teacher's statements are correct or incorrect and why. They calculate the grade for the work and return the paper to the teacher. In single or small group conference the instructor discusses the results.

Half Of Students Admit Cheating 'Very Seldom'

What would you think of a system where the schools were open 12 months (or 4 quarters) and each student could decide for themselves which 3-month period he wanted for vacation?	TOTAL	FR	SO	JR	SR
I would like it	44%	47%	42%	42%	44%
I would not like it	47	43	49	50	47
Don't know	9	10	9	8	9
	100%	100%	100%	100%	100%

What do you feel would be the best grading system?					
Current system (1 through 5)	38%	41%	39%	35%	36%
Current system plus personal comments	24	23	24	24	26
Only "pass" or "fail"	18	16	16	20	20
No grade at all	13	12	13	14	11
Other (please specify)	3	3	4	3	4
Don't know	4	5	4	4	3
	100%	100%	100%	100%	100%

Do you cheat on school homework or tests?					
Never	19%	20%	17%	17%	22%
Very seldom	50	53	50	49	47
Occasionally	28	24	28	31	29
Regularly	3	3	5	3	2
	100%	100%	100%	100%	100%

If you cheat, why do you?	TOTAL	FR	SO	JR	SR
It's easier	19%	19%	20%	18%	18%
I didn't study	43	39	46	47	45
Class boring/worthless	18	17	20	20	18
Pressure (parents, friends, self)	19	19	20	22	18
I feel incapable of pssing the course	18	21	20	18	14
Other	14	16	15	13	13
Don't know	7	9	7	6	6
	100%	100%	100%	100%	100%

In which of the following fields do you plan to make your career:					
Business (trades and services, finance, manufacturing, etc.)	19%	12%	16%	21%	25%
Education (teaching, administration)	6	7	6	5	6
Professional (lawyers, doctors, etc.)	17	18	19	17	17
Science, research	5	5	5	4	5
Sports	7	11	8	6	3
Arts (music, theater, etc.)	7	7	8	8	7
Government	2	2	2	2	2
Agriculture (forestry, farming, etc.)	4	4	4	4	4
Other (please specify)	14	14	14	14	15
Don't know	19	20	18	19	16
	100%	100%	100%	100%	100%

---

1. The year-round school plan met with the disfavor of 47 percent of the freshmen.
2. The current system of grading is still popular with more than half the youths questioned.
3. Less than eight students out of ten cheat on tests or homework.
4. More sophomores cheat than freshmen, juniors, or seniors.
5. A fourth of the students were undecided about career choices while 20 percent preferred career areas not specified by the survey.*

*Phoenix Newspapers, Inc., conducted a survey of 10,000 high school students, and the results were printed by *The Phoenix Gazette* and in the booklet, *Tip-Off III*, 1974.

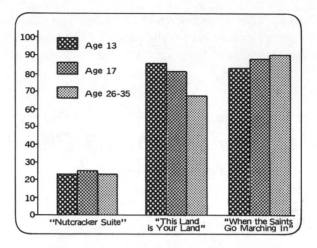

1. Only a minority of all age groups recognized American tunes like "This Land Is Your Land" and "When the Saints Go Marching In."
2. Fewer of the seventeen year olds recognized "Nutcracker Suite" than those younger and older.
3. The vertical axis of the graph represents the actual number of persons being questioned.
4. One age group led the two other age groups in recognizing the three pieces of music.
5. This graph shows that the persons questioned were more familiar with classical music than with popular music.*

*The graph appeared in the September-October, 1974 issue of the *NAEP Newsletter.*

▶SUBJECT AREA

Math in General

GRADE LEVEL

7–12

NAME OF ACTIVITY

Make the Match (Symbols and Definitions)

OBJECTIVE OF ACTIVITY

To provide practice for learning common, essential mathematical symbols.

STUDENT PREPARATION

The player has been introduced to the symbols and their meanings prior to participating in the activity.

TEACHER PREPARATION

Make a set of symbol cards, one symbol per card, for each player.

For example:

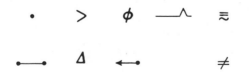

Make a set of definition cards, one definition matching each symbol per card, for the player-monitor. For example: less than, greater than, congruent, not equal, point, not an element.

PROCEDURE

There may be two, three, or four players plus the player-monitor. Each player receives a set of symbols, and the player-monitor has a set of definitions. As the player-monitor exposes the definition, the players find the correct symbol. The first student to match the definition receives three points; each of the other players who displays this correct symbol receives one point. The player who gets forty-five points first is the winner.

SUBJECT AREA

Math in General

GRADE LEVEL

9–10

NAME OF ACTIVITY

Math Symbols Wheel

OBJECTIVE OF ACTIVITY

To cope with the nonverbal symbols of mathematics. To assist students in retaining definitions of symbols.

STUDENT PREPARATION

Students should be familiar with the nonverbal symbols of math through daily problem-solving activities containing some or all of these symbols.

TEACHER PREPARATION

Prepare the math symbols wheel. (See the accompanying illustration.) The teacher prepares the students by presenting each of the symbols with sufficient practice so that students will find the Math Symbol Wheel a means of remembering as they match symbols with definitions.

PROCEDURE

One, two, or three students may work with the wheel at a time. All of the pins (with symbols attached) are removed from wheel. One student at a time may select from the pile of pins just one pin at a time. He then attempts to match it to the correct definition. If he succeeds, he makes 5 points. If he is unable to match his symbol with a definition, he must replace his pin on the pile and await another turn. The player with the highest number of points is the winner.

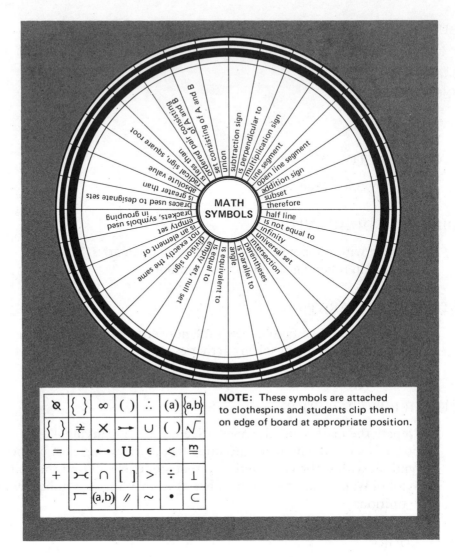

NOTE: These symbols are attached to clothespins and students clip them on edge of board at appropriate position.

Math Symbols Wheel.

General Math

SUBJECT AREA

General Math

GRADE LEVEL

7–9

NAME OF ACTIVITY

Classified Christmas

OBJECTIVE OF ACTIVITY

To provide practice time in problem solving, evaluating, and making judgments, assessing monetary value of goods, and interpreting abbreviated forms of communications in classified ads.

STUDENT PREPARATION

None.

TEACHER PREPARATION

Clip classified ads offering items that would be of interest to a forty-two-year-old father, thirty-nine-year-old mother, and teen-age children, two boys and a girl. Ditto enough copies to provide a set for each group of five to seven students. Ditto instructions sheet. (See examples.)

PROCEDURE

Each group shops the classified ads for Christmas presents for a needy family. The total cost may not exceed $125. At the completion of the task, each group reports its decisions to the class, and discussion follows.

530—Sporting

Goods and Services

USED Spalding golf clubs, includes bag and cart. Best offer. 266-5077.

SMITH & Wesson 357, model 27, 8⅜. Mint. Accessories. $260. 265-3990.

44 MAGNUM S&W model 29, 6½" barrell, $350. 938-5573.

SLATE pool table, coin and antique type in real good shape, will take best offer before Monday noon, 274-8485.

SCUBA equipment, tanks, regulators, wetsuit, miscellaneous. 838-5029. 5622 South Hurricane, Tempe.

Hanglider. 948-7243.

PARACHUTES; Jumping equipment. Hang glider. 268-9319.

SCUBA gear. 948-5619.

TOBOGGAN, new. 265-9449.

WANTED 22 Bretta. 937-7592.

NEW Wilson 1200. $135. 943-2517.

CHEAP SNOWMOBILES!
3040 N. 27th Ave. 254-0103

OPEN—HARCO—7 DAYS

Handguns & ammo discounted
4229 N 7th St. No. 106. 265-8666

WINCHESTER 74, 22 semi-automatic. Mint condition. Extras inclu[illegible] gun case, 600 rounds of long rifle ammo, and cleaning kit. Asking 266-4109; 266-3135.

S&W .44 magnum. 938-2760.

15' CANOE/trailer. Best offer. 969-8401 or 945-6103.

GOLF clubs, bag, cart. Guns, warehouse dolley. 956-2137.

POOL table Brunswick Professional Gold Crown, cost $1500. Sacrifice. 959-5098.

12 Piece Ram golf set and bag; 10 speed bike, $45. Both like new! 937-9308.

HANG GLIDER - Seagull III, 19', never used. Cost $590, Sell $490. 254-9550.

300 MAGNUM, new scope, perfect condition, $150. 12 gauge Fox double barrel in new condition, $120. 1208 North Oak Leaf Drive.

RELOADS, 38 special, $3.80. .357 JHP, $5.25. 44 Special, $4.90. .44 magnum JHP, $6.00. 45 auto, $4.35. Prices for 50. Discount Shooters Supply, 51st Avenue-Thunderbird. 938-5430.

PRIVATE party will buy antique guns or collections. 931-1442.

NEW shotguns for home or sport Hi Standard 18" or Smith-Wesson 20" $105, 18" or 20" coachguns $125. Also have long guns. Call Any day 1 to 9 p.m. 967-0763.

S&W Model 19, 357 mag, 4", excellent condition, dies, brass, miscellaneous. $200. May consider trade for Ruger rifle with scope. 967-3046.

REMINGTON 513T, Winchester model 61 ½. Interested parties only. Gemtop camper for LWB. 955-5672.

TRADE 357 for automatic or double barreled shotgun. 949-9552.

WILL trade new S&W model 66 for new Colt AR-15, high standard HD military 22 long rifle pistol, $75. 949-8924.

551—Clothing

Uniforms, Etc.

MENS suits and sport coats. 42-43 long. 942-4442.

MENS Clothes, coats size 44, slacks 40-34. 956-1877.

SALE: Save up to 50%. Ladies blouses, pants, jackets, long dresses. Continental Boutique, 5620 North 7th Street. Closed Mondays.

CANVAS SHOES

Various styles, priced from 69c to $2.49 pr. for men, ladies, boys & girls. No better bargains on these shoes can be found. Come in & save at YATES STORES, 3931 E. Thomas and 4750 N. 16th St. Open 'til 9:30 daily, and 'til 5 p.m. on Sundays.

MEN'S suits, nearly new. Newest fashion, good quality, reasonable. 7243 N. 16th St. 944-1802.

NEW clothes. Shirts, lots of 100, $1 each. Pants, lots of 100. $2.50 each. Sportcoats, lots of 25, $5 each. Leather belts, lots of 100, $1 each. J. Pidd, 35th Avenue / Bethany Home.

MEN'S and women's clothing, like new. 5607 West Pierson.

MENS suits nearly new. Newest fashion, good quality, reasonable. 7243 N. 16th St. 944-1802.

ESTATE FURS slightly used by fashionable ladies. Many styles. Low prices. Lorraine Black Furs. Town & Country Shopping Center. 955-1221.

575—Sewing Mach.

And Vacuums For Sale

Golden Dial-A-Stitch

'74 YEAR-END CLEARANCE
These touch-o-matics are still in the original factory cartons & have the famous push to wind auto bobbin, also they are jam packed with these built-in features. No attachments needed for zig-zag, button holes, overedge, stretch, blind hems, sews buttons, embroiders, darns, monograms & much more. $68 each while they last. Hurry for best selection. Full guarantee.
HOUSE OF SEWING
Mon. Thurs- Fri- 10 till 9
Tue- Wed- Sat- 10 til 5
15 yrs serving the valley
Tower Plaza Mall 38th St & Thomas
Valley West 57th Ave & Northern

USED vacuum cleaners from $9.95 up. Used zig zag sewing machines from $19.95 & up. New Pfaff sewing machines from $99.95 & up. House of Vaccums, 4232 N. 7th Ave. 279-4968.

1975 RICCAR'S

MODEL	1010 AKA-1020	$179
MODEL	888N AKA-889	$219
MODEL	510 AKA-520	$119

Why Pay More
SMD 2744 W. Camelback 249-0449

CABINETS $35 new, $25 used. Carter's 272-6431.

Vacuums, Sewing Machines
WOOLCO DEPT STORE
33rd Ave. at Grand Ave.

WE RENT VACUUM CLEANERS & SEWING MACHINES. (RENT CAN BE APPLIED TO PURCHASE)
HOUSE OF VACUUMS
4232 N. 7TH AVE, 1441 E. CAMELBACK
15 E. 6TH ST. TEMPE

KIRBY'S

Still in boxes, New 5-year warranty. S. M. Dist. 2744 W. Camelback Rd.
$79.50

SEW parts-needles, feet, etc. Freight Sales, 2424 N. 16th St.

"WE HAVE THEM ALL"

New-Floor Models-Demos-Trades
SAVE 30%-40%-50%
ELNA—VIKING BERNINA
PFAFF — NEW HOME — RICCAR

SINGER TOUCH N'SEW	$48
GOLD TOUCH N'SEW	$100
ZIGZAGS	$38

TOTEM SEWING CENTER
3219 E. Thomas 956-4231 955-8375

588—Home Furn.

For Sale

9x12 USED RUGS $5

CARPET HOUSE 1516 E. Van Buren

36" ELECTRIC stove, kingsize bed. 967-1571.

MAPLE dinette, with leaf, 36x48. $135. 267-7968.

70 YEAR old couch, carved legs, very good condition, $75. Child's desk and chair, $20. 956-1169.

10 FOOT couch, loveseat, need reupholstering, cheap. 247-2074.

BY owner. Mark Coomer exquisite painting "Maria Con Sus Parajitos," $3000. Call collect 213-793-3306.

STROLL-A-Chair, complete set, one year old, $175. Baby crib, $30. 849-6408.

18' COPPERTONE refrigerator also matching stove and oven other miscellaneous household items. Will trade for 15' or 16' upright freezer. 967-3825.

OWNER transferred. Must sell house full of mediterranean furniture this weekend! Including bedroom - living room - dining room and kitchen furniture - sewing machine - miscellaneous. This is high quality furniture. Cash - certified check only. Sat/Sun. 553 North Hobson Plaza. Mesa. 834-0542. Private parties.

DISPLAYED but never used — elegant 2 pc. Velvet Sofa & Love Seat $225. Herculon 2 pc Sofa & Chair $165. Beautiful chrome tables with smoked glass tops. Myer's Construct. Co. 266-6090, 263-8598.

SOLID MAPLE CHEST $65

Brand new, 6 drawer, 50" high, reg. price $109. Guaranteed in writing lowest prices in town. On maple.
GOBINS, 1635 N. 7th St. 254-7071

ONE pair custom made lemon color casement draperies, 118x94. Two pair custom made oyster colored draperies 40x60 and 58x92. Nubby textured beige divan 100". One lounge chair. 949-9470.

600—Dogs

Supplies and Services

LIKE to find good home for puppy, free. 997-6031.

GERMAN Shepherd pups and mother. 247-1922.

COCK-A-POO pups, Sheep/Shepherd mix. 993-8567.

AKC SHEPHERD, female, adult, obedience trained. 938-9876.

FREE to good home amiable black male cockapoo, 2, loves children, housebroken, good watchdog. 264-4547.

GREAT Dane male, also Beagle mix male. 937-3990.

AKC Miniature female poodle. 9 months, silver beige, 996-9089.

PIT Bull Terrier, female, papers, all shots. 992-4942.

FREE three year old German Shepherd, female. Good watchdog, great with children. Needs yard. 992-8704.

SIBERIAN Husky puppies. AKC. See parents. 938-6672.

AKC Registered Pekingese puppies. Home raised. 266-3596.

AKC Weimaraner puppies. 267-1056.

AUSTRALIAN Shepherd puppies, $20. 992-4527.

SILKY. 1-585-4659.

AKC Siberian Huskies for sale or trade. 969-8573.

AKC COLLIE pups. 992-6221.

AFGHANS by champion Coastwind Abraxas. 943-1940.

WIREHAIRS. 938-2320.

WHITE Pekingese. 1-982-4634.

SHELTIES. Puppies. Studs. 971-1400.

LHASA Apso stud service. 966-7807.

BEAGLES, show puppies. 276-0622.

CHIHUAHUA puppies. 997-0429.

WANTED: Mixed Litters of Pups. Good homes guaranteed. 276-2151.

GOLDEN Retrievers male and female. AKC, 6 months. Like to sell as pair. $200. 938-2936.

601—Cats

Supplies and Services

PERSIANS at stud, Kittens. 967-6720.

SIAMESE all colors, 244-9628. Also foreign shorthairs.

NEED home for kitties. 247-4851.

PERSIANS, 247-1444.

HIMALAYANS. 971-3975.

PERSIAN male cat, 2 years, shots, neutered, $20. Must sell. 838-6563.

BEAUTIFUL calico spayed female, can be shown as household pet, $15. 276-7869.

FREE: two silly affectionate inseperable house-broken male cats to responsible home only. 265-2658.

GO CAT GO HOME DEL
50 LBS. $2.50 C.O.D.
CAT LITTER, VERY ABSORBENT. REC. BY VETS & CATTERIES. ARIZ. MINING. 273-0608.

603—Birds, Fish

And Supplies

SUPER SPECIALS

SILVER ANGELS	4/$1
ALBINO TIGER BARBS	$.79ea.
ARTIFICIAL PLANTS	40c & up

PHOENIX TROPICAL
3148 N. 37th Street
1 Block North of Tower Plaza

FIVE Parakeets, four males, one hen, $9 each. Eight zebra Finches, three hens, five males, $9 each. Four Finch cages, $15 each. 7233 North 31st Drive.

FISH tank, fish, and accessories, $30. 247-4851.

NEONS, 5 for $1. White Clouds, 4 for $1. Cherry Barb, 4 for $1. Breeder Angels, $5, your choice, some mated pairs. Large fish shipment just arrived. THE TROPICAL HUT, 828 North Country Club, Mesa. 964-4647.

NEONS 9C

MED. REDTAIL SHARKS	$1.19
5" ARAWANNAS	$6.99
5" PEACOCK EELS	$1.09

(No Limit—Sale Ends Tues.)
ISLE O' FISH
PARADISE VILLAGE CENTER
Between Cactus & Thunderbird Rds
On 19th Avenue 997-9707

616—Poultry

And Rabbits

GEESE, ducks, chickens, rabbits, cages. 936-3671.

MALLARDS, pigeons, and one Japanese rooster. 265-6568.

RABBITS. 947-9705.

BUNNIES, rabbits. 938-0444.

LAYING hens. 832-2664.

PIGEONS for sale. Nuns, fan tails, powders, trumpeters and so forth. Also cage and nest. 973-5147.

DUTCH rabbits wanted. 955-3377.

BUNNIES, rabbits. 252-2691.

ROOSTERS, $1 each. 243-2743.

BABY turkeys and ducks, pullets, meat chicks. Pigs, calves. Lord's Farm, 412 West Carefree Highway. 1-465-7734. 992-3486.

RABBITS, cheap. 997-4344.

CHICKENS, 932-3517.

LAYING hens, $4 each. 268-5068.

RABBITS. 992-3656.

CAGES. 275-9710.

INCUBATORS and brooders. 243-2743.

ROOSTERS, 6 months, $2. 933-0507.

SACRIFICE. PIGEONS & rabbits. 892-0460

TURKEYS, chickens, rabbits. Several varieties. 992-2007.

PIGEONS. 971-2005.

RABBITS. 276-8029.

BUNNIES, cages. 971-3975.

RABBITS. 277-7745.

BANTAMS, Rabbits. 955-4542.

BUNNIES, 993-1134.

RABBITS. 955-7652.

PIGEONS, 944-2735.

CALVES $50. Pig $15. Geese $8. Mallards and Bantams $1. 838-2558.

CHICKEN cages, $7 up. 276-7869.

RABBIT pellets $4.45. Reddoes cheap, Satins Rex. 846-8104.

DUCKS - cheap. 273-0268.

DRESSED rabbits, bucks, bunnies and junior does, also one triple hutch. Reasonable. Scottsdale. 946-0682.

RABBITS, bunnies, ducks, fertile eggs. 937-3166.

PIGEONS for sale. Nuns, fan tails, pouters, trumpeters and so forth. Also cage and nest. 973-5147.

621—Fruits

And Produce

ARIZONA Navels. $2.50. 247-7300.

GRAPEFRUIT good quality, 3c. 277-9072.

DELICIOUS hydroponic tomatoes. Pick your own! 87th Avenue/Olive. Open daily 10-4:30, Sundays 1-4.

FRESH-Picked citrus and pecans. Bare-root shade and fruit trees. Bare-root roses and rose trees. Open Saturday and Sunday. Gilbert Nursery. 2301 West Southern Avenue. 276-1529.

DATES and Oranges. 956-9621.

GRAPEFRUIT 3c. 279-8863.

U-PICK-IT, Citrus. 964-3853.

U-PICK-IT
ORCHARDS

Lemons	40 lb	$1.95
Grapefruit	40 lb	$1.95
Sweet oranges	40 lb	$2.95
Red Grapefruits	40 lb	$2.95

80 acres to pick in. Bring own containers. 2 miles south of Beeline on Gilbert Rd. 3300 N. Gilbert Rd, Mesa. 964-3853. FREE USE COMMERCIAL JUICER.

DATES & Citrus. Dolson's. 937-9159.

CARMICAL's. Juice oranges. Approximately 65 lbs/$4. 3601 East Baseline. 268-7619.

625—Food & Meat

Products

CHOICE beef halves, hanging weight, custom cut, wrapped, frozen and delivered. Unconditionally guarnteed, financing available. 264-1329.

HALF beef, hanging weight, processing incl. U.S.D.A. good and choice. T&S Meats, 937-7572.

GRAIN fed beef. 937-7569.

INFORMATION, free survival ki[illegible] no purchase necessary. Food for storage. Easy terms. 994-1258.

HEAVY beef sides, 59c lb. Freezer packs any size you want. Six months to pay available. The Meat Block, 6546 West Indian School 846-7658. Open Sunday. We take food stamps.

SELECT freezer beef, 75c pound hanging. Cut, wrapped, frozen, delivered. 978-1524.

Classified Ads for Christmas Shopping.

Example of instructions sheet:

Classified Christmas

Your group has raised $125 to buy Christmas presents for a less fortunate family. The family consists of the father (age forty-two), mother (age thirty-nine), two boys (ages seventeen and fifteen), and one girl (age fourteen). Make a list of what you would buy from these classified ads. You should all review the ads and contribute your suggestions. Use all the money, if possible, but do not go over $125. The secretary of your group will report to the class when all groups have completed the problem.

Choose a chairperson and a secretary. The chair should see that all committee members contribute to the discussion and that they all agree on final decisions. The secretary acts as the recorder. The final list may be in any form you choose.

► SUBJECT AREA

General Math

GRADE LEVEL

7–10

NAME OF ACTIVITY

Do-It-Yourself Crossword

OBJECTIVE OF ACTIVITY

To stimulate students to gain a knowledge of the unique vocabulary of mathematics and to strengthen the use of an index in a textbook.

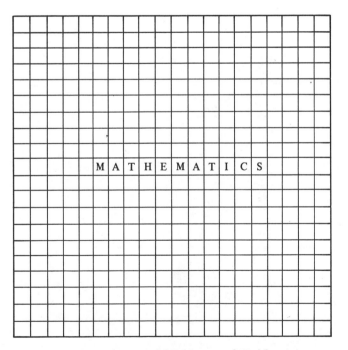

Do-It-Yourself Crossword Grid.

431

STUDENT PREPARATION

The student has read the text and auxiliary materials and has access to words from which to build the puzzle.

TEACHER PREPARATION

Prepare a crossword grid on a ditto master and print the word MATHEMATICS in the middle squares (see the example).

PROCEDURE

Working alone or in small groups, students begin by forming words with the letters in MATHEMATICS. All words used must relate to mathematics and must be accurate, so students should be encouraged to use their text index. The last stipulation is that students be able to show they know the meanings of the words used, perhaps in a group competition when the crosswords are completed.

SUBJECT AREA

General Math

GRADE LEVEL

7–10

NAME OF ACTIVITY

Guesstimating

OBJECTIVE OF ACTIVITY

General math students often lack the ability to estimate an answer before computing a problem. Consequently, they submit their papers to the teacher with outlandish, impossible answers and are unaware that their solutions are mathematically impossible. This activity gives students practice in guesstimating measurements, working with tangibles to get the concept of estimating. It also fosters the skill of observing.

STUDENT PREPARATION

None.

TEACHER PREPARATION

Display ten or more objects of varying weights, lengths, and sizes. For each object prepare one question and ditto a copy for each student.

Examples:

1. Bundle of spaghetti. How many ounces does it weigh?
2. Clear plastic bag of jelly beans. How many pieces of candy?
3. Picture. How many inches wide? How many inches deep?
4. Log. How many feet long?
5. Long balloon. How many inches long? How many inches around?

6. Empty glass jar. How many cups of water will it hold?
7. Newspaper. How much does it weigh?
8. Unabridged dictionary (closed). How many pages?
9. Sack of oranges. How much does it weigh?
10. Large bowl of cooked popcorn. How much does popcorn weigh?
11. 6 oz. can tomato juice. How many cups?

PROCEDURE

Students observe each object and estimate answers to the questions. (Teacher may or may not permit them to handle the realia.) They record each answer. After the guesstimation is completed, students check their answers by measuring, counting, weighing and enter results next to their guesstimates. As a final activity, they eat the popcorn, jelly beans, and oranges.

SUBJECT AREA

General Math

GRADE LEVEL

7–10

NAME OF ACTIVITY

Add It in Your Head

OBJECTIVE OF ACTIVITY

To provide practice in the skill of estimating in an everyday situation.

STUDENT PREPARATION

None.

TEACHER PREPARATION

None.

PROCEDURE

The student makes arrangements to go shopping with a parent or relative when numerous small items are being purchased in a drug, variety, or grocery store, for example. Without paper and pencil, the student keeps a running estimate of items as they are collected. He includes a tax estimate and allows for round-off errors. When the shopping is completed, the student tells his companion the estimate, and it is written on the back of the cash register receipt. On a target date the class and teacher discuss what type of estimation errors were made most often and why. The teacher collects the cash register slips to study the errors and to identify students who need additional help.

▶SUBJECT AREA

General Math

GRADE LEVEL

7–12

NAME OF ACTIVITY

Coupon Clipping

OBJECTIVE OF ACTIVITY

To increase students' skill in computing percentages in an everyday situation.

STUDENT PREPARATION

None.

TEACHER PREPARATION

Scan newspapers and magazines for coupons offering refunds on purchases of grocery items. Clip thirty to forty and paste each on an index card. Prepare a ditto instructing students what to do with the store coupons. (See examples.)

PROCEDURE

This activity is designed for the individual student who needs practice in computing percentages. The teacher gives him seven to ten coupons and a sheet of instructions. In the company of the shopper in the family, the student examines the products for which he has coupons, enters their prices on his sheet and also lists the amounts of the refunds on each item. He computes his percentages of savings and writes a statement on the value or nonvalue of being a coupon clipper. Coupons are to be returned to the teacher when the activity is handed in.

Coupons for Grocery Items.

437

Example of assignment sheet:

Student's Name:
Name of Store:
Date:

	Name of Item	Price of Item	Amount of Refund
1.			
2.			
3.			
4.			
5.			
6.			
7.			

1. How much actual money did you save on Item 1? _____ Item 2? _____ Item 3? _____ 4? _____ 5? _____ 6? _____ 7? _____
2. What is the percentage of money saved on Item 1? _____ Item 2? _____ Item 3? _____ 4? _____ 5? _____ 6? _____ 7? _____

3. How much money did you save on the entire bill? _____
4. What percentage does the savings amount to on the entire bill? _____

5. Is it worth it to the shopper in the family to clip store coupons? Why?

SUBJECT AREA

General Math

GRADE LEVEL

7–10

NAME OF ACTIVITY

Lead Them On

OBJECTIVE OF ACTIVITY

To increase skill in recognizing relevant data and in disregarding extraneous material in word problems.

STUDENT PREPARATION

After studying the example given by the teacher, each student writes a short vignette, containing data both relevant and irrelevant to solving a word problem. The question for the problem need not be an expected one.

TEACHER PREPARATION

Write an example which would help clarify the assignment without limiting imagination.

Example:

> Betty's parents own a bakery. Their business income is approximately $12,000 per year. Both of Betty's older brothers have part-time jobs. Ted earns $20 per week at a drug store, and Chuck has a paper route which nets $14 a week. Of the four Baker children, Betty and her younger sister are the only two who are unemployed. Q. How many people in Betty's family are older than she?

PROCEDURE

The vignettes are passed out randomly, and each student works the problem presented to him or her. When everyone has finished, the student who wrote the problem joins the student who worked it, and they discuss the results. The procedure is repeated several times.

General Math

GRADE LEVEL

7–9

NAME OF ACTIVITY

Bargain Paperback Day

OBJECTIVE OF ACTIVITY

Page after page of arithmetic workbook problems could be one of the factors in the presence of weak math skills of junior high students. For a remedial teacher to give them more of same compounds the problem. This activity is a sample of the kind that enables students to discover that fractions and percentages are operational in their everyday world. An additional goal is to encourage reading.

STUDENT PREPARATION

None prior to assignment.

TEACHER PREPARATION

Announce the date for Bargain Paperback Day, when the classroom will be turned into a used bookstore. Students will need time to decide which of their paperbacks they are willing to sell. Have a supply of change.

PROCEDURE

On the day set for the used paperback sale, prices are set according to the original price of book and its present condition. Guidelines are on the blackboard:

Good Condition	1/3 off original price
Average Condition	1/2 off plus 5 cents
Poor Condition	2/3 off original price

Students buy and sell their paperbacks, comic books, and magazines. Sellers compute the sale price and mark their wares accordingly; buyers doublecheck the computations. After the sale, the rest of the class period is spent reading.

SUBJECT AREA

General Math

GRADE LEVEL

7–9

NAME OF ACTIVITY

Everyday Math

OBJECTIVE OF ACTIVITY

To provide opportunity for students to discover the relationship
between classroom math and math as it is used daily in the non-
school world.

STUDENT PREPARATION

None.

TEACHER PREPARATION

Prepare as many math puzzlers (examples below) as there are
students in the classroom so that each student has his or her own
task. The tasks should range from simple to complex ones to provide for individual differences. Place each task in its own envelope
and then distribute all of them to the class.

Examples:

1. Picture of a clock with the question: "What does a clock have to
   do with math?"
2. Picture of a baseball diamond with the question: "What does a
   baseball diamond have to do with math?"
3. Picture of a table (or other piece of furniture) with the question:
   "What does a table have to do with math?"
4. On a slip of paper type: "Clip an article from the newspaper in

which some type of mathematics is discussed, for example, statistics or comparison of numbers. Report the math operation required."

5. On a slip of paper type: "Visit the highway department and get statistics for auto accidents which resulted in the loss of human lives for one week (or month). Compute the percentage of increase or decrease of fatalities over the same week or month last year. Estimate what the year's fatalities might be based on month-to-month statistics from the previous year."

PROCEDURE

Each student works on his puzzler for X amount of time and prepares himself to share his findings with the rest of the class.

►SUBJECT AREA

General Math

GRADE LEVEL

7–10

NAME OF ACTIVITY

Which Are the Better Buys?

OBJECTIVE OF ACTIVITY

To give practice in comparing, evaluating, and making judgments.

STUDENT PREPARATION

None.

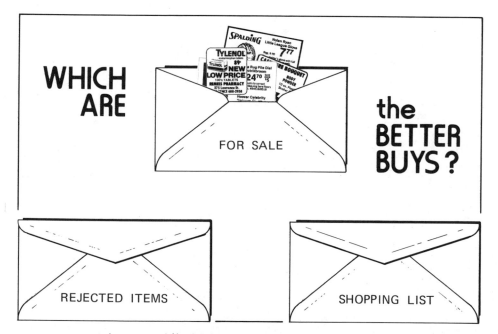

Diagram of "Which Are the Better Buys?" Board.

445

TEACHER PREPARATION

From E.O.M. sales ads in newspapers clip two ads for each of twelve
non-food household items, such as brand-name small appliances,
linens, and accessories. Mount each on 3 X 5" index card. For each
pair mark a + or a − on the backs of the cards. Prepare a board
similar to the one shown.

PROCEDURE

The students shop through the sales items as they would through
the newspaper. They choose twelve items that they would buy
because of either their superior quality or quantity and place the
cards in the "Shopping List" envelope on the board, depositing the
remainder in the "Rejected Items" envelope. When each student has
finished the activity, she checks her judgment against the teacher's
by checking the +'s and −'s on the backs of cards and discusses
discrepancies.

Algebra

Algebra

GRADE LEVEL

9–12

NAME OF ACTIVITY

Poker Chip Formulas

OBJECTIVE OF ACTIVITY

To foster the recognition of area (A) formulas and volume (V) formulas.

STUDENT PREPARATION

The student has worked with the various formulas and has some knowledge of the rules of poker (or other game requiring chips).

TEACHER PREPARATION

Provide a deck of fifty-two playing cards, card game rules, as well as fifty-cent size and silver-dollar size cardboard chips. On both sides of each of the fifty-cent size chips, print an area formula, such as square, circle, triangle, parallelogram. On the dollar size print formulas for volume, such as cone, cube, sphere, cylinder.

Examples:

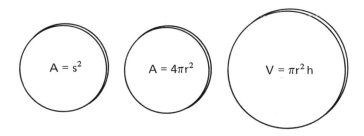

$A = s^2$ $A = 4\pi r^2$ $V = \pi r^2 h$

PROCEDURE

Four or five students follow the conventional rules of poker and use the formula chips to ante and raise the pot. They must identify each formula on the chip they use before putting it in the pot. The player with the best hand must identify all the formulas printed on the chips before he takes the pot. If he cannot, the player with the second best hand has an opportunity to do so. The student with the most chips at the end of the activity period is the winner.

SUBJECT AREA

Algebra

GRADE LEVEL

9–12

NAME OF ACTIVITY

Reverse Crossword Puzzle

OBJECTIVE OF ACTIVITY

To enhance vocabulary building, to increase spelling accuracy, and to encourage use of the glossary.

STUDENT PREPARATION

The student has been introduced to the concept or unit whose terms are used in the puzzle.

TEACHER PREPARATION

The language of mathematics, like the language of science, is precise, strictly fixed. Consequently, mathematical terms usually have no simple synonyms, and alternate learning techniques need to be designed to aid students in mastering terminology. The reverse crossword, one such aid, is made by selecting terms important to or contributing to a concept under study. The concept of the hyperbola has been chosen for demonstration. When you have chosen the terms, fill them into spaces, crossing letters of words where you can find overlaps. Prepare a set of instructions. Make a copy of the puzzle and directions page for each student (see examples) since this activity is used for a reinforcement early in the study of a particular concept.

PROCEDURE

With the completed puzzle in front of him or her, the student writes the clues or definitions, using the glossary or a dictionary when necessary.

Reverse Crossword Puzzle

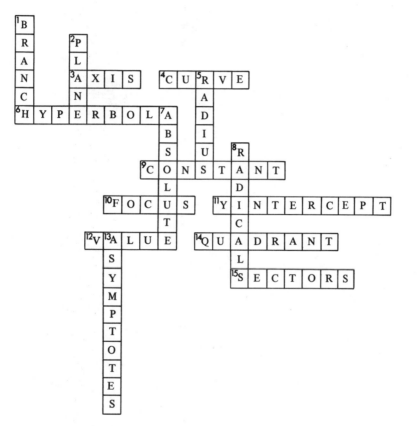

DIRECTIONS

In this puzzle the words, relating to the hyperbola, are already filled in, but there are no definitions. Look at each of the across and down words, note its position, and write a meaning by the word's corresponding number. Check your text if you get stuck.

Down	Across
1.	3.
2.	4.
5.	6.
7.	9.
8.	10.
13.	11.
	12.
	14.
	15.

Geometry

SUBJECT AREA

Geometry

GRADE LEVEL

10–12

NAME OF ACTIVITY

What's-its-name?

OBJECTIVE OF ACTIVITY

To reinforce the association of geometric figures and their names.

STUDENT PREPARATION

The student has had instruction and has used figures in daily assignments. This activity is a pleasant method of further helping students master the vocabulary of geometry.

TEACHER PREPARATION

Prepare dittoed copies of a square divided into twenty-five sections. Sketch a geometric figure in each section. (See example.) Print all possible terms for the figures on a transparency.

PROCEDURE

The teacher exposes a term on the transparency and pronounces it. Students find the figure and pencil its name across the appropriate drawing. They copy the spelling from the transparency if they do not know how to spell the word. Thus, three learning avenues are used: students hear the term, see it, write it. There may be more than one term for figures. For example, the sketch in the upper right hand corner may be called an inscribed polygon, an inscribed quadrilateral, or a circumscribed circle. If the term parallelogram is given, students may write it on a square, rhombus, rectangle, or any other parallelogram as long as they can justify the response. But

What's-Its-Name?

they may not use the term on more than one figure. As students identify all twenty-five figures, they drop out of the activity. The teacher continues until all of the terms have been used. The class discusses the responses as each student checks his or her own work.

SUBJECT AREA

Geometry

GRADE LEVEL

10–12

NAME OF ACTIVITY

Volume Poker

OBJECT OF ACTIVITY

To help students learn to cope with mathematical formulas.

STUDENT PREPARATION

The student has had instruction in finding volume.

TEACHER PREPARATION

Provide suitably marked deck of cards and rules. (See Procedure.)

PROCEDURE

Formulas may be made from cards of any suit. However, any formula made from one suit will beat the same formula made from a mixed suit. A formula made from one suit will also beat all formulas above it on the following chart. The joker is wild and can be used for any card.

Play any poker dealing game.

ORDER OF RANKING

Volume	*Formula*
Cube	$s^2 s$
2 cubes	$s^2 s, s^2 s$
rectangular solid	lwh
right circular cylinder	$\pi r^2 h$

pyramid	1/3 bh
sphere	$4/3\pi r^3$
right circular cylinder	$1/4\pi d^2 h$
right circular cone	$1/3\pi r^2 h$
rectangular solid and cube	lwh, $s^2 s$
right circular cylinder and cube	$\pi r^2 h$, $s^2 s$
pyramid and cube	1/3bh, $s^2 s$
sphere and cube	$4/3\pi r^3$, $s^2 s$

SUBJECT AREA

Geometry

GRADE LEVEL

10–12

NAME OF ACTIVITY

Syllable Cards

OBJECTIVE OF ACTIVITY

To improve math vocabulary by reconstructing four-syllable words broken at the syllable on four separate cards.

STUDENT PREPARATION

The student has been introduced to the geometric terms.

TEACHER PREPARATION

On each of four pieces of cardboard, print one syllable of a four-syllable math word. Make as many different sets as there are words that remain "sticklers" for some students. Examples:

Card 1	Card 2	Card 3	Card 4
hy	per	bo	la

PROCEDURE

After cards are shuffled well, student puts four cards together to form one word correctly. On his paper he draws or defines the term and consults textbook to check his accuracy.

If you are starting the book here, you are coming in on the middle of the act. Part I is the curtain raiser; it builds up to the use of the physical education section.

While some instructors have a blind spot where reading training in physical education is concerned, others are well aware that not only does the general subject of physical education have its own language but also that each sport and game has its own language. They also know that when those languages are committed to print (in manuals, handouts, directions, written tests), reading skills need to be merged with content.

It is for the latter physical education instructors that this section has been written. If you have read this far, you are among those who find ways to help students with the vocabulary and comprehension skills just as you help them with physical skills.

Among the skills demonstrated in physical education activities are some involving specialized vocabulary, interpreting medical information,

CHAPTER 12

Physical Education

459

relating factual information with concept, following directions, applying ideas. Activities relate specifically to gymnastics, volleyball, and dance, but can be generalized to other areas. Other activities are useful in all areas of physical education instruction. You will find that many of the activities in the health and science sections will supply useful learning experiences for physical education students.

Physical Education

GRADE LEVEL

9–12

NAME OF ACTIVITY

Hit or Miss

OBJECTIVE OF ACTIVITY

This game can easily be used as a part of the regular instruction of any sport or physical activity. Its objective is to assist students in reinforcing their knowledge of specialized vocabulary.

STUDENT PREPARATION

The student has been introduced to the terms to be reinforced.

TEACHER PREPARATION

Make the board illustrated, the markers (round pieces of cardboard numbered 1, 2, 3, 4, 5), and the spinner. Type a set of instructions (see model).

PROCEDURE

The game, designed for two or more players, is played according to the set of instructions.

Hit or Miss Board.

Hit or Miss
(For two or more players).

DIRECTIONS

The first player spins and enters his marker on any letter along the outside path. He writes this letter on a piece of paper, then moves his marker in any direction the total number of spaces indicated by the spinner. He continues spinning and moving his marker for ten turns, writing down the letter(s) of each space on which his marker stops.

The object of the game is for a player to move his marker into varied lettered spaces, so that at the end of his ten turns he will have enough letters written on his piece of paper to form the greatest number of words having to do with the sport or physical activity being studied in class. The player forming the greatest number is the winner.

►SUBJECT AREA

Physical Education

GRADE LEVEL

7–12

NAME OF ACTIVITY

Time Out for Health

OBJECTIVE OF ACTIVITY

To foster interpretation of medical information written for laymen.

STUDENT PREPARATION

None.

TEACHER PREPARATION

A healthy body is as much the concern of physical education instructors as an active body. Aids to health are in the media. Clip articles concerning health from newspapers and magazines. Among the resources are question-and-answer columns written by physicians, information disseminated by local, state, and federal health agencies, and syndicated cartoons that are commentaries on health. Make transparencies for an overhead projector.

PROCEDURE

This type of activity can be a class starter. Using the overhead projector, the teacher devotes the first five or so minutes of a class to one clipping. The instructor points to the main ideas of the article, formulates questions, and elicits responses from the class, both objective and subjective. The latter clues the teacher in on myths that need to be corrected.

NOTE

The instructor may wish to have students scour newspapers and magazines for materials. The student who brings the clipping conducts the class starter.

SUBJECT AREA

Physical Education

GRADE LEVEL

7–12

NAME OF ACTIVITY

Win—How Many Ways To Say It?

OBJECTIVE OF ACTIVITY

Within the context of physical education and sports, the coach has means especially favorable to the success of students' increasing their reading vocabulary. The objective of this activity is to have students study the use of synonyms for the word *win* by reading the alternatives used by sports writers.

STUDENT PREPARATION

None prior to assignment.

TEACHER PREPARATION

Sports writers are adept at taking everyday language and applying it in a colorful way to sports. For example, the word *sting* usually is associated with the bite of an insect. In a sports headline, it means win. Hammer calls to mind a carpenter's tool, but to a sports writer it's a synonym for win. Give students three or four models (see examples) and assign them to clip verbs in sports headlines that mean win. Prepare a ditto from which students work (see example).

PROCEDURE

Students clip twenty to twenty-five synonyms for win and paste them on an 8½ X 11″ sheet of paper. On the ditto they write each of the verbs, the sport, the score, and the degree of the victory suggested by the word. For example, if the student uses the word *hammers* and the score is 48–7, the student might describe the degree implied in the verb this way: "Big win—six touchdowns."

Example of ditto prepared by the coach:

Win—How Many Ways to Say It?

After you paste the words meaning *win* from sports headlines, write each on this sheet. In the next column identify the sport; next put the score because it often has a clue to help you answer the last

Examples of Words Sports Writers Use When They Mean Win.

column. Then describe the amount of the win that the word implies. Three examples are given to get you started.

Word	Sport	Score	What Term Implies
1. hammers	football	48–7	Big win—6 touchdowns
2. nips	basketball	117–115	Just got by—close one
3. blanks	football	14–0	Didn't let other team score
4.			
5.			
6.			
7.			
8.			
9.			

VARIATION

Television and radio sportscasters also are masters in varying their use of verbs that are equivalents for the word *win*. Variety can be added to this activity by having students study announcers' choices. (English teachers say "Thanks," Coach.)

SUBJECT AREA

Physical Education

GRÁDE LEVEL

9–12

NAME OF ACTIVITY

Vocabulary Agility

OBJECTIVE OF ACTIVITY

These several activities have as their objective strengthening students' ability

1. To cope with the specialized vocabulary of gymnastics,
2. To derive the meaning of gymnastic terms from context clues,
3. To relate factual information with the concept.

STUDENT PREPARATION

None.

TEACHER PREPARATION

1. Make a large display for the gym wall using configuration clues to illustrate specialized gymnastic terms (see examples).
2. Devise puzzles that demand recognition of specialized terms (examples of scrambled words and square puzzle given).
3. Devise puzzle that provides context clues to define terms (see example of cross-clue puzzle).
4. Print instructions for stunts on 12 × 18″ cards and print the terms for the students on separate cards (see examples). Distribute the cards to students and have them walk around and find their "match," then perform stunt.

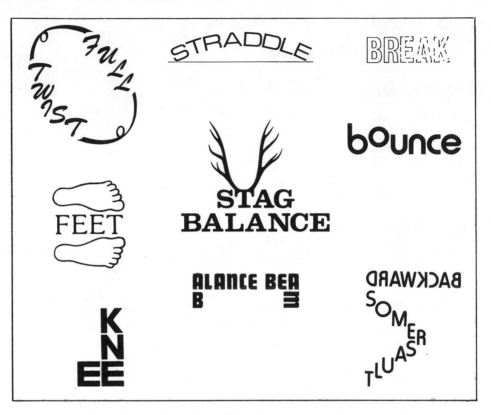

Examples of Configuration-Clue Illustrations for Large Display on Gym Wall.

PROCEDURE

These methods of teaching vocabulary within a physical education class can be easily integrated into the regular instruction of the sport.

Example of Scrambled Words Puzzle

BALANCE BEAM VOCABULARY

1. GIHH CNABELA   _____
2. VIPOT   _____
3. ENEK ACBLANE   _____
4. TSI V   _____
5. GATS NABECLA   _____
6. KDCU KLWA   _____
7. NADIGLOA ECBLAAN   _____
8. MRA STOPIINGS   _____
9. ENITUOR   _____
10. TONUM   _____
11. KLWA ROFARDW KWDBACRA _____
12. RUTN IHHG RO WLO   _____
13. TDIOUSMN   _____
14. TSNEREP   _____
15. NOE OFOT CELBNAA   _____
16. WLO BLEANAC   _____
17. UAQTS NABECLA   _____
18. MJUP MDITNUOS   _____
19. LVTUA NTOUDIMS   _____
20. LBNACAE MBAE MTRSE _____

Answers:

1. High Balance
2. Pivot
3. Knee Balance
4. V Sit
5. Stag Balance
6. Duck Walk
7. Diagonal Balance
8. Arm Positions
9. Routine
10. Mount
11. Walk Forward Backward
12. Turn High or Low
13. Dismount
14. Present
15. One Foot Balance
16. Low Balance
17. Squat Balance
18. Jump Dismount
19. Valut Dismount
20. Balance Beam Terms

Example of Square Puzzle

VOCABULARY FOR TRAMPOLINE

```
I  D I S M O U N T E K I P T M I  S  S  C
S  N S T B L G A C D B J N O K L P L O
O  B O I F O O U A R U R U E E O S B M
M  C N R T T U V R M S N Y P T T T D B
E  C O L A L C W P I T O L T S S R A I
R  F R O S B M A C L U U E T K I A G N
S  K N E E D R O P E V R N N A W D T A
A  T O P B O T L D H B S R U T T D N T
U  H E L P N F B T P S R F T B F L E I
L  I W S E B A S L O E F E S D L E C O
T  O L S H L I T R R A U M A L A B N N
W  A E M A W S O N D T L A W K H O U E
B  R N N T E U R Y T D L D O Y G U O S
P  D C L B T B D B N R T B D A V N B T
N  E L D I R U C Y O O W P L U O C K T
A  U I N T U R N R R P I F I P T E C A
F  O E M T H D C A F D S E A L B H U P
E  N I L O P M A R T Y S J O R F P T C
```

TRAMPOLINE	SOMERSAULT	TURN
FRONT DROP	ROUTINE	BALANCE
SEAT DROP	HALF TWIST	STUNT
BOUNCE	SPOTTER	JUMP
(and) BREAK	KNEE DROP	COMBINATION
BARONI	PIKE	FULL TWIST
TUCK BOUNCE	FLIP	PRESENT
DISMOUNT	STRADDLE	
MOUNT	BOUNCE	

Key to Square Puzzle on Page 475.

Example of Cross-Clue Puzzle

Gymnastics

Key to Cross-Clue Puzzle on Page 475.

Put the missing word in the correct spaces on the cross-clue puzzle.

A = Across   D = Down

Did you know that the word, __7A____, originally meant "in the nude?" It comes from the Greek word *gymnazo*, which meant "__8A____ train naked." The early ___11D___ believed that nudity was good for your health. They thought that the warmth ___5A___ the __4A____ was good for the ___10A___ in your back. In

___6D___, some of the early Olympic ___14A___ meets were ___3A___ in the ___2D___. Today modern gymnastics are usually performed in a ___1A___, and the ___7D___ wear clothes. Three common types of equipment are the horse, the ___13A___ and the balance beam. When ___1D___ ___9D___ the horse, it is called a ___12D___ horse.

Examples of stunt cards (make one set of cards for every two students, directions card, 12 × 18″; term card, smaller):

1. Let yourself down easily with arms, ducking head. Land on neck and shoulders. Tuck tightly. Roll like a ball. Hold the tuck until you come to balance on feet. Keep heels wide and close to buttocks.

FORWARD ROLL

2. Sit down backward just behind the heel so you lean backward. Place hands on mat to break fall. Place hands behind shoulders, palms up. Tuck. When weight of body is on hands, push up to relieve neck strain.

BACKWARD ROLL

3. Turn head and shoulder under and to side. Break fall with arm, turning elbow in. Land on back of shoulder blade. Roll diagonally over back and buttock muscles. Roll to stand.

SHOULDER ROLL

4. Take short run. Turn sideways. Make arms and legs resemble spokes of wheel. Arch back keeping head up and hips straight. Your side, not front, should be toward mat when you land on feet.

CARTWHEEL

```
I D I S M O U N T E K I P T M S S C
S N S T B L G A C D B J N O K L P L O
O B O I F O O U A R U R U E E O S B M
M C N R T T U V R M S N Y P T T D B I
E C O L A L C W P I T O L T S S R A N
R F R O S B M A C L U U E T K I A G N
S K N E E D R O P E V R N N A W D T A
A T O P B O T L D H B S R U T T D N T
U H E L P N F B T P S R F T B F L E I
L I W S E B A S L O E F E S D L E C O
T O L S H L I T R R A U M A L A B N N
W A E M A W S O N D T L A W K H O U E
B R N T E U R Y T D L D O Y G U O S
P D C L B T B D B N R T B D A V N B T
N E L D I R U C Y O O W P L U O C K T A
A U I N T U R N R R P I F I P T E C A
F O E M T H D C A F D S E A L B H U P
E N I L O P M A R T Y S J O R F P T C
```

TRAMPOLINE	SOMERSAULT	TURN
FRONT DROP	ROUTINE	BALANCE
SEAT DROP	HALF TWIST	STUNT
BOUNCE	SPOTTER	JUMP
(and) BREAK	KNEE DROP	COMBINATION
BARONI	PIKE	FULL TWIST
TUCK BOUNCE	FLIP	PRESENT
DISMOUNT	STRADDLE	
MOUNT	BOUNCE	

Key to Square Puzzle.

Key to Cross-clue Puzzle.

Physical Education

GRADE LEVEL

7–12

NAME OF ACTIVITY

Volley-Scotch

OBJECTIVE OF ACTIVITY

To reinforce learning the rules of volleyball and the movements of individuals on the court as a result of compliance with such rules.

STUDENT PREPARATION

The student has studied the rules of the game.

TEACHER PREPARATION

Make a hopscotch diagram on a piece of cardboard with two small holes bored in each space. Mount on a piece of wood for durability. Make wooden pegs that fit in the holes and color-code them so players can identify their pegs. On 3 X 5" cards type situations involving rules that could occur on a volleyball court (see examples) and an answer sheet.

PROCEDURE

Volley-scotch is designed for two players. A player takes a card from the stack that is piled face down. If the player answers correctly, he advances one position on the hopscotch board. If the answer is incorrect, the peg remains in the square on which it had been. The player who advances to the top of the hopscotch board and back first is the winner. Students decide how many rounds they wish to play.

Volley-Scotch Board.

Examples of situation cards:

1. While the server is serving the ball, the RF of the serving team steps off the court in order not to be hit by the ball.
   Indicate the official's decision:
   P—point
   SO—side-out
   L—legal, or play continues
   R—repeat the serve
   TO—team time-out
2. Team A serves. The ball hits the ceiling twenty-five feet above the court.
   Indicate the official's decision:

P—point
SO—side-out
L—legal, or play continues
R—repeat the serve
TO—team time-out

3. Two opposing forwards play the ball at the same time above the net, and the ball falls back on the receiving team's side. The player from the receiving team who just played the ball contacts it again, sending it over the net.
Indicate the official's decision:
P—point
SO—side-out
L—legal, or play continues
R—repeat the serve
TO—team time-out

4. What is the procedure when the serving team, after having had two time-outs for rest, consumes one minute for substitution?
    a. Legal
    b. Team is warned
    c. Side-out
    d. Point for opponents

5. When shall it be necessary to declare a game defaulted?
    a. A team fails to list all team members and substitutes in the scorebook one minute prior to game time.
    b. A team fails to be in proper serving order when the official blows the whistle for the second game.
    c. A team has only five members on the court for the second game because of injury to the sixth team member.

6. The ball is in play when a player on the serving team is injured. What is the correct procedure?
    a. Call time-out immediately; the receiving team puts the ball into play.
    b. Call time-out immediately; the serving team puts the ball into play.
    c. Wait until the ball is dead to call time-out; the receiving team puts the ball into play.

7. After Team A has started serving, it is discovered that the last member of Team B to serve was serving out of turn.
    a. Foul called on Team B and a point awarded to Team A.

    b. Points scored by player serving out of turn are cancelled and game continues with Team A serving.

8. Which official may recognize substitutes?
   a. Referee
   b. Umpire
   c. Scorer
   d. Either the referee or umpire

Physical Education

GRADE LEVEL

9–12

NAME OF ACTIVITY

Newspaper Choreography

OBJECTIVE OF ACTIVITY

Ideas for the creation of a dance come from the least expected places. An everyday resource like the newspaper can trigger ideas, for instance. The objective of this activity is to encourage students to interpret and to apply ideas from newspaper articles by improvising a dance.

STUDENT PREPARATION

None.

Phase I

TEACHER PREPARATION

Select words from newspaper headlines from which students can improvise a dance. Display them in some fashion on an overhead projector, in a montage, or on slips of cardboard. (See the example.)

PROCEDURE

If the words have been placed on individual slips of cardboard, the students choose one sight unseen, are given time to create their improvisation, and then perform for their classmates. As students deliberate their creation, they should consider the meaning of the word, its sound, and its rhythm. This idea might lend itself to a production number for a student assembly, props being enlarged words from newspaper headlines and actions being individuals' concepts of the word in dance form.

energy

Lively

Regal Satin

sophisticated

kidnap

posh

ECHO

winner

optimistic

antisocial

incognito

Crowding

MINK

Apathy

threat

Headline Choreography Words.

Phase II

TEACHER PREPARATION

Clip articles from the newspaper that lend themselves to the creation of a dance. The articles might be about a person who would serve as a character to be portrayed in movement, a place which would stimulate a student to improvise in dance a first visit, or a thing which could be brought to life rhythmically. (See examples.) Laminate the articles for durability.

PROCEDURE

Students shop through the newspaper articles that are displayed and choose one that triggers an idea for a dance. Each student reads and interprets his or her article. After a time limit, members of the class take turns briefing classmates on the gist of the article and dancing their interpretation.

Lowell Parker

Shapely Pearl Hart was the 'Bonnie' of pioneer Arizona

Part 1 of a three-part series.

She was the "Bonnie" of her day, a tough little broad whose dubious fame as a gun gal preceded that of another Bonnie by some 30 years. Her "Clyde" was a slob named Joe, who in no way measured up to the desperado qualities of the later Bonnie's boy friend. But that's another part of the story.

She was only 5 foot 2, and she weighed in at around 110. Nobody ever described her as pretty, but a lot of men thought she was sort of cute. She had a lush little figure that drove the boys crazy, and she knew it.

HER NAME WAS Pearl Hart, an appellation that fitted neatly into headlines, and she was a real tiger of a gal. She could be mean enough to shake up the strongest of men, or she could be coy, flirtatious, sweet and very feminine, according to demands of the moment. When she was good, like after having a morphine fix, she was very, very good. And when she was bad, no morphine fix being available, she was horrid.

Pearl was in her very early 20s and already rather wise in the more wicked ways of the world when she arrived in Arizona somewhere in the neighborhood of 1892. Having served an apprenticeship in the oldest profession during a year or so in New Mexico, she had no difficulty in

finding work in Bisbee, Tombstone, Tucson and finally Phoenix.

Little did anyone then realize that Pearl Hart, baby-faced with pouting lips, sullen eyes and, of course, that shapely figure, some day would be famous or infamous and would make Arizona famous or infamous, depending upon how you looked at it.

* * *

THOUSANDS OF WORDS have been written about Pearl since that afternoon of June 5, 1899, when she and Joe held up the Globe-Florence stage. Most stories vary in details about her antecedents, lovers and adventures prior to robbery. But they all add up to the fact that Pearl for several years was a national figure every bit the headline equal of a later-day Bonnie.

She was the darling of the Hearst press. Reporters had little trouble coming up every day with something new about her, for Pearl had an imagination equal to that of Jules Verne. Of course, you couldn't believe a word she said, but the fact that she said it was good enough.

Although the stage holdup, a bungled and not-too-profitable job, was Pearl's only venture in armed robbery, it made her, so to speak. Before that she was just another floozy, a little female bum living in a world of small-time bums publicized only on the police blotter.

Originally Pearl Taylor, daughter of a Canadian family said to be religious and well-do-do, she was only 17 when she ran off with a gambler and race track tout named Hart. It took her two years to learn that Hart was not the man she thought he was. A self-reliant kid, she took off on her own and wound

up in El Paso, where she became a hash slinger in a sleazy cafe frequented by equally sleazy characters.

Pearl always maintained that her intentions in El Paso were honorable; she hoped to marry a cattleman and settle down. But no marriage-minded cattleman came along and Pearl took up part-time free-lance prostitution as a means of augmenting her income.

One story has it that about that time she became acquainted with a musician and tin-horn gambler appropriately named Dan Bandsman, a handsome — aren't they always? — man of the world who introduced her to the joys of opium smoking in El Paso's little Chinatown. This same story has it that Pearl came to Arizona with Bandsman.

Another story has it that she arrived alone after having turned pro in a Silver City, N.M., bawdy house. Her story, probably untrue, was that she finally wound up in Phoenix for a reconciliation with her husband, presumably the aforementioned Hart.

Whatever the truth, the Bandsman-Hart romance, if there was one, didn't last long. Bandsman, apparently not all bad, enlisted at the start of the Spanish-American War and was never seen or heard of again.

As for the reconciliation, if it actually took place, it wasn't blissful enough to last; for soon thereafter Pearl found herself in the Mammoth mining camp and back in business with another girl in a canvas bawdy house. And there she found her "Clyde" in the form of one Joe

Boot, a would-be fancy man but a tin-horn at everything he tried.

Production at the mine dropped off with the usual disastrous effect on appurtenant businesses. Pearl and Joe headed back to Phoenix, but found the going tough in even such comparatively metropolitan surroundings.

One source of trouble was Pearl's habit. She had switched from opium to morphine, an opium derivative then easily obtained without prescription in any drugstore. Basically, Pearl was a mean-tempered little minx; when she wasn't turned on, she quarreled and fought with everyone around her, a failing that barred her from employment in any parlor house.

* * *

JOE DID HIS BEST for Pearl, but they just couldn't make it. No money for rent. No money for morphine. Not even any walking-around money for Joe.

It was then that the subject of stage robbery came up. Joe later maintained that it was all Pearl's idea, that she wanted to raise money to open her very own bawdy house down in Mexico. Not so, said Pearl, the whole fiasco was all Joe's fault.

No matter whose idea it was, the couple finally agreed that a holdup was the only way out. They picked a spot near Kelvin on the route of the Globe-Florence stage, an area with which they were familiar, as the ideal spot for the heist.

TOMORROW: The not-so-great stage robbery and its gaudy aftermath.

Jungle conceals plantation efficiency

LA LIMA, Honduras—The banana plantation is just as lushly verdant, and jungle-y close and humid as one would expect. Vines are planted to cover the crop and shade it, so grass will not grow.

The cutters work in teams; one stalking through the sweet-smelling shade to a banana-hand previously marked for cutting. One man, the hauler, props his pillowed shoulder under the huge hand of fruit, 85 to 100 pounds.

His partner, the cutter, arches swiftly with a long, glittering machete a n d whacks off the limb. After each cutting he sheaves his knife. This disinfects the blade, we were told, and prevents spreading of any disease.

This team can cut up to 250 stems per day, in this section.

The hauler than hooks the bagged bananas onto the overhead wire cables that criss-cross t h e plantation. They are hauled to the road and positioned with others in long lines. Soon a cable man riding a small tractor, moves them along to the packing house.

This farm has 917 acres; some 3,800 stems are cut per day. This (and 57 other plantations) are owned by United Fruit Company.

A banana plantation is a beautiful sight. The "trees" strong and tall, are not trees at all, but giant herbs. The leaves furl one atop the other to form the "trunk".

The blossom is a single fuschia-colored bud in the center of the leaf cluster. It has brilliant purple bracts in an exotic abstract pattern.

Under each bract is a double row of small flowers,

each of which will become a "hand" or cluster of bananas. Ten or more hands grow on each stem. Each hand has 10 to 20 "fingers," or bananas. The small green fingers point downward, but soon grow out, then turn up.

A banana plant bears only one stem of fruit; then it is cut down. But each rhizome (root) produces many shoots, each of which take over in turn. Thus the plantation has a continuous crop, making bananas not seasonal, but available all year round.

WALKING from plant to plant, we could see almost every stage of development:

Here the buds, just born today. At another plant, tiny banana fingers, only 2 days old.

All the bananas are in transparent protective plastic bags. This protects the fruit from insects, birds a n d against scarring by t h e heavy green leaves, 8 to 10

feet long, as they are blown by tropic winds.

Each plant is tagged for identification and research experiments, and even the tags must be in plastic bags, or the bugs would eat the information right o f f of them.

EVEN IN this jungle irrigation is necessary, but here it is the overhead type, sprayed in a misty circle that covers four acres at a time. The spray mixes fertilizer into the water, and is costly, we were told.

In this remote outpost, American efficiency is applied to an area that was

all jungle before being planted with bananas. Now, only the atmosphere is romantically jungle-esque. There is only the look, shade and scent of the tropics. Behind the facade, is a successful commercial enterprise that provides the world with one of its cheapest fruits.

Newspaper Articles Supplying Background for Choreography.

CHAPTER 13

Science

If you are starting the book here, you are coming in on the middle of the act. Part I is the curtain raiser; it builds up to the use of the science section.

Probably the most difficult of all the languages in the upper-grade curriculum is that of the various sciences, botany, biology, chemistry, and physics. Despite the fact that these courses draw the better student, language continues to be a problem. For those who elect the course known as general science, the language barriers are sometimes insurmountable.

Like mathematics, the language of science is precise. Dimethylsulfoxide is dimethylsulfoxide, and there's no short, simple word that is an adequate synonym. And the island of Langerhans is not a misplaced geography term.

Before functions and factors, comprehension in other words, can be dealt with, the science student must cope with an inflexible vocabulary. Some activities in this section and teaching techniques in part I underscore the advantages of direct teaching and learning of word

484

parts, a technique that helps students deal with the dimethylsulfoxide-y words. Another technique, almost always pleasurable to students, helps take the mystery out of terms like island of Langerhans, Fahrenheit, laser, and cebar. (See part I, Who Dreamed That Word Up?)

More than half the activities in this section aid students toward vocabulary growth. Other activities have their reading/thinking skills in mind, such as interpreting visual materials, observing with the senses, determining acceptability of claims, classifying, using the library, and problem solving.

General Science

SUBJECT AREA

General Science

GRADE LEVEL

7–9

NAME OF ACTIVITY

Contamination

OBJECTIVE OF ACTIVITY

To foster interpretation of visual materials and to alert students to recognize clues to food contamination.

STUDENT PREPARATION

The student has had classroom instruction and has read materials on bacteria that cause food poisoning.

TEACHER PREPARATION

Obtain enough copies of the illustration and checklist for each student in the class. The name of the four-page brochure is "Sanitation Follies," and the source is The Environment and Health Committee of the Single Service Institute, Inc., 250 Park Avenue, New York, N.Y., 10017.

PROCEDURE

The line drawing shows fifty-nine violations of the rules of safe food service. The student is to circle each violation and check his or her count against the list that accompanies the drawing. Classroom discussion follows.

REMEMBER THE FUNDAMENTAL 5 OF SAFE FOOD SERVICE

• CLEAN HANDS — Dirty hands spread germs. Hands and fingernails should be washed thoroughly with soap and water before work, after using toilet and everytime they are soiled.

• CLEAN SERVICE — Handling utensils the wrong way may spread disease. Single-service is clean and should be handled carefully to keep it sanitary. After use, other utensils should be scraped, washed clean in hot water, sanitized as required by the health department, then carefully stored and handled.

• HEALTHY WORKERS — Food workers must be healthy, for colds and other diseases may be passed to others. Germs from infected cuts, pimples or boils may cause food poisoning.

• RIGHT TEMPERATURE — Cold stops germs from growing; heat kills them. Cold foods should be kept chilled, hot foods should be kept hot. Prepared food never should be left standing at room temperature one unnecessary minute.

• CLEAN FOOD — Food may be infected by coughs, sneezes, handling, dirty equipment, vermin, animals, and wastes. It should be protected during storage, preparation, display and service.

Sanitation Follies.

CHECK YOURSELF AGAINST THE EXPERTS. THIS IS THEIR LIST.

IF YOUR SCORE IS:

56 Plus — You can call yourself an expert.
46-55 — You're better than average.
36-45 — With a little more study you would be good.
25-35 — It's time you brushed up on food service facts.
Under 25 — Tsk! Tsk! You'd better try again.

- ☐ Dripping pipes above food
- ☐ Broken plaster walls
- ☐ Food exposed in open packages
- ☐ Mice
- ☐ Spiders and spiderwebs
- ☐ Tools and tacks kept near food
- ☐ Uncovered garbage cans
- ☐ Garbage on floor
- ☐ Insecticide sprayer on food shelves
- ☐ Sugar sack stored on floor
- ☐ Fly swatter on work surface
- ☐ Food delivery crate on work surface
- ☐ Cockroaches
- ☐ Food worker scratching head while on duty
- ☐ Food worker seated on work surface
- ☐ Puddings held without refrigeration and exposed to contamination
- ☐ Cleaning materials and insecticides left near foods
- ☐ Poison stored with foods
- ☐ Utensils improperly stored
- ☐ Spilled liquids on floor
- ☐ Refrigerator door left open
- ☐ Refrigerator overcrowded
- ☐ Improper storage utensils in refrigerator
- ☐ Exposed pipes in food preparation area
- ☐ Common drinking cup over sink
- ☐ Single pan for dishwashing
- ☐ Dishes put in pan without scrapping
- ☐ Unsafe dishhandling
- ☐ Employee washing in dishpan
- ☐ Improperly racked clean dishes and utensils

- ☐ Cleaning mop in kitchen
- ☐ Smoking while at work
- ☐ Dishwiping with soiled apron
- ☐ Cat in kitchen
- ☐ Street clothing hung in kitchen
- ☐ Food exposed to animal contamination on preparation surface
- ☐ Flies in kitchen
- ☐ Screen door wedged open
- ☐ Hole in screen door
- ☐ Tasting food with mixing spoon
- ☐ Bottles of milk set next to hot stove
- ☐ Stove hood missing
- ☐ Sweeping during food service
- ☐ Sweeping floor without sweeping compound
- ☐ Food server wearing brooch and loose bracelets
- ☐ Thumb in soup
- ☐ No sneeze guard on cafeteria line
- ☐ Dirty cleaning rag on service counter
- ☐ Sneezing on food
- ☐ No self-closing door to washroom
- ☐ Door to washroom opens directly to food service area
- ☐ Handwashing facilities not in working order
- ☐ No cap or hair net worn
- ☐ Dangling earrings
- ☐ No uniform or apron
- ☐ Side towel tucked under arm
- ☐ Knives and forks held by eating ends
- ☐ Fingers inside drinking glasses
- ☐ High heeled shoes

ENVIRONMENT AND HEALTH COMMITTEE
SINGLE SERVICE INSTITUTE

250 PARK AVENUE
NEW YORK, N.Y. 10017

Sanitation Checklist.

▶SUBJECT AREA

General Science

GRADE LEVEL

7–12

NAME OF ACTIVITY

Spelling Puzzle

OBJECTIVE OF ACTIVITY

To provide a means by which students can improve their spelling of words in a lesson or unit.

STUDENT PREPARATION

Previous study of words.

TEACHER PREPARATION

Choose key words from a lesson or unit whose spelling will be difficult for some students. Using a piece of graph paper with fairly large squares, write the longest word in the center of the sheet. Select another word that has a letter in it the same as one of the letters in the first word.

```
                                        T
                                        O
                                        R
            K A N G A R O O R A         T
                                        O
                                        I
                                        S
                                        E
```

Proceed until all of the words have been placed in this fashion on the graph paper. Shade all of the boxes not being used. This becomes the key to the puzzle. Place the key on top of a ditto, enter the initial word only and shade the appropriate boxes. (See result.)

PROCEDURE

Students, needing additional practice in spelling words in the lesson, fit the words appropriately around the initial word given. The activity reinforces correct spelling because

1. students have the correct spelling before them as a model,
2. they have to look at words closely to find matching letters,
3. they say the letters to themselves as they enter words in the puzzle,
4. the act of printing is an additional mode of learning.

Students can check their accuracy against the key. Since the objective of this activity is a concentration on spelling, meanings of the words are not included. A different activity should be designed for the objective of defining words.

Plants and Animals Spelling Puzzle

Across
MESQUITE
LIZARDS
KANGAROORAT
PALOVERDE
CACTUS
OCOTILLO
SAGEBRUSH
SCORPIONS
GROUNDSQUIRREL

Down
SAGUARO
YUCCA
WREN
OWLS
ROADRUNNER
TORTOISE
RABBIT
CREOSOTE
SNAKES
KITFOX

General Science

GRADE LEVEL

7–9

NAME OF ACTIVITY

Gift of the Senses

OBJECTIVE OF ACTIVITY

To give students practice in observing with the senses; to expose students to what is going on every day and what can be gained by observing life. Comprehension of the written word is tied to experience; thus the link between this activity and reading.

STUDENT PREPARATION

None.

TEACHER PREPARATION

Materials are discussed in Procedure.

PROCEDURE

Sense of Touch

In the front of the room is a trash can filled with objects of differing shapes and textures, such as foods, jello, and water balloons, covered with dish soap. A hole has been made in the lid of the trash can. Each student comes forward and sticks his hand in the trash can. He returns to his seat and writes what and how he felt. After all the students have completed the task, discussion follows on why they got a particular feeling about certain objects.

Sense of Taste and Smell

Four of five blindfolded members of the class taste and smell two objects that have nothing in common; for example, they would taste chocolate and smell shrimp at the same time. The rest of the class observes and reports reactions. The exercise illustrates jumping to conclusions because students probably will not want to taste the candy, thinking it is the fish. After discussion, the same students react to another taste-smell test.

Sense of Hearing

Behind a screen the teacher or a student makes different sounds that would be unusual to the ear when the sense of sight is not in use. Some examples are

1. A spoon striking a glass half full of water
2. Broken glass being poured from one bucket into another
3. Two rocks being struck together
4. The opening of a pop bottle or can

Each sound should be produced twice so students have a chance to write what they thought they heard. Discussion of responses follows.

Sense of Sight

An object is in the center of a large circle formed by the students. The students observe and record exactly what they see. They exchange papers and critique their partner's power of observation, marking each entry with an F for fact or O for opinion. A variation is to have some students role-play a situation in the center of the circle.

SUBJECT AREA

General Science

GRADE LEVEL

7–9

NAME OF ACTIVITY

To Be—Sold, Or Not To Be—Sold

OBJECTIVE OF ACTIVITY

To foster recognition of advertising sales talk and to encourage experimentation to determine acceptability of manufacturers' claims.

STUDENT PREPARATION

None.

Phase I

TEACHER PREPARATION

Make a presentation to the class on the purposes of advertising. As a part of the introduction to this activity, have students speculate on whether or not advertising pays, discuss benefits of advertising to the consumer, and appraise advertisings' possible contribution to the national economy. It is important that students have this type of input before they engage in phase II.

Phase II

TEACHER PREPARATION

Prepare an assignment sheet for each student in the class (see example). Have each student gather information on one TV commercial paid for by a brand-name manufacturer and fill in the assignment sheet.

PROCEDURE

Each student selects a TV commercial on which to report and attempts to duplicate the TV demonstration at home. Then she records the requested information on the assignment sheet. After the teacher reads the reports, she selects five or more demonstrations that would be appropriate to repeat in the classroom. Discussion follows the demonstrations, and students try to reach a conclusion on ideal consumer behaviors relating to advertising claims.

NOTE

The teacher may wish to assign students to watch particular TV commercials instead of giving them their choice. There are more than enough to go around, such as the cooking oil that allows the egg to slip easily from the griddle; the paper towel that slurps up liquids not only faster but more thoroughly than its competitor; the candy that lasts longer than other bars; the paper plate that is stronger than others; the soap suds that leave eyeglasses with no film; the shampoo that holds a pearl longer than other brands; the liquid that causes a ball of hair to disintegrate; the dish-washing liquid that leaves no greasy film on hands; the dog food that beckons pooch to its bowl. (And if a cat does the cha cha, please write the author, whose cat never got beyond the two-step.)

To Be—Sold, or Not To Be—Sold

Directions: Watch a demonstration on a TV commercial and do the same demonstration yourself at home. Report your findings on this sheet.

NAME OF PRODUCT:

MANUFACTURER OF PRODUCT:

MANUFACTURER'S CLAIM ABOUT THE PRODUCT:

DESCRIBE THE DEMONSTRATION:

(Now conduct the experiment at home.)
MATERIALS USED:

RESULTS OF EXPERIMENT:

MY CONCLUSIONS:

SUBJECT AREA

General Science

GRADE LEVEL

7–12

NAME OF ACTIVITY

Hand in Glove: Does It Fit?

OBJECTIVE OF ACTIVITY

The objective of Hand in Glove is threefold, to help students

1. To identify main idea and supporting details,
2. To integrate factual information into concepts,
3. To classify information as a technique for study and review.

STUDENT PREPARATION

Since this is a review and reinforcement activity, the student should have previously studied the material.

TEACHER PREPARATION

Type or print selected concepts on orange cards. Type or print examples or supporting details on white cards. The white cards also can include diagrams and pictures if applicable. An answer key should also be made.

Example from Physical Science:

ORANGE CARD:
doldrums

WHITE CARDS: (Textbook and unabridged dictionaries are sources.)

1. A belt of calms north of the equator between the northern and southern trade winds in the Atlantic and Pacific oceans.
2. The weather prevailing north of the equator between the northern and southern trade winds in the Atlantic and Pacific oceans.
3. Light baffling winds north of the equator between the northern and southern trade winds in the Atlantic and Pacific oceans.
4. In the early days, sailors feared this region because there were no dependable winds.
5. The gentle rising of warm air near the equator creates a zone of general calm or shifting winds.

Other concepts that might be considered for orange cards are:

1. Prevailing Winds
2. Divisions of Atmosphere
3. Convection Currents
4. Why Air Pressure Is Important
5. Coriolis Effect
6. Trade Winds
7. Cumulus Clouds
8. Cirrus Clouds

PROCEDURE

The student spreads the sets of orange cards out on a flat surface. Then he places the white cards (which have been mixed up) under the appropriate orange cards. The student checks work from an answer key and makes any needed adjustments. The activity may also be used by teams by adding a scoring system.

VARIATION

Both the white and the orange cards are mixed.

SUBJECT AREA

General Science

GRADE LEVEL

7–12

NAME OF ACTIVITY

Parts and Wholes

OBJECTIVE OF ACTIVITY

To emphasize the important role of prefixes, suffixes, and roots in the meaning of scientific terms.

STUDENT PREPARATION

The students have had prior introduction to affixes that are important in various scientific fields.

Phase I

TEACHER PREPARATION

Prepare a booklet of prefixes, suffixes, and roots for each member of the class (see model in part I, Prefixes, Suffixes and Roots). Make up imaginative words and ditto copies.

Examples:

pseudocorpus	(false body)
nebulopsycho	(cloudy mind)
monorhodoped	(single green foot)
chlorohydrology	(study of green water)

PROCEDURE

Using their booklets, students decode the created words.

Phase II

TEACHER PREPARATION

None.

PROCEDURE

Students are divided into groups of four. Each team then puts together its own imaginative word, referring to the booklet for assistance. (Many of the words become whole sentences or short stories which make use of puns to complete the meaning.) As a team finishes its word, it is copied on a transparency so that the whole class can help break it down and read it.

Some examples of students' creations:

microchromogyneco	(small green woman)
decaoculanthropo	(ten-eyed man)
chromohemoichthyobioculohexapod	(green-blooded fish with two eyes and six feet)

Biology

SUBJECT AREA

Biology

GRADE LEVEL

10

NAME OF ACTIVITY

Cave Man's Barnyard

OBJECTIVE OF ACTIVITY

To reinforce prefixes, suffixes, and roots important for understanding difficult terminology in biology.

STUDENT PREPARATION

Prior instruction of prefixes, suffixes, and roots often used in the field of biology.

TEACHER PREPARATION

Prepare a booklet of prefixes, suffixes, and roots for each member of the class similar to the one discussed in part I, Prefixes, Suffixes and Roots. (There are many good sources for affixes; most English grammar and vocabulary books have lists of Greek and Latin prefixes and derived words. Another source is Dale, Edgar, and Joseph O'Rourke, *Techniques of Teaching Vocabulary* [Palo Alto, California: Field Educational Publications, 1971] .) The booklet should be slightly smaller than the biology textbook so students can keep it conveniently in the text for frequent reference. The teacher also should prepare several transparencies, each showing a prehistoric animal, such as a brontosaur, triceratops, or tyrannosaur, or a mythological figure such as Pan or unicorn. (Unabridged dictionaries are good sources for line drawings of appropriate animals.)

PROCEDURE

The class is divided into small groups. Observing the drawing and using their booklets, students in each group form the longest fictitious name possible for the animal, joining together appropriate prefixes, suffixes, and roots. The word does not need to be pronounceable, but it must be accurate, that is, each affix must describe a part of the animal. Each group writes its word and records the number of letters in it on a transparency. After a time limit, a spokesman for each group shows its transparency alongside the transparency of the animal, giving other students in the class an opportunity to challenge any of the prefixes, suffixes, and roots used. The group creating the longest accurate name for the animal is declared the winner.

SUBJECT AREA

Biology

GRADE LEVEL

10

NAME OF ACTIVITY

Big Words for Important Sciences

OBJECTIVE OF ACTIVITY

This activity has two objectives:

1. To show students the many varied subject areas that are within the field of the life sciences.
2. To familiarize students with the various study aids that are built into the textbook.

STUDENT PREPARATION

None.

TEACHER PREPARATION

Give an introductory lesson on the textbook's index and glossary and a standard dictionary. In addition, prepare a ditto, similar to the example, for each member of the class.

PROCEDURE

Using their textbooks and/or dictionaries, the students place the appropriate letter before each of the words in the left-hand column. They also write the number of the page on which they found the information that helped them make their choice and underline the source. As a final activity students write the vernacular label given to professionals in each of the life sciences.

Big Words for Important Sciences

1. ___ zoology

A. Study of plant life of the past
Page ___ (index, glossary, dictionary)
A person who works in this area is commonly called ____.

2. ___ botany

B. Study of bacteria and other micro-organisms
Page ___ (index, glossary, dictionary)
A person who works in this area is commonly called ____.

3. ___ entomology

C. Study of inland waters and waterways
Page ___ (index, glossary, dictionary)
A person who works in this area is commonly called ____.

4. ___ limnology

D. Study of classification of insects
Page ___ (index, glossary, dictionary)
A person who works in this area is commonly called ____.

5. ___ biology

E. Study of animal parasites
Page ___ (index, glossary, dictionary)
A person who works in this area is commonly called ____.

6. ___ genetics

F. Study of birds
Page ___ (index, glossary, dictionary)
A person who works in this area is commonly called ____.

7. ___ parasitology

G. Study of reptiles and amphibians
Page ___ (index, glossary, dictionary)
A person who works in this area is commonly called ____.

8. ___ embryology

H. Study of the function of the cell
Page ___ (index, glossary, dictionary)
A person who works in this area is commonly called ____.

9. ___ cytology

I. Study of fishes
Page ___ (index, glossary, dictionary)
A person who works in this area is commonly called ____.

10. ___ protozoology   J. Study of fungus as a disease of man
Page ___ (index, glossary, dictionary)
A person who works in this area is
commonly called _____.

11. ___ venomology   K. Study of plants
Page ___ (index, glossary, dictionary)
A person who works in this area is
commonly called _____.

12. ___ ornithology   L. Study of spores and pollens
Page ___ (index, glossary, dictionary)
A person who works in this area is
commonly called _____.

13. ___ ichthyology   M. Study of the environment
Page ___ (index, glossary, dictionary)
A person who works in this area is
commonly called _____.

14. ___ herpetology   N. Study of animals
Page ___ (index, glossary, dictionary)
A person who works in this area is
commonly called _____.

15. ___ paleobotany   O. Study of harmful poisons of animals
Page ___ (index, glossary, dictionary)
A person who works in this area is
commonly called _____.

16. ___ palynology   P. Study of heredity
Page ___ (index, glossary, dictionary)
A person who works in this area is
commonly called _____.

17. ___ microbiology   Q. Study of animal development
Page ___ (index, glossary, dictionary)
A person who works in this area is
commonly called _____.

18. ___ ecology   R. Study of bacteria
Page ___ (index, glossary, dictionary)
A person who works in this area is
commonly called _____.

19. ___ bacteriology   S. Study of protozoa
Page ___ (index, glossary, dictionary)
A person who works in this area is

commonly called ____.

20. ___ mycology   T. Study of both plants and animals and
                           their relationships
                           Page ___ (index, glossary, dictionary)
                           A person who works in this area is
                           commonly called ____.

AND THERE ARE JOBS IN EVERY ONE OF THESE FIELDS OF
LIFE SCIENCES

SUBJECT AREA

Biology

GRADE LEVEL

10

NAME OF ACTIVITY

Is There a "Right" Answer?

OBJECTIVE OF ACTIVITY

To foster the skills of problem solving and predicting.

STUDENT PREPARATION

The teacher has previously given classroom instruction in the skills.

TEACHER PREPARATION

Prepare mimeographed copies of an incomplete fictitious incident that relates to biology and to students' out-of-school world, as well as three or four different endings to the episode. (See examples.)

PROCEDURE

The students decide which of the endings the character would be most likely to choose and justify the answer. When each student has made his selection, he joins classmates who have chosen the same answer. The group prepares the rationale for that response and presents it to the class. The teacher is alert to the logic used by each group, and with questioning strategies leads each group to examine its justification.

Examples of incidents:

1. A large factory owner knows that the smoke stacks at his plant are pouring out black smoke into the air. He has heard a lot about

pollution and is aware of the governmental regulations on control of air pollution. However, his company has had financial setbacks, and he is cutting down on his expenditures.

a. He notifies his engineers to correct the problem.

b. He does nothing about it.

c. He calls the Environmental Protection Agency to look at the situation.

2. A bicycle rider has taken a shortcut through the park because he might be late to work for the third time that week. A strong wind is coming up, and he notices picnickers rushing for their car, leaving litter on the table they were using.

a. He hurries on to work.

b. He waits to see if they are coming back to pick up the litter.

c. He cleans it up himself.

SUBJECT AREA

Biology

GRADE LEVEL

10

NAME OF ACTIVITY

Prefix Vocabulary Cards

OBJECTIVE OF ACTIVITY

To help students learn the often-used prefixes in the area of life science.

STUDENT PREPARATION

The student has heard the words in class discussion or has read them in the textbook.

TEACHER PREPARATION

Make 3 X 5″ cards, writing a prefix on the front of a card and words including the prefix on the reverse side. Make as many cards as there are often-used prefixes under discussion.

Example:

Front of card:	bio
Back of card:	

1. biochemical	9. biologic
2. biocatalyst	10. biologist
3. biodegradable	11. biology
4. bioclimatic	12. bionics
5. bioecology	13. bionomic
6. biogenesis	14. biophysics
7. biographical	15. biopsy
8. biogenetic	16. biosphere

511

Example:
Front of card: exo
Back of card: 1. exobiologist   5. exoskeleton
2. exocrine   6. exosmosis
3. exodermis   7. exospore
4. exoenzyme   8. exosphere

PROCEDURE

The students work in pairs. They hold the front side of the card so each can see and take turns saying and writing a word that uses the prefix and define the word. When neither student can think of any more words, the partners check their accuracy by turning over the card. Spelling is important. A dictionary is available for checking conflicts and for finding other words to add to the teacher's list on the card.

▶SUBJECT AREA

Biology

GRADE LEVEL

10

NAME OF ACTIVITY

Can the World Live with Nuclear Energy?

OBJECTIVE OF ACTIVITY

This activity enables students to become involved in the problems that arise when two different areas of science, that of ecology and nuclear power or energy, conflict. The question is "Should a nuclear power plant be built in _____ (your state) near _____ (your town)?"

STUDENT PREPARATION

Previous instruction in problem-solving techniques.

TEACHER PREPARATION

As a resource person, supply handouts, films, materials, and information from which students can get additional data.

PROCEDURE

The class is divided into three groups: the environmentalists, the nuclear engineers, and the judges. The problem is to decide if a nuclear power plant should be built in _____ near _____. The two groups research their areas in order to make a convincing argument to the judges. Discussion follows the judges' decision.

Chemistry

SUBJECT AREA

Chemistry

GRADE LEVEL

11–12

NAME OF ACTIVITY

Dial an Ion

OBJECTIVE OF ACTIVITY

To give practice in the skill of coping with the word form and
symbol form of the special vocabulary of chemistry.

STUDENT PREPARATION

The student has studied ions, their symbols, and their charges.

TEACHER PREPARATION

From the ion chart in the textbook prepare interacting wheels such
as those in the example.

PROCEDURE

This is an individual activity in which the student lines up an ion
(outer wheel) with a symbol (middle wheel) and charge (inner
wheel). The chart in the textbook is used to verify accuracy, or the
teacher may provide a key.

Key:

Aluminum	Al +3
Ammonium	NH_4 +1
Barium	Ba +2
Calcium	Ca +2
Chromium (III)	Cr +3
Cobalt (II)	Co +2

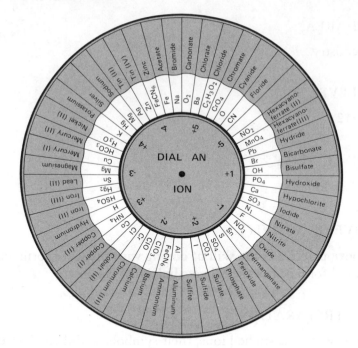

Dial an Ion Chart.

Copper (I)	Cu +1
Copper (II)	Cu +2
Hydronium	H_3O +1
Iron (II)	Fe +2
Iron (III)	Fe +3
Lead (II)	Pb +2
Magnesium	Mg +2
Mercury (I)	Hg +1
Mercury (II)	Hg +2
Nickel (II)	Ni +2
Potassium	K +1
Silver	Ag +1
Sodium	Na +1
Tin (II)	Sn +2
Tin (IV)	Sn +4
Zinc	Zn +1
Acetate	$C_2H_3O_2$ −1

Bromide	$Br -1$
Carbonate	$CO_3 -2$
Chlorate	$ClO_3 -1$
Chloride	$Cl -1$
Chromate	$CrO_4 -1$
Cyanide	$CN -1$
Floride	$F -1$
Hexacyano-ferrate (II)	$FeCN_6 -4$
Hexacyano-ferrate (III)	$FeCN_6 -3$
Hydride	$H -1$
Bicarbonate	$HCO_3 -1$
Bisulfate	$HSO_4 -1$
Hydroxide	$OH -1$
Hypochlorite	$ClO -1$
Iodide	$I -1$
Nitrate	$NO_3 -1$
Nitrite	$NO_2 -1$
Oxide	$O -2$
Permanganate	$MnO_4 -1$
Peroxide	$O_2 -2$
Phosphate	$PO_4 -3$
Sulfate	$SO_4 -2$
Sulfide	$S -2$
Sulfite	$SO_3 -2$

SUBJECT AREA

Chemistry

GRADE LEVEL

10–12

NAME OF ACTIVITY

What Is It?

OBJECTIVE OF ACTIVITY

To enable students to test themselves on their familiarity with the names of compounds that two or more elements form.

STUDENT PREPARATION

The student has previously studied names of compounds derived from the elements.

TEACHER PREPARATION

On a ditto prepare a list of several pairs (or more) of elements and a list of scrambled word forms opposite the paired elements (see example). Provide a key.

PROCEDURE

From the list of scrambled compounds and the names of the elements, the student figures out the name of the compound the two elements form. He checks his accuracy with the key.

What Is It?

1. hydrogen and oxygen   ydrxohedi   _____
2. copper, oxygen, and sulphur   pcepro lsuetaf   _____
3. silicon and oxygen   nosiilc xdoiied   _____
4. hydrogen and chlorine   chdoyrhorlci daci   _____

 5. boron and flourine
 6. magnesium, carbon, and oxygen
 7. boron and hydrogen
 8. carbon and oxygen
 9. lithium and flourine
10. hydrogen and oxygen

roobn dtiforureil _____
negsammui brcoaanet _____

robon dhryditeir _____
barcon xdodiie _____
tilhmui dforulie _____
rewta _____

Key:
 1. hydroxide
 2. copper sulfate
 3. silicon dioxide
 4. hydrochloric acid
 5. boron triflouride
 6. magnesium carbonate
 7. boron trihydride
 8. carbon dioxide
 9. lithium flouride
10. water

SUBJECT AREA

Chemistry

GRADE LEVEL

10–12

NAME OF ACTIVITY

Letter Cube Game

OBJECTIVE OF ACTIVITY

To help students learn to cope with the symbol form of chemical elements.

STUDENT PREPARATION

The student has studied the names and corresponding symbols of chemical elements from the Periodic Table of the Elements.

TEACHER PREPARATION

On all sides of six small wooden cubes print the single letters involved in the symbols for chemical elements. Provide a cup to hold the cubes. The Periodic Table is used by students to check their accuracy.

PROCEDURE

A student throws the cubes from the cup. Using the letters on the top surface of the cubes, he forms as many symbols for chemical elements as he can. If playing alone, he jots them down; if he is in a group, another student records. The player may use any letter more than once. For example, he throws C, S, A, T, U, and G. From these letters, he could make all of these symbols:

Ca = Calcium	Ag = Silver
Sc = Scandium	Cs = Cesium

Cu = Copper   Ta = Tantalum
Ga = Gallium   Au = Gold
As = Arsenic   At = Astatine
S = Sulphur   Ac = Actinium
C = Carbon   U = Uranium

The player receives one point for each acceptable symbol and the name of its chemical element.

▶SUBJECT AREA

Chemistry

GRADE LEVEL

10–12

NAME OF ACTIVITY

Symbol Poker

OBJECTIVE OF ACTIVITY

To help students learn the symbols of the different elements.

STUDENT PREPARATION

The student has a knowledge of the symbols of the common elements and the rules of poker (or other game requiring chips).

TEACHER PREPARATION

Provide a deck of fifty-two playing cards, card game rules, as well as fifty-cent size and silver-dollar size cardboard chips with the symbols of the elements printed on both sides.

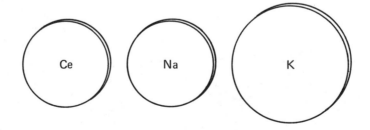

PROCEDURE

Four or five students follow the conventional rules of poker and use the symbol chips to ante and raise the pot. They must identify each element they use to stay in the game and put it in the pot. The player with the best hand must identify all the elements printed on the chips before he takes the pot. The student with the most chips at the end of the activity period is the winner.

SUBJECT AREA

Chemistry

GRADE LEVEL

10–12

NAME OF ACTIVITY

Element Trade

OBJECTIVE OF ACTIVITY

To help students learn the order and the elements of the Periodic Table of the Elements.

STUDENT PREPARATION

The student has studied the names of the elements and their locations on the Periodic Table.

TEACHER PREPARATION

On several sets of 3 × 5″ cards print the names of the elements.

Examples:

Hydrogen	Rubidium
Sodium	Cesium
Potassium	Francium

PROCEDURE

The class is divided into groups of five to seven, and each group is given a set of cards with the names of the elements on them. After being shuffled, the cards are dealt until all the cards are distributed. The dealer gives the players a minute to arrange the cards in their hands, and then the game begins. The object is to get in one's hand all the elements in a group (vertical row of Periodic Table) or family (horizontal row). The player keeps the "like" cards dealt and calls for the number of cards he wishes to trade until another player says he will trade the same number. When a player gets a complete group or family of elements, he lays his cards down and is declared the winner.

▶SUBJECT AREA

Chemistry

GRADE LEVEL

10–12

NAME OF ACTIVITY

Dictionary Search

OBJECTIVE OF ACTIVITY

To help students learn to use and become familiar with the dictionary or other reference book.

STUDENT PREPARATION

Students should have a basic knowledge of terms peculiar to or related to chemistry.

TEACHER PREPARATION

None.

PROCEDURE

Give the students a dictionary or other reference book they need to be familiar with and tell them to turn to a particular page, section or area of the book. They are to record every word or concept on the page or in the section which they can justify as having to do with chemistry in some way.

Examples from just one column on page 199, *Webster's New Collegiate Dictionary*, eighth edition, 1975:

1. chromate
2. chromatic
3. chromatic aberration

4. chromaticity
5. chromatics
6. chromatid
7. chromatin
8. chromatogram
9. chromatography
10. chromatolysis
11. chromatophore
12. chrome
13. chrome alum
14. chrome green
15. chrome red
16. chrome yellow
17. chromic
18. chromic acid
19. chromite
20. chromium
21. chromize
22. chromo
23. chromogen
24. chromolithograph
25. chromomere
26. chromonema
27. chromophil

When the students have made a list of the words, they return to each dictionary entry, read it, and paraphrase its meaning on their papers. Working in dyads enhances interest in this activity.

SUBJECT AREA

Chemistry

GRADE LEVEL

10–12

NAME OF ACTIVITY

Chemistry Treasure Hunt

OBJECTIVE OF ACTIVITY

To aid students in gaining a working knowledge of library research procedures.

STUDENT PREPARATION

The student is able to use the reference area and the stacks of the library or learns to use them in the process of the treasure hunt.

TEACHER PREPARATION

Find several articles related to chemistry in different books and magazines of the school library (or local library). Record the names of the articles selected for the activity and write a short synopsis of the content. Draw a map showing the location of each article in the library and write directions. (See example.)

PROCEDURE

Eight to ten students are given the map and directions. As noted, the directions tell them what the article is about but not its name, or the name of the article but not the name of the magazine or book, only its location. In this way the students will have to use the subject and title catalogues and the magazine index references.

Write directions like these on the ditto:

Find these articles or books. If the clue concerns an article, write
the author's name, magazine's name, month and year of publication
and page number(s) of the article. If the clue concerns a book, write
the author's name, the name of publisher, and the year of copyright.

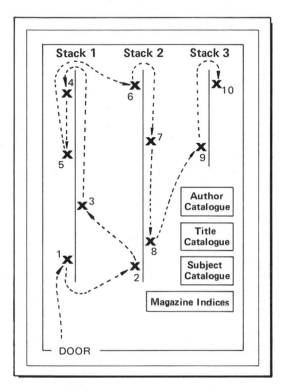

*Library Reference
Area Map.*

#1—4th row up. Article on gasoline distillation.

#2—Bottom row. Article on air pollution.

#3—2nd row up. "The Eagle and DDT."

#4—Top row. Book which tells about the discovery of oil in
     Oklahoma.

#5—3rd row up. Book which tells about the origin of gunpowder.

#6—5th row up. Autobiography of the discoverer of dynamite.

#7—Top row. Book on "tie dying" which tells about what makes a
     good dye.

#8—2nd row up. *Popular Mechanics,* 1970 issue. High altitude
     combustion in airplane engines.

#9—Bottom row. Article on the uses of calcium carbonate
   ($CaCO_3$) from seawater.

#10—3rd row up. Article on the development of the antibiotic
   tetracycline.

Physical and Earth Sciences

SUBJECT AREA

Physical Science

GRADE LEVEL

7–12

NAME OF ACTIVITY

Science Sequences

OBJECTIVE OF ACTIVITY

To aid students in safely and successfully performing a laboratory experiment. Other skills involved in this activity are following directions, collecting and organizing data, hypothesizing and problem solving.

STUDENT PREPARATION

The student has had a tour of the lab and has received an introduction to the course.

TEACHER PREPARATION

Prepare three sets of activity materials:

1. Comic Sequences
   Six or more sets of cards containing individual frames from the Sunday comics.
2. Science Sequences
   Six or more sets of cards containing individual steps of general instructions for performing a laboratory experiment (see sample set).
3. Sequences for Success and Safety in the Lab
   An individual copy for each student of detailed laboratory instructions and safety rules (see example).

PROCEDURE

The class is divided into six groups, and each group is given a set of the comic strips that are out of their sequential order. The group task is to put the frames in proper order. The cards are numbered on the back to allow students to check their results. Each group should work on three different sets to get the feeling for sequencing. Then the groups are given the sets of science sequence cards and instructed to put them in the order they think an experiment should be performed. Each group must explain the sequence it chose. As a final activity, each student is given a copy of Sequences for Success and Safety in the Lab. The teacher reads the sheet step by step and elaborates on it and answers any questions the students pose. The students place the sheet in their notebooks for use during each lab session.

Sample set for Science Sequences:

· Read experiment. (#1 is on back of card.)
· Ask questions about experiment. (#2)
· Put on safety glasses. (#3)
· Gather all necessary equipment and materials. (#4)
· Follow steps of experiment. (#5)
· Record data. (#6)
· Check to make sure you have completed entire experiment. (#7)
· Return equipment. (#8)
· Clean up work area and wash hands. (#9)
· Finish work in notebook. (#10)

Model for Sequences for Success and Safety in the Lab:

Sequences for Success and Safety in the Lab

1. Read over the entire experiment before coming to class.
2. Ask the instructor any questions you have concerning the experiment.
3. Put on safety glasses.
4. Gather all necessary equipment and materials.

      a. Set up equipment at your work area.

      b. Check that equipment is in working order.

5. Follow the steps of experiment carefully.

      a. Measure accurately.

      b. Light burner with caution.

      c. Wipe up all spills immediately and wash your hands.

      d. Time exactly.

6. Record all data in your notebook.

7. Read over the steps of the experiment to make sure you have collected all of the necessary data.

8. Return all equipment to its proper place.

      a. Wait for glassware to cool before touching.

      b. Wash glassware before storing.

      c. Return safety glasses to their storage drawer.

9. Wash off work area and wash hands thoroughly.

10. Return to your work area and complete the work in your notebook.

REMEMBER!

Wear safety glasses.
Wipe up spills.
Be careful with burner.

►SUBJECT AREA

Earth Science

GRADE LEVEL

7–9

NAME OF ACTIVITY

Go Dig

OBJECTIVE OF ACTIVITY

To develop the skills of classifying and comparing as students increase scientific vocabulary.

STUDENT PREPARATION

The student has read the text and has participated in class demonstrations and lectures.

TEACHER PREPARATION

Make a deck of cards comprised of four suits, each of which is a general geological classification. Each suit contains seven pairs of rocks which fit into one classification. (See examples.)

PROCEDURE

Students play this game in small groups according to the rules of the game called Go Fish. They are dealt five cards and must make pairs by asking the person on the left for a specific rock or mineral. If the person doesn't have a match, the student is told to "Go Dig," meaning to take a card from the top of the deck. The student who lays down all of his cards in pairs first wins the game.

Earth Science Cards for "Go Dig."

If you are starting the book here, you are coming in on the middle of the act. Part I is the curtain raiser; it builds up to the use of the social studies section.

CHAPTER 14

Social Studies

All classes in the social studies curriculum have human behavior as the focal point of study. How people behaved yesterday is told on the pages of history. How they interact with other people, with their environment, with their problems today leaves inky traces across daily newspapers and weekly news magazines. Through these media, parallels, examples, comparisons, contrasts—all current—can be made with history, the yesterday which was once today. Likewise, inspecting yesterday's geography, economics, and government from today's viewpoint releases them from the immobility of textbooks.

Words hold humanity still long enough for study. The specialized language of the social studies— whether it is the language of geography, history, government, or ecology—is ever present and sometimes presents difficulties for students. While vocabulary is not important for its own sake, concepts are, and concepts ride on the backs of words.

Several of the activities in this section have vocabulary growth as their target, but more of them have been designed to exercise students' reasoning powers: making relationships, discerning fact from opinion, selecting the main idea, recognizing important details, interpreting graphics, drawing conclusions.

Everything that's fit to print is fair game as a teaching tool: auto brochures, for example, restaurant ads, foreign correspondents' stories, crossword puzzles, telephone books, bumper stickers. They are all worthy supplements to the textbook.

Geography

►SUBJECT AREA

Geography

GRADE LEVEL

7–12

NAME OF ACTIVITY

Foreign Cars

OBJECTIVE OF ACTIVITY

To increase map-reading skills and to facilitate the use of a gazetteer.

STUDENT PREPARATION

None.

TEACHER PREPARATION

Obtain pictures of foreign cars from automobile dealers. Print the name of the car and the city of manufacture (but not the country) on the picture and paste on cardboard for durability. (See partial list.) Have small pennants and some modeling clay available. Several gazetteers and a globe of the world should also be accessible.

PROCEDURE

The picture cards are distributed to the students, who use the gazetteer to locate the countries of the cities of manufacture. To insure that they turn to the map in the gazetteer, the students make a record of the sectional location of the city.

Example:

AUDI—Munich, West Germany, located in the southeastern part of the country.

The picture cards are rotated until all have completed this part of the activity. For the last picture card in her possession, the student prints the name of the automobile on a pennant. Using clay, she plants the pennant on the proper city on the globe.

Partial List of Foreign-Made Cars

ALFA ROMEO
AUDI—Munich, West Germany
AUSTIN MARINA
B.M.W.
CAPRI
CITROEN
COLT
COURIER
CRICKET
DATSUN—Yokohama (main plant), Japan
FIAT—Turino, Italy
HONDA
JAGUAR—Coventry, England
LUV
M.G.
MAZDA—Hiroshima, Japan
MERCEDES-BENZ—Sindelfingen, West Germany
OPEL
PEUGEOT
PORCHE—Stuttgart, West Germany
RENAULT
SUBARU
TOYOTA—Takaoka (main plant), Japan
TRIUMPH—Coventry, England
VOLKSWAGEN (bug)—Stuttgart, Germany
VOLVO

Geography

GRADE LEVEL

7–9

NAME OF ACTIVITY

Eating Our Way through Geography

OBJECTIVE OF ACTIVITY

Using restaurant ads to motivate students as they study countries in World Geography.

STUDENT PREPARATION

Before each new country is introduced, students bring restaurant ads from newspapers and the Yellow Pages of the telephone book, and menus.

TEACHER PREPARATION

Using the ads/menus as catalysts, the teacher prepares questions. (See examples.)

PROCEDURE

When introducing the country, the teacher uses the ads/menus and questions in his or her presentation. Some questions can be answered at time of introduction; others serve as starting points for individual or group study.

· Is Emperor's Garden appropriate as a name for a Chinese restaurant? Why?
· What is meant by Triple Crown?

- What do you think Hong Kong Style is? How about Cantonese Style? What if the ad said Mandarin Style?
- Locate China on the map.
- Is the food served in this restaurant the same as food the natives of China eat?
- Describe farming in China.
- Where are the largest settlements of Chinese and Chinese-Americans in the United States?
- Would there be a difference between food served in Nationalist China and in Communist China? Explain.
- What is the capital of Nationalist China? What is the capital of Communist China?

Emperor's Garden
WORLD FAMOUS
CHINESE CUISINE
SERVING
Chicago—New York—Hong Kong Style
THIS WEEK'S SPECIAL
TRIPLE CROWN
Fresh Lobster Kew, Roast Pork and Chicken blended with Bamboo Shoots, Water Chestnuts, Snow Pea Pods and Imported Mushrom.
· · 7228 E. 1st Ave., Scottsdale   946-6564
Cocktails ● Lunch ● Dinner

- Locate Mexico on the map.
- What language is spoken in Mexico?
- Have you eaten these foods? What do their names mean?
    tortillas
    enchilada
    albondigo
- In what states would we probably find the largest number of Mexican restaurants?
- What kind of government does Mexico have?
- In what city do Mexican government officials work?
- How many Americans live in Mexico? Why would they wish to live there?

544

SUBJECT AREA

Geography

GRADE LEVEL

7–9

NAME OF ACTIVITY

Places in the News

OBJECTIVE OF ACTIVITY

To familiarize students with places in the United States where news is happening and to give them practice in locational skills.

STUDENT PREPARATION

Students clip stories from newspapers that have datelines in any of the fifty states and paste each on an 8½ × 11″ sheet of paper. (A dateline is the place of origin of a news story. See examples.)

TEACHER PREPARATION

When an average of ten news stories per student has been accumulated, give ten stories, each numbered from one to ten, to every student. Provide a clear piece of plastic to each student.

PROCEDURE

The students cover the map of the United States in their textbook with the plastic. Then they locate on the map each of the datelines on their stories and enter the number of the story on the plastic, connecting the number to the city with a line. Two students exchange stories and repeat the process using a different colored felt pen or crayon. The two students check each other's work. Then in quiet conversation, they discuss one or two of the news stories which interest them most.

New Orleans bowling captured by Helling

Associated Press

NEW ORLEANS — Don Helling of St. Louis outscored Jay Robinson of Los Angeles 237-213 in the championship game Saturday to win the $80,000 New Orleans Open Bowling Tournament.

Helling averaged 251 pins Saturday afternoon in finals play to earn $10,000 and take his fourth career title.

He struck in the first frame, spared in the second, then came up with five consecutive strikes. Robinson spared, struck three times, but trailed by 21 in the sixth frame.

Although leading most of the way in match play, Helling had lost his advantage to Robinson in the final game of head to head rolling Friday night, and had to defeat two straight opponents Saturday in the finals lineup.

Dick Weber of St. Louis defeated Ralph Hartmann of New Hyde Park, N.Y., 198-194 in the first match, then fell to Earl Anthony of Tacoma, Wash., in the second, 216-159.

Helling began with seven straight strikes and coasted to a 265-226 victory over Anthony before meeting Robinson.

Robinson won $6,000, Anthony $4,000, Weber $3,200, and Hartmann $2,600.

Bears pull out win after trailing Army

Associated Press

BERKELEY, Calif. — Chuck Muncie and Howard Strickland ran for touchdowns and Steve Bartkowski threw a 7-yard scoring pass to Steve Oliver to bring the California Bears from behind in the second half to a 27-14 victory over Army Saturday.

The Bears, 22-point favorites, were outplayed in the first half, trailing 14-0 at intermission. But Cal broke the game open in the second half as its offense began to roll and its defense came alive.

The defense stopped a last-quarter Army drive on the Cal six, and also accounted for the final Bears' score when Karl Crumpacker intercepted a pass by Army sub-quarterback Greg McGlasker and carried it 45 yards for the final Cal touchdown.

Texas wedding is 1776 replica

Associated Press

DE SOTO, Tex. — The groom wore long, white stockings, his dark pigtail bound with a ribbon.

His father wore a powdered wig.

The bride, swaying in a red, white and blue hoop skirt, blushed. The setting Saturday was the wedding of Marcus Skierski and Sandra DelaVega which they dedicated to the De Soto Bicentennial '76 observances in this Dallas suburb.

The couple read their vows from an original 18th Century prayer book.

"It was my idea to dedicate the wedding to the Bicentennial," said Skierski, an 18-year-old college student. "It was Sandra's idea to dress everyone in colonial era costumes. She was pretty enthused when we started talking about it."

The couple and the entire wedding party donned costumes, either rented or homemade. Hundreds of persons, including state officials, turned out for the wedding, and reception where buckwheat cakes, apple cider and other old recipes were served.

The ceremony was held at the Nance Farm main house, a 126-year-old structure designated as a De Soto historical site.

An English major, Skierski said he would liked to have had horses and carriages at the wedding but "it's the money thing. It cost more to arrange for horses and carriages nowadays than it did back then."

The young couple found one way to deal with the current recession, however.

"The prayer book called for only one ring in the ceremony. At least Sandra didn't have to buy me one" he quipped.

History

SUBJECT AREA

American History

GRADE LEVEL

10–11

NAME OF ACTIVITY

Puzzle, Puzzle on the Wall

OBJECTIVE OF ACTIVITY

To stimulate learning and recalling significant facts (names, dates, places, and events) in American history and to encourage use of the dictionary and other reference material.

STUDENT PREPARATION

The student has read (or reads as he needs puzzle answers) the text and has listened to discussions in class.

TEACHER PREPARATION

The giant crossword puzzle is made on a washable mat three feet square (four eighteen-inch mats taped together also will serve for construction). Paint the crossword puzzle on the mat (see model). In addition the game requires four different colored water-based felt-tip pens, four word definition booklets (see model), one book of answers (see model), and a sponge for washing off the mat so it can be reused. Staple the sheets of puzzle clues to some kind of firm backing to construct the booklet. Mount the giant puzzle on the wall.

PROCEDURE

The game is for two, three, or four players who race to fill in the most words on the puzzle. Each student, in turn, uses his or her own particular colored felt-tip pen to fill in a word. Five points are given for each word defined. The players are urged to use the text, dictionary, and other reference materials. (Clues to puzzle begin on page 550; the Key is on page 554.)

American History Puzzle.

Prosperity to Depression: Language of the '20s and '30s

Across
1. Key word in 1920 election
6. Financial condition of 1920s
11. Dislike strongly
14. Article
15. And not
16. Liquid used for road-laying
17. Tilt
18. Turn over and over
20. Alone
22. Native mineral from which metal is taken
23. Where (Latin)
24. Act of extending favors
25. Political dexterity
27. Sphere
28. Light talk
29. W. A. _____, editor during depression years
30. Car
33. General term for stock or bond
37. Nickname for Aristotle Onassis
38. Al _____, Democratic candidate for president, 1928
39. United States (abbr.)
40. To be
42. Pronoun
43. Bed
44. Toy
46. Something kept concealed
47. Note on musical scale
48. Preposition
50. Robert _____, noted poet who wrote about the industrial city
53. Hindu prince
54. _____ Court of International Justice
55. Skill
58. Form of I
59. Twice five

60. Single
61. Inside of
64. Hail
65. Member of National Socialist Party of Germany, 1922–45
66. Council of ministers who advise chief executive
67. Russian leader
69. Negative
70. Belonging to
72. Combine of business firms
74. Pad
78. Vehicle
79. Sweet potato
80. 1924 law that reduced quota of immigrants
84. Form of music popular in '20s
85. Civil War General Robert E. _____
87. Nothing
88. Address for woman
90. Remove gently
92. Henry _____, pioneer of assembly line production
93. Concerning
94. Light tune
97. Yet
98. Smooth
99. Aged
100. Indianapolis is its capitol
101. Firearm
102. State of being poor
104. Girl's name
106. Pronoun
109. Large
110. Combine of commercial or industrial firms
112. Payments to make amends for war losses
115. To exist
116. President Warren G. _____, 1921–23
120. A direction
121. Chooses
122. Slump in trade
123. Insecticide
124. Near

Down

1. Belonging to a nation
2. Referring to a major political party founded by Jefferson and Madison
3. Science of farming
4. To fall in
5. Suffering from lack of food
6. Rind of a fruit
7. Preposition
8. Call of distress
9. Forbidden by law
10. Three times
11. Injure
12. Tract of land
13. Without difficulty
16. Also
19. Destiny
21. Lyric poem
26. Willa _____, novelist of 1920s who wrote about rural America
31. Groan
32. Belonging to us
34. Ready money
35. Fast driver
36. Nevertheless
41. Very
45. Person in political office
49. Sudden terror
50. Harding administration legislative group favoring farmers
51. Principle person holds as true
52. 20th _____, 1933, provided change of inauguration date
54. _____ Rogers, cowboy humorist of 1920s
56. Pact
57. Reduction of military weapons
59. Slim
62. Declare positively
63. Finish
68. Organ of sight
70. Grain of common cereal plant

71. President _____ Roosevelt, 1933–45
73. State of not being employed
75. Form of to be
76. _____ _____ Scandal
77. Observe
78. President Calvin _____, 1923–29
81. Happy
82. Social reforms in 1933 campaign of Franklin D. Roosevelt
83. Female head of country
85. Place where wild animals are kept for showing
89. Deceased
91. Bias
92. Good time
95. Even if
96. _____ Long, who promised every man an income of $5,000 a year in 1930s
97. Pieces
103. Wooden peg used in golf
105. Male child
107. Energy unit in metric system
108. President William A. _____, 1909–13
109. Same as 115 across
110. Fine rain
111. Babe _____, baseball hero
113. Similar to
114. To prosecute
115. School _____, introduced in 1920s, brought about central schools
117. Bright color
118. Father
119. Pronoun

VARIATION

A teacher who has multiple sections of American history may wish to assign a particular colored pen to each section. The sections compete against each other before the bell, after the bell, and during roll call.

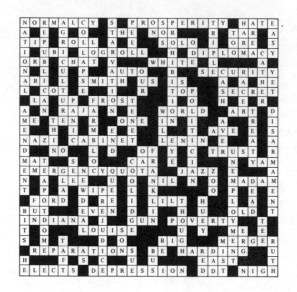

American History Puzzle Key.

SUBJECT AREA

History

GRADE LEVEL

7–12

NAME OF ACTIVITY

Clue Cards to Historical Figures

OBJECTIVE OF ACTIVITY

To help students practice skills of recognizing important details and of reasoning deductively.

STUDENT PREPARATION

Previous study of the historical figures featured in the activity.

TEACHER PREPARATION

Initially the teacher makes the cards, then students can make sets to be used by their peers. Each set contains five 3 X 5″ cards, each of which gives a clue(s) to the identity of a historical figure. (See examples.) Each card is assigned a point value of from five to one, and the value is printed on a corner of the card. On the reverse side of the card worth five points is printed the name of the person in history about whom the clues have been written.

PROCEDURE

Two or more students may play. One person reads the five-point card (with the character's name on the back). The other player tries to identify the historical figure from the clues. If he is correct, he receives five points. If wrong, the first player reads the clues on the four-point card, and so on until the one-point card is reached. Roles are reversed on the next set of cards.

Examples of clues to be typed on 3 × 5″ cards (numerals are point values):

Set 1:
- 5 Secretary of State for Wilson until he resigned this office, he was unwilling to press the reprimand of Germany for the sinking of the Lusitania.
  (On back of card: William Jennings Bryan)
- 4 Nominated but not elected to Presidency in 1896, 1900, and 1908.
- 3 Democrats nominated him on a platform of "free and un-limited coinage of both silver and gold" in 1896.
- 2 Delivered the "Cross of Gold" speech.
- 1 Attorney for the state in 1926 Scopes (monkey) trial.

Set 2:
- 5 Before the age of thirty he was Tennessee's first Congressman.
  (On back of card: Andrew Jackson)
- 4 At the age of thirteen he served in the Revolutionary War.
- 3 As President he was faced with the threat of disunion, and he was ready to take up arms again to defend the union of the states.
- 2 His political adversaries called his personal friends the "kitchen cabinet."
- 1 At his inaugural reception the exuberant but uninvited crowds broke china and furniture, and the press around this man became so great he had to escape through a back window.

Set 3:
- 5 He narrowly missed two elections to the Presidency and a conviction for treason.
  (On back of card: Aaron Burr)
- 4 Sometimes he talked of the conquest of Mexico with himself as emperor.
- 3 He planned at one time to desert the Republican party and run for governor of New York as a Federalist candidate and, once elected, to detach his state from the Union.
- 2 Alexander Hamilton criticized him in a widely publicized Albany newspaper, and he demanded that the criticisms be

retracted or they would be regarded as a challenge to a duel.
- 1 After fatally injuring Hamilton in a duel, he was indicted for murder, but he escaped from New York.

Set 4:
- 5 He served in the Black Hawk War of 1832 with Jefferson Davis.
  (On back of card: Abraham Lincoln)
- 4 He discussed the power of the Constitution to control slavery in the territories in his Cooper Union speech.
- 3 Johnson ran as his Vice President in 1865.
- 2 Johnson took over the Presidency when he was assassinated.
- 1 "A house divided against itself cannot stand."

Set 5:
- 5 On Dec. 3, 1868, trial began for teason against the United States. On Dec. 25, 1868, charges were dropped as a consequence of unconditional pardon and amnesty for rebels.
  (On back of card: Jefferson Davis)
- 4 He introduced a Senate resolution calling for a Federal Slave Code for the protection of slaves as property in the territories.
- 3 Died in 1890, an ex-President once tried for treason.
- 2 Was a President at the same time as Abraham Lincoln.
- 1 Elected President of the Confederacy in 1861.

Set 6:
- 5 He believed that "sheer honesty and even unselfishness . . . should prevail over nationalistic self-seeking in American foreign policy."
  (On back of card: Woodrow Wilson)
- 4 As President he failed to recognize the dictatorship of Huerta of Mexico.
- 3 As Europe was plunged into turmoil, he vowed that Americans would remain "impartial in thought as well as action."
- 2 They reelected him on the slogan, "He kept us out of war."
- 1 He entered WWI, calling the participation a "war to end all wars."

Set 7:
- 5 As an economy move, he ordered all federal agencies to curtail

new personnel and construction and requested recommenda-
tions for ways to reduce former President Truman's budget.
(On back of card: Dwight D. Eisenhower)

- 4 He asked Congress to authorize use of American troops to
  meet Communist aggression in the Middle East and to appropriate funds to aid in the development of the area. The docu-
  ment, a "doctrine," bears his name.
- 3 As a popular general, he campaigned for the Presidency.
- 2 Supreme Commander of NATO forces in WWII.
- 1 Richard Nixon was elected as his Vice President in 1952.

Set 8:

- 5 He escaped an assassin's bullet which fatally injured Mayor
  Cermak of Chicago.
  (On back of card: Franklin D. Roosevelt)
- 4 "Let me assert my firm belief that the only thing we have to
  fear is fear itself."
- 3 "I pledge you, I pledge myself, to a new deal for the American."
- 2 He was stricken with polio in the midst of his political career.
- 1 He approved the Senate's declaration of war on Japan.

Set 9:

- 5 He ran on McKinley's platform as Vice President of "the full
  dinner pail."
  (On back of card: Theodore Roosevelt)
- 4 Many feared a "damned cowboy in the White House."
- 3 Not yet forty-three years old, he was the youngest President
  in the White House.
- 2 He was leader of the Rough Riders.
- 1 Deep in the wilderness on a camping trip, a guide informed
  him that McKinley was dying from an assassin's bullet and
  that he was to return to take the office of President.

Set 10:

- 5 He was the tenth child in a family so poor that he had to go to
  work at the age of ten after only two years of school.
  (On back of card: Benjamin Franklin)
- 4 His publication, the *Pennsylvania Gazette,* was a popular
  paper because he criticized British officials.

- 3 Next to the Bible, his *Poor Richard's Almanac* became the most widely read publication in the colonies.
- 2 "God helps those who help themselves."
- 1 He created the lightning rod, bifocal lens, and a stove that bears his name.

Government

U. S. Government

GRÁDE LEVEL

11–12

NAME OF ACTIVITY

Move Over, Mr. Gallup

OBJECTIVE OF ACTIVITY

It is not surprising that some upperclassmen find graphs visual hindrances rather than visual aids when one considers that many adults are unable to interpret diagrams. This activity suggests that if students have not learned to interpret graphs and charts by this grade level, a different approach is needed to help them understand the statistical data in government books. The approach offered involves personal experience in gathering data on which graphs are made. It hypothesizes that a logical way to learn to read graphs is to make graphs.

STUDENT PREPARATION

None.

TEACHER PREPARATION

Confer with the journalism teacher to plan a series of articles that discuss preferences of the student body. Each article is to be prepared by a newspaper staffer and one of the students in government class.

PROCEDURE

As the government teacher detects weakness in graph reading, he or she has a conference with that student on doing a survey that will be the basis of an article in the school newspaper. The student is given instructions on how to conduct an opinion poll and then reports to the journalism teacher to meet the reporter who is to write the story. Together they plan a question of interest to the student body. The government student conducts the survey, prepares the visual for the reporter's story and enjoys seeing his or her name in print. The government teacher is ready to assist in the selection of type of visual, in the display of data gathered, and in the application of the skills learned to a visual in the government book.

Government

GRADE LEVEL

11–12

NAME OF ACTIVITY

Think about It

OBJECTIVE OF ACTIVITY

To apply the thinking skill of drawing conclusions to phenomena in students' everyday world.

STUDENT PREPARATION

Students collect advertisements from telephone books, newspapers, magazines and newspaper articles about businesses in the community which market foreign-made products. For example, ads for

· A garage that services foreign cars
· A car dealer who sells foreign cars
· A boutique that specializes in jewelry, leather goods, artifacts made in another country
· A salon whose dresses are exclusives from European designers
· A shop whose lines of watches are exclusively Swiss-made
· A delicatessen which imports wines, cheeses, sausages, pastas

TEACHER PREPARATION

Prepare a display for the students' clippings. The area should be divided in order to facilitate classifying the ads and articles. One way to classify would be the countries from which the U. S. imports goods. Another way would be to set up classifications for goods themselves regardless of origin: automobiles, foods, household items.

PROCEDURE

As the students bring their ads and articles to class, they thumbtack them in the appropriate category. At the end of the time limit, study revolves around questions suggested by both teacher and learners, particularly the latter.

Examples:

1. Why is there a market for such products in our particular community?
2. What contribution does the marketing make to our community's economy?
3. What implications are there for the same (or similar) product that is American-made?

The appropriate closure for this activity is to have students draw conclusions based on the data collected. The activity also should be a catalyst for the class to examine the concept of export.

SUBJECT AREA

U. S. Government

GRADE LEVEL

7–9

NAME OF ACTIVITY

Gold Talk

OBJECTIVE OF ACTIVITY

To enable students to associate the common terms in gold dealings with their meanings.

STUDENT PREPARATION

None.

TEACHER PREPARATION

Prepare two sets of cards, typing the terms on one set (use card in vertical position) and meanings on the other set. (See examples.)

PROCEDURE

Two students participate in the activity, taking turns playing the role of leader. The leader places the cards containing the meanings face up on the table in front of him and gives the terminology cards to his partner. The leader reads each definition, and the partner selects the card with the appropriate term and hands it over. (If the leader isn't sure of accuracy, he checks on the back of the definition card.) If the student is correct, the card is laid aside. If he is incorrect, the card is returned face down on the table. The activity is completed when responses have been given correctly for all definitions. When the leader has read all the definitions through once and disposes properly of the cards, the partner picks up those term cards which were incorrectly given. The leader then reads definitions randomly. If the partner does not have a match, he says so. If he does, he gives the leader the appropriate card. Students reverse roles.

Examples of term cards and definition cards based on an Associated Press story:

Term	Definition
Bullion	Gold in bar, wafer, or other unworked form, valued for itself rather than for its decorative or coinage worth.
Troy ounce	Standard measurement of gold bullion, equal to 1.097 regular ounces. The standard gold bar is 400 ounces; anyone purchasing less than 400 ounces must pay a charge for fabrication of the gold into smaller sizes.
London fixing	A twice-daily setting of gold prices by five major bullion dealers who meet at a London bank in the morning and afternoon and agree on a basic gold price after consulting their clients to determine demand. Trading generally begins at this level, and many American dealers link their prices to the London fixings.
Futures	Contracts promising delivery at a later date at a price that is agreed on at the time of sale.
Ingot	A bar of gold or other metal.
Assay	A test to determine the purity of gold.
Purity	A measurement of how much gold is in an item.
Planchet	A tiny wafer of gold.

Current Events

▶SUBJECT AREA

Current Events

GRADE LEVEL

9–12

NAME OF ACTIVITY

Bumper Stickers

OBJECTIVE OF ACTIVITY

To strengthen students' ability to select main idea or message from a subjectively written newspaper article.

STUDENT PREPARATION

The student has been instructed in the skill of identifying main idea.

TEACHER PREPARATION

From the newspaper clip an editorial, by-line column, or feature story. (Straight news stories should not be used in this activity.) Duplicate a copy for each student in class. Display several examples of bumper sticker sayings in the classroom, such as:

- MIAs—I Want Them Accounted For!
- Eat Candy. Your Friendly Dentist Needs the Money.
- Your Money Worthless? Give It to Me.

PROCEDURE

Divide the class into small groups. It is the task of each group to read the article and co-author a bumper-sticker-type saying that embodies the main idea or message of the writer. When the groups have completed the task, each saying is read to the entire class. Each group also must express why the particular saying is a concise statement of the main idea or writer's message.

Joe Cole
Business and financial editor

'Buy now' theory drives prices up

For the consumer caught on the inflationary balloon ride, the trip isn't much fun.

The most exciting part is anticipating how the descent — inevitable — is going to be.

| Inflation
The big
balloon
ride |

The confusing aspect right now is that although the recessionary signs indicate that the descent may have started, prices aren't coming down.

They're keeping the inflation balloon on the rise, and the consumer-passenger can't be blamed for having that "the higher we go the farther and faster we'll fall" feeling.

The consumer's reaction could make it worse.

If the reaction is "Let's buy it now because it's going to be, 15 per cent higher next year," it's feeding inflation.

The economists refer to this as "inflationary expectations," and such an approach can of itself sustain inflation on its own.

It could well be that such expectations on a major business level have aggravated the inflationary trend by companies' borrowing money or exercising credit lines sooner than they might have ordinarily in order to beat anticipated price increases.

Both the consumer and the business who borrow to beat possible cost increases may be saving money at the moment, but their actions are inflationary.

They generate demand that produces the pressure that strains supply and forces costs even higher.

The frequent comeback to this line of argument is that the spending can't be postponed — the consumer has to have a new and bigger refrigerator or camper or house now, or the business has to expand its capacity to stay in competition.

That's valid — as long as the need really exists.

The line of argument is extended often in terms of credit use in general.

If there is a strong expectation that inflation will continue, with purchasing power declining correspondingly, the reasoning goes, it is wiser to use credit now and pay back debt with cheaper dollars later.

The kink in that approach is in knowing when to stop using it. If inflation breaks, and particularly if the reversal is sudden and harsh, those with their credit necks 'way out could find themselves missing something.

Some economic analysts already are talking in terms of conditions being right for just such a reversal — they're speculating on a return to a dollar pegged somehow to a non-monetary standard such as gold.

Even if such a reversal comes, inflation's balloon won't be deflated overnight. Everyone will be caught in a tug-of-war between recession and inflation for some time.

Consumer and business alike, indications are, will be playing their cards, credit and strategic, much closer to the chest than they were even two years ago.

One might wager with confidence that last year's definition of "need" won't hold up in next year's economy.

The economy clearly is moving from "stagflation" to "inflacession," a combination of inflation and recession, and the threat is that recession will become depression.

A great danger of the moment is that political reflexes will force overreaction to negative economic circumstances, shutting off anti-inflationary thrust and re-triggering inflation.

It's small consolation, but 20 to 25 per cent of the nation's work force was unemployed in the Great Depression. Because of population growth, that's fewer in numbers than the less than 6 per cent unemployed now, but it shows how bad things aren't yet.

The inflation balloon ride is by no means over.

It has to end sometime, and that time may be near.

For the long run, Arizona can consider itself fortunate. Its growth record and capacity for more growth should provide some buffer for the ride down.

Let's hope it doesn't end with a bang.

Current Events

GRADE LEVEL

7–12

NAME OF ACTIVITY

Is That a Fact!

OBJECTIVE OF ACTIVITY

To give experience in discerning fact from opinion.

STUDENT PREPARATION

Class instruction on fact versus opinion.

TEACHER PREPARATION

Clip articles written by a news columnist and mount each on an 8 1/2 X 11″ sheet of paper. Attach a tally sheet to each set (see

Michael Padev
Republic foreign editor

Inadequate help is sometimes worse than no help at all

WASHINGTON — The prominent British diplomat, journalist and writer, Harold Nicolson, who died recently, made a special study of great power policies toward smaller states. He used to tell his friends "an Oriental story," in an effort to illustrate how great powers should not treat small countries. Nicolson's story comes vividly to my mind as I read the news of the Vietnam tragedy.

• • •

ONCE UPON A TIME, Nicolson used to relate, a young peasant woman was trying to wade through a small river near her village somewhere in the Far East.

The river was shallow and the current not too strong, so the peasants had no difficulty in walking across from one bank to the other.

But the young woman was hesitant and somewhat afraid to put her bare feet into the water. She had an additional burden — she was carrying her newborn baby in her arms.

All of a sudden help came to the young woman in a miraculous way. A young stranger, and a giant of a man, appeared from nowhere. He was tall, muscular and confident. He said he would carry in his arms both the baby and the young woman across the river. He started with the baby.

Somewhere in midstream the young giant, strong and powerful as he was, lost his balance and fell into the water. Before he could get up, the baby had slipped from his hands. It soon disappeared down the river and drowned.

Facing the horrified and tearful mother the young man said: "I am terrible sorry. It was not my fault, really. I must have stepped on the wrong stone."

Great powers, Nicolson would add, should never behave like that young and confident man.

Unless a great power is absolutely certain that it can carry the burden of a small nation to the very end, it should never attempt to do so. Half-help is worse than no help at all.

• • •

THIS IS ESPECIALLY true when great powers operate in distant foreign lands without first-hand knowledge of local conditions and realities.

The young man in Nicolson's story was strong enough to help effectively the mother and her baby.

But he knew nothing about the small river near that village. It was, therefore, none of his business to try to help.

Every peasant in the area could wade successfully through the river because he knew what stones to step on and what stones to avoid.

The young man, for all his strength, proved a dismal failure. He was thus directly responsible for the baby's death — he stepped on the wrong stone.

Years ago, we could have helped the Vietnamese defend their independence and reorganize their war-shattered economy. We tried, but we failed.

We stepped on the "wrong stone," and now the baby is down the river and dead.

It is futile to debate the question as to who is really responsible for this American foreign policy disaster — what president, which Congress, the press, the military, public opinion?

• • •

IN THE FACE OF the ghastly Vietnamese tragedy, such debates are, frankly, rather irrelevant.

Next time we are urged to help someone wade across a river we had better think twice before stepping into strange waters. If that man had not been so eager to help — in Nicolson's story — the baby would not have perished, as the young mother, perhaps with the help of some local peasants, would have managed somehow to get across to the other bank.

It is sad to say it, but it is true: the Vietnamese would have been better off without Uncle Sam's help. .

example) and place it in a folder. Repeat this procedure for articles from several columnists, e.g., Reisel, Harris, Buckley, Goldwater.

PROCEDURE

The student reads the articles and as he meets a fact he tallies it in the "fact" column; as he identifies an opinionated statement, he tallies in the "opinion" column. After the student completes the operation for each writer's column, he draws conclusions that seem indicated and discusses his judgment with the teacher. After he works through several columnists, he uses his tally sheets to compare and make additional judgments.

TALLY SHEET FOR MICHAEL PADEV

Date of Column	Fact	Opinion

Social Studies in General

Social Studies in General

GRADE LEVEL

7–9

NAME OF ACTIVITY

Slip of the Prefix

OBJECTIVE OF ACTIVITY

The importance of the role of affixes, particularly prefixes, in comprehension should motivate teachers to give students repeated experiences in discovering how word meanings are altered by changing prefixes.

STUDENT PREPARATION

None.

TEACHER PREPARATION

Clip newspaper headlines containing words with a prefix. Identify by number, mount them on a sheet of paper and make transparency (see example). Ditto a handout that asks students to manipulate the words and prefixes (see example). Provide dictionaries and a list of commonly used prefixes. Prior to giving the assignment, demonstrate on an overhead projector the procedure students are to use.

Example:

Hong Kong gives tourist a variety of attractions

Word containing prefix: attractions
Prefix used: at
Meaning of word: something that draws a
                              person to
Meaning of prefix: to

Prefixes that change meaning of word, new words, and meanings:

1. *dis*traction   draws away from
2. *re*traction   draws back
3. *pro*traction   draws forward

Which of these words might make sense in this headline?

Distractions might work. The headline would mean taking the tourists' minds off routine they have back home.

Place transparency of headlines on overhead and distribute handouts.

PROCEDURE

In dyads, students work through the prefix words in the headlines, consulting list of prefixes provided by teacher and dictionaries.

Example of handout:

Headline #1
    Word containing prefix:
    Prefix used:
    Meaning of word:
    Meaning of prefix:
    Prefixes that change meaning of word, new words, and meanings:

    Which of these words might make sense in this headline?

Headline #2
    Word containing prefix:

Prefix used:

Meaning of word:

Meaning of prefix:

Prefixes that change meaning of words, new words, and meanings:

Which of these words might make sense in this headline?

Example of transparency.

1. # Dems in House lead party with reforms

2. **Vegetarians fight meat promotions**

3. ## *'Gold rush' to resume after break for holiday*

4. # Consumer neglect is charged

5. *Westinghouse to sell major appliance plants*

6. *Extension of revenue sharing urged*

▶SUBJECT AREA

Social Studies in General

GRADE LEVEL

7–12

NAME OF ACTIVITY

Auto Tales

OBJECTIVE OF ACTIVITY

Automobiles are a revealing aspect of modern life. This activity allows students to make a relationship between Americans' principal means of transportation and the names selected by auto manufacturers.

STUDENT PREPARATION

None at first, then visits to auto dealers for brochures.

TEACHER PREPARATION

Collect brochures from one auto dealer, enough for each student in the class. Borrow several word history books from the library and provide dictionaries. (For a bibliography of these resources see part I, *Who Dreamed That Word Up?*) Design a list of questions that will guide the student in discovering why and how manufacturers select names for makes and models.

Examples of guide questions:

1. What does the name mean?
2. Where does it come from?
3. What does the name mean to you?
4. What image do you visualize when you see or hear this word?
5. Do you think the name is appropriate for this auto? Why or why not?

6. If you have seen, ridden in or driven this car, what name would you give it?

Demonstrate, using the brochure from the auto dealer.

Example of demonstration on the name of one Ford:

Mercury

1. What does the name mean? (Have students use dictionaries and word history books. Mercury, in all of its meanings, has to do with speed.)
2. Where does it come from? (The mythological Roman god who was a messenger of the gods.)
3. What does the name mean to you? (Elicit responses from students. They will volunteer answers such as barometer, thermometer, U. S. spacecraft, planet.)
4. What image do you visualize when you see or hear this word? (Elicit.)
5. Do you think the name is appropriate for this auto? Why or why not? (Elicit.)
6. If you have seen, ridden in or driven this car, what name would you give it? (Elicit.)

Since all branches of the social studies deal with man, draw conclusions from students as to the reason manufacturers chose the names they have for one of people's most expensive possessions.

PROCEDURE

After the demonstration, students visit auto dealers or search newspapers and magazines for brochures or ads on automobiles. On their return to class they follow the guide questions, using word history books and dictionaries. Since the names of so many makes and models come from mythology, some students may appreciate these legendary stories for the first time.

A Look Forward

To some, *A Look Backward* or *In Retrospect* might seem to be more appropriate titles for the closing pages of a book than *A Look Forward.* However, the title is prompted by the positive kinds of learning experiences that result for students when classroom teachers plan for teaching process as well as they plan for teaching content.

You have examined many and varied techniques for merging the teaching of process, reading/thinking skills, in other words, and teaching content. You have singled out some exercises that fit your classroom style, your purpose, your particular learners. Possibly you already have tried out a few. You also have found that when there is not an exact fit between a technique or activity and the givens of your teaching situation, some simple amendments and/or adaptations help you meet the objectives of the technique.

As you make further decisions for incorporating the practices in this book into your daily plans, the premises on which the concepts in the book are based can serve as guidelines.

Each Discipline Has Its Own Language . . .

Every content area has a specialized language of its own, and success in understanding the concepts of the discipline is directly tied to the learner's ability to cope with the language, to read it, to write it, to speak it, and to make sense of it when he or she hears it.

. . . And Language Is a Two-fold Concept

The term language has a two-fold implication. It is a body of words, a vocabulary. But the term also stands for the use to which a writer or speaker puts words, the way he strings words together to accomplish his purpose for communicating, whether that is to inform, to persuade, to explain, to entertain.

Language-Coping . . .

Language-coping—reading—thinking, whatever you may wish to label the concept, is a skill. It can be learned. If it can be learned, it can be taught. Better yet, the content of any discipline can be taught *through* its specialized language.

Whatever Its Demands . . .

Specialized language sometimes includes vocabulary terms totally unknown to the learner. In other instances, equally hindering to comprehension, are words for which the learner has a different referent.

. . . Can Be Taught

Paired association is a time-honored learning technique. Every time a teacher can couple a new vocabulary word or concept or comprehension skill with an experience already in the learner's repertory, chances for success improve. A learner's nonacademic world, regardless of its circumstances, is a storehouse of correlates with the academic world. Your goal is to find ways to make the new familiar and the familiar new.

Important Learning Theory . . .

Growth in a skill, in this instance, language-coping skills, takes place when the teacher:

1. Identifies the skill,
2. Demonstrates how it operates, and
3. Provides practice time.

. . . Coupled with Student Needs . . .

Some students need assistance with making sense of the printed page most of the time. Most of them require help much of the time. Even the best of them need your guidance some of the time.

. . . And Teacher Competency . . .

It is the classroom teacher who can best help students learn and refine language-coping skills (process). It is you for several reasons. First, you are there when the help is needed. In addition, you know more about the language of your subject area than any other person on campus. And, make no mistake about it, you have the competency.

. . . Pays Off for a Lifetime

Students skilled in making sense of symbols, particularly printed symbols, become adults who can solve problems and make decisions. To adults who have learned the process by which learning takes place, learning is a comfortably manageable lifetime habit, pursuit, and pleasure.

A Look Forward

Index